Dirty Work

Dirty Work
The Social Construction of Taint

Shirley K. Drew
Melanie Mills
Bob M. Gassaway

editors

BAYLOR UNIVERSITY PRESS

Cover Design by Steve Sholl, Waterstone Agency
Book Design by Diane Smith

Library of Congress Cataloging-in-Publication Data

Dirty work : the social construction of taint / edited by Shirley K.
Drew, Melanie Mills, and Bob M. Gassaway.
p. cm.
Includes bibliographical references and index.
ISBN-13: 978-1-932792-73-7 (pbk. : alk. paper)
1. Work--Social aspects. 2. Stigma (Social psychology) 3.
Occupational prestige. 4. Occupations--Psychological aspects. 5.
Work--Psychological aspects. 6. Quality of work life. I. Drew,
Shirley K. II. Mills, Melanie, 1958- III. Gassaway, Bob M. IV. Title:
Social construction of taint.
HD6955.D57 2007
306.3'61--dc22
2007015611

This book is dedicated to the following individuals

James R. Triplett

Tim Mills

Cheryl Gassaway

And to the memory of

James R. Wilcox
1942–2006
mentor and friend

Contents

Acknowledgments

It has been a pleasure working with the authors who contributed their fine work to this edited volume about dirty occupations. We appreciate the weeks or months they spent in the field to gather the data for their chapters about the people who work in interesting and important occupations.

With respect to the entire volume, we would like to thank Carey Newman at Baylor University Press for his enthusiasm for and belief in this project. We owe Diane Smith and Ellen Conduit at Baylor a debt of gratitude for "cleaning up" our manuscript (editorial dirty work). This book is better for their efforts. We would also like to acknowledge those individuals in the Ethnography Division of the National Communication Association who have provided ongoing inspiration as well as guidance over the last several years . . . not to mention a "third space" for ethnographers to "be."

Shirley K. Drew
Bob M. Gassaway
Melanie Mills

I want express my deep appreciation to my husband and partner Jim. He listened to me talk endlessly about the work, read every version of what I wrote, and has encouraged me every minute. I want to thank my father, Roger Drew, from whom I inherited my love for learning and for books. I am grateful to the many people who have influenced me in my work as a teacher, an ethnographer, and as a person. First, to my wonderful students (past and present) and colleagues at Pittsburg State University who make my work life a joy and a privilege. Thanks to Tina Allen and Janelle Iley for help with the editing. For inspiration to do the work, either by example, through personal conversations or both, I want to acknowledge the following people: Bob Gassaway, Patricia Geist, Bud Goodall, Bob Krizek, and Melanie Mills. To my good friend, novelist Max McCoy, whose support in the early stages of this project means more than he knows. Finally, thanks to the many individuals who agreed to let me "hang out" with them, ask questions, and generally just pry into their lives in order to better understand the work they do. Particularly I would like to express my appreciation to Judge Donald Noland, Chief Mendy Hulvey, and Sgt. Roger Rajotte.

Shirley K. Drew

This work would not be possible without my husband and partner, Tim, doing the family dirty work while I disappeared for days at a time in front of the computer, on the road, or hanging out at the hospital. You are a treasure. I am also grateful for my parents, James and Ruth Bailey, and the dirty work they did so that I wouldn't have to. Big thanks go to Martha, Katie, and Lauren (my other cheerleaders at home), who also gave me space and support to complete this project. Working with Shirley and Bob was a pleasure (most of the time!). This book is a testament to good collaborative work. My writing is richer for personal conversations with (and encouragement from) Jim Wilcox, Mark Borzi, Tim Mills, Sherry Walker, Bud Goodall, Jack Berghorst, Lois Lyons, and Ramona Tomshack (along with the other hik'rbabes!). I wish Jim were still here to celebrate its conclusion. Finally, I would like to thank the participants in my research projects (you know who you are) for sharing your stories and giving me insights into your work lives that are reflected here.

Melanie Mills

I greatly appreciate the access that the crime scene investigators of the Albuquerque Police Department granted me and their willingness to answer questions about their work and their thoughts about their work. Similarly, I received excellent access from the physicians and staff at the New Mexico Office of the Medical Investigator, which I greatly appreciate. The people in both organizations taught me a great deal. I also am grateful for the support of my wife, Cheryl, the nicest person I have ever known. She lived with the telephones that rang at all hours of the day and night and understood when I was on a crime scene all night. She also tolerated my tales from the field and my excitement about the fascinating cases I encountered during my research. And I appreciate Ken Benson and Robert W. Habenstein, who showed me the fascination of studying occupations and professions.

Bob M. Gassaway

Introduction

Melanie Mills, Shirley K. Drew, & Bob M. Gassaway

Many jobs, and even the ordinary lives of most people, have some level of dirty work in them. For most people, however, the dirty work in their lives is limited to changing diapers, carrying out the trash, or cleaning an occasional toilet. But dirty work is at the heart of a number of occupations and professions. It is often work that is not talked about in polite company, yet it is labor that allows many of us to live in a way to which we have become accustomed—without a lot of muss and fuss. Those who do dirty work make it possible for other people to take it for granted.

In this volume, we do not assume that dirty work denigrates the people who perform it, but dirty work does take people in a wide range of jobs into situations that most of us would prefer to avoid. Further, these dirty jobs, while absolutely necessary to continue civilized life as we know it, tend to be relegated to the low end of occupational social hierarchies—with some exceptions, such as, attorneys and judges. Despite its fundamental nature, dirty work seldom makes it into "polite" public conversation. There is an apparent understood obligation to protect society from its dirty work, and this stigmatizes (taints) its dirty workers. Through a series of ethnographic studies, this volume explores the workaday lives of people in ten occupations who come into frequent and persistent contact with dirty work. We studied these occupational cultures to learn how the people who perform dirty work talk about their jobs, their coworkers, and the foul aspects of their occupations. Each chapter studies an occupation, the people who perform that occupation, and how they communicate at and about work. We focus especially on how they manage the taint of their dirty work.

Evolution of a Concept

The study of organizational cultures went mainstream in the early 1980s with the publication of Deal and Kennedy's *Corporate Cultures* and Peters and Waterman's *In Search of Excellence*. The idea that social or community issues could significantly affect not only employee morale but also the proverbial bottom line was an idea ripe for public consumption. There was a good bit of popular as well as scholarly attention to the concept of *using* (in the very manipulative sense of the word) culture to improve the success of organizations. A new occupation, corporate anthropology, was developed in response to this new wisdom. Communication scholars and other social scientists produced much literature about how culture is created, transmitted, and maintained. While subsequent publications minimized the effect of culture as an economic indicator, the language of culture still became a part of the public talk about how we understand organizational behavior.

So what is organizational culture? A definition we like comes from Pacanowsky and O'Donnell-Trujillo (1983, p. 123) who say culture is a "reality as it is constructed of particular jokes, stories, songs, myths, polite exchanges, and so forth . . . which give substance to what would otherwise be insensate behavior." When individuals interact in organizations, their medium of exchange is in units of culture (Conquergood, 1984). That is how we learn the rules of being in a group. It is how we understand the values of a group, along with how to express them appropriately. It goes beyond the formal structure of the organization identified in documents like procedures manuals and into the everyday performance of working.

Not only do people perform, transmit, and move in organizational cultures—they also identify with their occupational roles. An occupational community is a "group of people who consider themselves to be engaged in the same sort of work, whose identity is drawn from the work, who share with one another a set of values, norms, and perspectives that apply to but extend beyond organizational matters, and whose social relationships meld work and pleasure" (Van Maanen & Barley, 1984, p. 287). There is a layering of organizational and occupational cultures such that each contributes uniquely to individual worker identities. The differences are important to note.

The organizational perspective of culture often accentuates the meaning of work for others (i.e., what is the role of this work/job in the organizational system?). The occupational perspective concentrates on the meaning of work for those who do it (i.e., what moves individuals to "be" in this line of work?). Both provide interesting yet different frames for understanding the experience of work that are not mutually exclusive and create interesting spaces for investigation. Some of the organizational culture theories and models can be meaningfully extended to the occupational context to give us a richer understanding of relationships among cultural identities.

While organizational identification has been the object of much scholarship (e.g., Barker & Tompkins, 1994; Cheney, 1983; Cheney & Tompkins, 1987; Gossett, 2002; Scott, 1997), changing career dynamics encourage a renewed focus on occupational identity, considered to be a set of central, distinctive, and enduring characteristics that typify a line of work (Van Maanen & Barley, 1984). Eisenberg and Goodall (2004) refer to this as the new contract. We do not "do" work the way it was done by previous generations in which people spent entire careers in the employ of the same organization. Because workers are likely to be employed by six to eight employers in their careers, we need to shift focus from organizational to occupational identities to understand them. Workplace trends and technological advances have made it increasingly likely that people will more strongly identify with an occupation versus an organization, and that makes it more important than ever to understand occupational work cultures. Further, in an increasingly fragmented society, as occupational identities become more salient, they also become more contested (Gergen, 1991), because the social value of occupations varies from context to context. For example, college professors (our occupation) can be viewed as self-sacrificing martyrs, pretentious elitists, or glorified babysitters, depending on the context of the observation. College professors, however, seldom qualify as dirty workers, although there are certainly those who do not like us.

There is considerable utility to examining work through this larger occupational lens, especially as we try to understand the social nature of workgroups. That is one intention of some of the work represented in this volume.

Doin' the Dirty Work

Another intention is to look at occupational identity management in stigmatized jobs. Hughes (1951) invoked the term *dirty work* to refer to tasks and occupations that are likely to be perceived as disgusting or degrading. He further observed that society delegates dirty work to groups who act as agents on society's behalf, and that society then stigmatizes these groups, effectively disowning and disavowing the work it has mandated (1962). Ashforth and Kreiner (1999) argue that the stigma of dirty work fosters the development of a strong work-group culture and defense mechanisms that transform the meaning of *dirt* and moderate the impact of social perceptions of dirtiness. Dirty jobs, those whose stigma would seemingly threaten the ability of occupational members to construct esteem-enhancing social identities, foster very supportive occupational communities, which at first may seem to be a counterintuitive discovery. The following chapters describe what kinds of taint-management strategies may be found in a variety of dirty occupations. Taint management occurs through everyday practices that reframe dirty tasks as valuable and focus on positive aspects of the job, allowing members to derive satisfaction and pride from their work.

Ashforth and Kreiner (1999) identify dirty work by physical, social, and moral taint. Physical taint takes place in jobs associated with dirt, garbage, sewage, death, bodily fluids, or dangerous conditions. Employees face social taint when their work requires a servile relationship to others (e.g., a maid) or regular contact with stigmatized people (e.g., criminals). Moral taint occurs when an occupation is generally regarded as somewhat sinful or of dubious virtue, like that of a pawnbroker or stripper. These taint categories are not mutually exclusive. Ashforth and Kreiner suggest that many occupations appear to be tainted on multiple dimensions. For example, prostitutes qualify as tainted by all these conditions, while construction workers qualify only by physical conditions. Each of the occupations included in this volume qualify as tainted on at least one of these dimensions. Taint does not include actual job task descriptions, but instead depends on the disgust people have for the jobs: "dirtiness" is therefore a social construction rather than an objective work feature.

Ashforth and Kreiner (1999) make a distinction between dirty work occupations with high versus low prestige. Higher prestige occupations require advanced education and carry some status and power; they also command higher salaries than those of lower status occupations. Higher prestige occupations include attorneys, judges, and physicians, for example. While these jobs are esteemed, they are tainted by virtue of their social associations with criminals and people with tainted illnesses (e.g., AIDS, sexually transmitted diseases, etc.). Taint reduces the prestige of and stigmatizes these occupations. Lower prestige occupations include sanitation workers, bill collectors, telemarketers, and tabloid reporters. Taint in these occupations is more readily apparent.

Whether occupations are high or low prestige, the dirty workers respond to stigma by creating a strong occupational culture. Ashforth and Kreiner explain that despite the stigma, workers "do not tend to suffer from low occupation esteem . . ." (1999, p. 417). In fact, they construct a self-esteem enhancing identity that is part of a strong culture. Through their interaction with other members, workers create rituals, traditions, collective values, languages, and meanings that identify the individuals as well as the work in more positive terms than society might assign to them. This reframing allows workers to wear their dirtiness as a badge of honor. We honor these professions with recognition of their critical place in our communities. It's dirty work, but somebody's gotta do it!

Doin' the Dirty Work: A Social Construction Approach

The world of work—like all other aspects of our social worlds—is not static nor is it experienced and understood in the same way by all participants. Rather, the people who work in particular occupations construct, reconstruct, and coconstruct their understandings of their jobs, how the work should be done, and the value of their occupations. People think and talk with others about their work in an effort to understand and deal with the problems they encounter. It was our job as researchers to unpack and make sense of these understandings through careful observations and interactions with the people we studied. We have tried to represent these understandings in a fair and consistent manner.

The research in this volume represents an immersion in the work environment, all longitudinal, ranging from weeks to years. This makes it more likely that we were able to represent multiple occupational realities as understood by the participants in these social worlds. While individual research approaches vary, all the work is ethnographic. As such, this kind of research is not a laboratory undertaking in which we garbed ourselves in sterile suits to avoid the taint inherent in the jobs we studied. We spent time in prisons, courtrooms, fire stations, and trucks, to name only a few places. We went to murder scenes and suicides, truck stops and accident scenes, and we walked next to the people we studied to try to understand what they see as well as how they talk about and make sense of their lives at work.

Sometimes the people we studied made their understandings and emotions readily observable. Otherwise, we learned much of what we understand about their worlds through our interactions with them (e.g., in interviews and conversations), as well as through other textual analysis in the form of written documents and material culture. We paid close attention to the many relevant contexts, including but not limited to the socio-historical and cultural frames.

Evolution of a Book Idea (Our Story)

The editors of this book (and one of our authors) met at a writing workshop sponsored by the Ethnography Division of the National Communication Association in New Orleans in 2002. Bob was a speaker at the workshop. Melanie and Shirley were friends from graduate school who share a mutual and longstanding interest in ethnography as a way of knowing and being. They also shared a history of attending ethnography pre-conference meetings. When Bob began to speak about his work with crime scene investigators, the women looked at each other and smiled. It was the beginning of the journey toward this book.

A smile is a good way to embark. We met Sarah in a small group the same day. Not only did we happily discover a common interest in writing about occupational cultures, we also found we were interested in occupations that qualified as dirty work. The four of us, along with Cliff, a colleague of Sarah's, corresponded after the meeting to coordinate a panel for NCA 2003: "Crime, sex, diesel, and fire: Examining the occupational cultures of dirty workers." Steve May, our respondent, provided useful feedback toward expanding this project beyond the convention. Panelists and interested friends met for brunch following our session to discuss ideas for pursuing a book on occupational cultures. Eventually, at NCA 2005 we pitched our ideas to Carey Newman at Baylor University Press, who enthusiastically embraced our concept and encouraged us to submit a book proposal . . . and here we are.

How We Collected Essays

While waiting approval of the book proposal, we scouted out (hand-picked, if you will) researchers who have been working in fields that are consistent with our conception of dirty work. Many of our occupational fields overlap and interact.

What we discovered is that there is great potential for an interdisciplinary series on this topic, which may be our path from here. All of our authors have published or publicly presented research in their area of occupational interest, which means that they have taken the opportunity to live in the work, the way you do when you write steadily about it. We think that is important. Finally, we note (with another smile) that our own work as ethnographers is stigmatized in the communication discipline (see Fine, 1994 and Shields, 2000) and qualifies as dirty work. We think that irony enhances our abilities to do our work well. See what you think.

Part I

TAINT MANAGEMENT ETHNOGRAPHIES

1

Doing Justice

Shirley K. Drew

*[As an attorney] you get more cynical and jaded. . . . Criminal law is a
pretty cutthroat business; you are a bottom feeder or you're the top
guy in the area.*

John Gutierrez, County Attorney

Girard, Kansas, a town of about 2,800, is the county seat of Crawford
County. The downtown is built around a traditional courthouse
square with many turn-of-the-century buildings. A Vietnam-era
Huey helicopter serves as the centerpiece of the square along with
the Veterans of Foreign War memorial to the veterans of Girard. The
courthouse was built in the 1920s, and has undergone a long-term
restoration. The restoration brings the building up to current standards for use, yet it retains its traditional flavor, with wide corridors
and high ceilings.

Judge Donald Noland's office and courtroom are on the third
floor of the building, and I walk up the marble staircase, hearing my
footsteps echo around me. The building seems strangely empty.
Though I have been to Girard and to the courthouse several times
before, I see it with new eyes on the first day I come to meet with the
judge about my research. I am anticipating the question that several
of my friends and colleagues have asked me: "Why are you interested in this topic?" I'm not sure what I will say, and only hope the
right response will come to me when I need it.

After some initial small talk in the court offices, the judge sits down with me and gives me a brief review of how the judicial system works. He has clearly done this before, and I realize that he has probably had many college students as interns in his court. Still, I'm grateful that I do not have to ask questions about things I don't remember from my high school civics and history classes.

Next, he leads me into the courtroom. It is impressive in a traditional sense. The high ceilings and formal columns fit my expectations of what a courtroom should look like. Interestingly, the judge sits in the chair on the witness stand, and I sit casually on the short marble ledge framing the jury box, prepared to question him. He begins by talking about the process of jury selection and of instructing the jury for trials. "Some people clearly don't want to serve," he says. "But I remind them, as nicely as I can, that it is their civic duty. I think people who serve come out of the experience with a much greater appreciation of the legal system and how it works. When they complete the job, I tell them that they are now qualified to criticize the system." How does the system work? This is, at least in part, what interests me.

He asks about my research. I tell him that I want to know about the daily work lives of lawyers and judges. I tell him that I want to observe courtroom proceedings, everyday interactions between him and the attorneys, conduct interviews, read whatever I can, and just hang around. It may take several months. He says he will do whatever he can to help. As I leave the courtroom and start down the marble staircase, I realize that he never asked me why I was interested in knowing more about lawyers and judges.

Opening Remarks

I have often thought that everything I know about the law, I learned from *Law and Order*. This television series, and all its franchises, would have us believe that working within the criminal justice system is challenging, dramatic, and even glamorous. While the work is challenging, and often rewarding, it is rarely as dramatic or glamorous as television portrays it. I suppose this dramatic portrayal is one reason I was interested in learning more about the legal professions. I wanted more than a fictionalized account of the professions; I wanted to know the stories of the people who really do the work.

The work of judges, prosecutors, and defense attorneys is often "dirty work." Judges and attorneys in the criminal justice system are often viewed as dirty or tainted. The taint on these occupations is both social and moral. Dealing with society's undesirables, including murderers, drug users, and child abusers, these individuals are often asked the familiar question, "How can you do it?" (Ashforth & Kreiner, 1999).

In this chapter I use a layered account to describe, and to some extent explain, a "slice of life" of some of the attorneys and a judge who work in the criminal justice system in southeast Kansas. "The layered account draws on many points of view and presents them to the reader as representations of lived experience. . . . [It is] a narrative form designed to loosely represent to, as well as produce for, the reader, a continuous dialectic of experience, emerging from the multitude of reflexive voices that simultaneously produce and interpret a text" (Ronai, 1995, p. 396). Specifically, I examine the performances and roles of the people who do these jobs in an effort to understand the culture of this community. More specifically, I look at the cultural performances of the people in these occupations. These performances are evidenced in the rituals, role enactments, storytelling, humor both in and out of the courtroom, and the everyday conversations between the people in this community. I spent eight months as a participant observer—sitting in court, hanging around the court offices, and talking informally with the people who work in this setting. I examined court documents, newspaper articles, and some case law in order to gain a very basic understanding of the system and culture in which these people work. I conducted twenty semi-structured and unstructured interviews of county and defense attorneys, as well as one of six presiding judges in the 11th District of the Crawford County Kansas criminal courts. I was afforded access through Judge Donald Noland, who has served this district since 1991.

Performance as Culture

Goffman's (1959) notion of human performance in everyday life paints a picture of life as a stage, and people as actors playing various roles, wearing masks to manage the impressions others have of them. Performances vary from the more formal front region (or onstage) to the less formal back region (or offstage). The assumption is that the roles onstage are more scripted than those backstage. This has been a fruitful way to view human interaction, and I will borrow some of his language to describe what I observed in this courtroom community.

Some scholars, however, object to the idea of human perform-ance as playacting. Turner (1980) views human performance as the completion or accomplishment of our culture; it is these perform-ances that not only constitute, but reveal our cultural realities to us. Pacanowsky and O'Donnell-Trujillo (1983) view the notion of com-municative performance similarly to Turner and extend it as a way to understand organizational culture. The performance view acknowledges the processual nature of communication and "culture as a social construction [that is] continually reconstructed" (p. 127). Performances in organizations are "those situationally relative and variable interactions by which organizational members construct organizational reality" (p. 128). They do not see these performances as playacting but as interactions that bring organizational reality into being.

One particular type of performance is the organizational ritual. "Organizational culture is, in large part, constituted in the various rituals which members regularly or occasionally perform. . . . [They provide members] access to a particular sense of shared reality" (Pacanowsky & O'Donnell-Trujillo, 1983, p. 129). In the criminal jus-tice organization, the rituals are determined by occupation rather than by organization alone.

Ritual and Tradition

Scholars have noted the confusion surrounding the loosely defined nature of ritual (Wolin & Bennett, 1984; Troll, 1988). However, there are three points upon which most agree. Troll (1988) explains these three characteristics as involving repetition, serving to maintain continuity in a system, and as "relatively more formal than infor-mal" (p. 621). The system-maintaining function of ritual is particu-larly relevant to the criminal justice system. Behaviors and speeches used by the judge and attorneys maintain the link to the traditions of the court (a tie with the past) and maintain the current system of rules and roles. Since rituals necessarily involve others, it reinforces the roles other individuals perform in the ritual.

Ritual strengthens the structure of the institution of the criminal justice system; it affirms interpersonal bonds between coworkers, recognizes positions of members and membership changes, and transmits elements of the culture to new members. In addition, it validates the meanings that people have for the culture through the repetition of the rituals. It connects the past to the present through the enactment of many traditions.

The rituals in court are evidenced in the language, nonverbal behaviors, and dress of those who participate in the process. The symbol system is highly structured and part of a history of courtroom traditions. Traditions in the legal process are elegant and dignified performances, a form of civilized behavior that is in obvious contrast to the cases the judge hears. It is these traditions that maintain order in the courtroom. The rituals and traditions of the justice system are the mechanisms that protect individual rights, as well as the legal process as a whole.

The judge describes his mental preparation for going into court as "putting on his game faces." The first formal ritual of the day is when the clerk announces, "All rise." The judge enters the courtroom, and once he is seated at the bench he says, "Thank you, please be seated." And the main performance begins. Another daily ritual begins with the attorneys formally stating their appearances. The judge asks, "Will you please state your appearances?" The county attorney stands and responds, "May it please the court, the state appears by and through John Gutierrez." The defense attorney responds similarly. The *court* is synonymous with the *judge*, who is the formal representative for the court. The defendant only speaks when spoken to. Most of the interaction occurs between the attorneys and the judge, and the attorneys always refer to him as "Your Honor" or "Judge." In turn, the judge nearly always refers to the attorneys as "Mr.", "Ms.", or "Counselor." This ritual establishes and demonstrates the credibility of the judicial process for the defendant and for the public. Variations in the judge's address usually occur when the hearings are relatively informal or the attorneys are standing at the bench during first appearances. In this case, the judge occasionally refers to attorneys by first names, though the attorneys still refer to the judge as "Your Honor" or "Judge." I found it interesting that these attorneys nearly always addressed him or referred to him as "Judge," even when offstage. Because it was the norm, I began addressing him in the same manner. In an archive of newspaper clippings in the court office, I found the following article:

From *The Morning Sun*, Pittsburg, Kansas, March 27, 1991

"Who Gives a Hoot"
by Vern Grassie

What would you do if you came home some night and found that your spouse had been replaced?

> . . . I recently underwent such a shock, not with my wife of 34 years, but with my judge of 34 years. I knew he had resigned . . . I went to his going away party at the courthouse . . . I read in the paper that he had been replaced . . . I knew the replacement because he had been my summer intern when I was County Attorney a hundred or so years ago. But, it didn't really hit me until I walked into the courtroom and found this young whipper-snapper sitting in MY judge's chair. . . .

> . . . So here was this new "kid" on the bench, who I kind of bottle fed for the first few years of his practice. . . . He was still just a kid to me.
>
> "Everyone rise!" said the clerk. And the new kid entered the courtroom in his black robe and sat in MY judge's chair.
>
> "Are both parties ready to proceed?" the kid asked.
>
> "Yes, your honor," said the other attorney.
>
> "Don," I said, "I have a couple of things I need to talk about before we do this."
>
> The kid looked me in the eye and softly asked, "Will counsel approach the bench?"
>
> We walked up to the bench and the kid whispered, "Mr. Grassie," (sounding a lot like MY judge used to sound) "YOU WILL address THIS court in an appropriate fashion, you WILL NOT refer to me in THIS courtroom in any inappropriate fashion. Do you understand that, MR. GRASSIE?"
>
> "Yes, your honor," I squeaked as I walked back to the counsel table. I was thinking that this kid maybe wasn't a kid anymore when he put on that black robe. . . ."

The black robes worn by the judge are as much a part of courtroom tradition as the specialized language. While they are not absolutely required (at least not in all courts), they are a physical representation of the judicial role and the legal system. Judge Noland told me:

> When I first became a judge 12 years ago, I decided not to wear the robes. I thought it would be less intimidating and pretentious. After hearing a case involving a violation of a restraining order (the couple were in the middle of a divorce), I came back to my office. Shortly after, Vern Grassie, an attorney for one of the parties, came in and told me that the couple had asked, "Don't we get a real judge?" After that, I started wearing the robes. (paraphrased)

During one of my observations, the judge explains to the defendant the consequences of pleading guilty. He tells him that if he pleads guilty, the court will move to sentencing. If he pleads not guilty, the court will appoint an attorney if he cannot afford one. Then the case will move to trial. It is one of the standard speeches, a "tightly scripted" performance (Pacanowsky & O'Donnell-Trujillo, 1983), and it is routine for the judge and court officers. It plays an important role in maintaining order and ensuring that the rights of the defendant are protected. The plea has to be voluntary and knowing, and the judge must inform the defendant of this or the plea might be invalidated in the appellate courts. In effect, it maintains the integrity of the judicial process.

The judge has a standard script for hearings, sentencings, and pleas. Sometimes he will step outside those scripts (is more improvisational) when he has something he wants to say to defendants. At a sentencing for a rape case I observe, the defendant insists he is not guilty but pleads out. His sentence is 120 months (ten years). The judge asks if the defendant has any statement and he says "No." Judge Noland looks at the defendant and says, "I'm disheartened to see that you continue to assert that you are not guilty. I regret that you're not remorseful. The case against you is very strong."

It occurs to me that the symbolic rituals used by the court are similar (at least in form) to those used in the Catholic Church. Though no longer a practicing Catholic, I still find the ritualistic aspect of the church, and now the court, intriguing. Judge Noland is the priest, the defendants the sinners. The judgment is penance. You know, "I order you to secure detention (jail or prison)," rather than, "Say two 'Hail Marys' and three 'Our Fathers.'"

Many times a defendant will stand at the bench, and the judge will tell him to "stand up straight, sir," or to "pay attention." While he is always respectful to people who come into his court, his message is clear: "You *will* have good manners in this court . . . you *will* show respect for the court and this process." And, with the judge symbolically placed at the highest point in the room, his comments are rarely ignored.

However, not all behavior in the courtroom is as formal as I expected. As I sit in the jury box one afternoon waiting for the next case to begin, I notice that the defense attorney Steve Angermeyer, sitting next to me, is reading a guitar magazine. I find it interesting that the professionals sitting in the gallery waiting for their cases to be heard frequently pass the time reading or talking quietly to one another. It does not fit my image of how I expected people to behave in a courtroom. It is oddly casual. Too many reruns of *Law and Order*,

I think. The professionals seem only mildly interested in what is happening at the bench, if at all. No doubt it becomes routine.

On occasion, the back region and front region performances cross (Goffman, 1959), resulting in light humor in the courtroom or serious conversations in the "inner sanctum" of the court offices. One morning John Gutierrez, the county attorney, while prosecuting a felony DUI, is describing the facts of the case. His humor is always present, even in court, though it is a bit more restrained there. He is talking about the defendant, who is accused of driving extremely fast and drunk on a motorcycle on a major street in nearby Pittsburg. He describes the driver as pulling a "Steve McQueen-type move" to get away from the police. When he says this, I smile and the judge tries not to smile.

Humor and Work

Humor serves important functions within occupational groups. Pogrebin and Poole (1988), in their study of police humor, they explain that it serves to create social meanings, as well as to support group values, beliefs, and behaviors. Members use humor to share common experiences and to raise group concerns that might not be expressed otherwise. It helps to promote group solidarity and allows members to laugh at each other without ill intent, because the members share a communal relationship. It serves as a coping strategy. It allows members to normalize crises, to laugh at their dilemmas, and to foster group cohesion. Pogrebin and Poole (1988) argue that both members and organizations benefit from institutionalized humor because it preserves the status quo. Additionally, it is a means of transmitting group culture to new members.

Back in the court offices, the attorneys remove their jackets, the court officers relax their poses, and the judge removes his robe, speaking amicably to his colleagues. They joke with one another, sometimes at the judge's expense. He is very good-natured about it, giving it right back, enjoying the repartee. While it's clear he takes his role as a judge seriously, he doesn't seem to take himself seriously. This occurs before, between, and after the formal performances that are first appearances, hearings, and trials. Humor is an important part of these back-region performances, a sharp contrast to the more formal front-region performances. Goffman argues that these back-region performances serve to "sustain one another's morale and maintain the impression that the show that is about to be presented will go over well or that the show that has just been presented did not really go over so badly" (1959, p. 130).

Not all the attorneys I observed participated in humorous exchanges. One of the deputy county attorneys maintained his formal demeanor both in and outside of court for the most part. He told me that he does not get involved in the camaraderie (in or out of the office) because it is important to him to "maintain the office's integrity." While I cannot say that I never saw him smile, I did observe a consistent seriousness about him that I did not see in others except in the courtroom.

Back-region performances include lunch at their favorite hangout—an old- style "Mom and Pop" diner called the B & S Café. Other aspects of the culture stretch beyond the organizational setting and are a part of these individual lives outside work. For example, nearly everyone I talked to had some experience with firearms, not only as part of the job, but as part of their leisure activities. They spend much of their social time together as well. They frequently get together on weekends or evenings to fish in the judge's pond or to shoot targets. Michael Gayoso, a defense attorney, summed it up best. His first experiences practicing law were in a large city. He said the environment was hostile and tense in and out of the courtroom. He explains, "[There] you attack everything, the prosecutors, the whole system. Attorneys here are very personable; we argue like hell in court, but are sincere and kind outside of court. [We] talk, have a drink, and socialize after work with one another."

Stories

Stories allow members of a community to make sense of their experiences; the sense-making occurs *in the creation and telling* of the story. Narratives portray a shared collective history that defines relationships among the members. They are used to orient new members by providing history, cultural information, and guidelines for expected behavior. Storytelling is a performance that is often part of groups' interactions, and usually involves anyone in the proximity of the storyteller. Like humor, the storytelling ritual allows us to communicate ideas in acceptable ways. Lawyers and judges often deal with people who are at their worst, so stories are the mainstays of offstage conversations. The listeners join in. "As listeners, we are co-producers with the teller of the story . . ." (Boje, 1991, p. 107). We create these joint performances through subtle utterances or other nonverbal cues such as head nodding (p. 107).

I heard many stories during the months I spent with the judge
and the attorneys. After hanging around them for a while, it became
difficult to shock me and I sometimes joined in the creation of the
story. One day after the morning hearings were over, the judge told
me a story about a man who was on probation for using crack
cocaine. Apparently he and his girlfriend were at his place and his
gun was lying on the kitchen table. "She picks it up, starts playing
with it, twirling it, etc. He tells her not to do that. She says, 'Oh, it's
not loaded' and shoots him in the head and kills him. She goes nuts.
[It was] truly an accident. She gets voluntary manslaughter. [They
do] an autopsy on him because it was a violent crime. When they
remove his clothes, they find in his pants pocket a condom, a probation officer's card, and a vial of crack." The judge adds, smiling rue-
fully, "That's his legacy."

"Sort of a metaphor for his whole life," I say.

"Exactly," he says, and nods.

I heard several stories about how misinformed the general public is regarding how well attorneys are paid. "People think we're rich
. . . rolling in it," one told me. He explained that the only wealthy
attorneys were those that worked in the large law firms in the bigger cities. One day at lunch, the judge told a story about his first
murder case as a court-appointed attorney:

> It was the late 1980s and I was paid $20 an hour. I spent endless
> hours and more than six months on this case—and lost. In the end,
> I billed the state $12,000. I got paid $6,000. By the time I paid my
> clerical staff and my overhead, I didn't even make minimum wage.
> (paraphrased)

He laughs as he tells this story and the other attorneys at the table
nod their heads in understanding. Other similar stories follow; stories like this unite members of a group through shared understanding. Stories like this are instructive to new members, as well as
researchers who are only temporary members.

We learn *local knowledge*, in Fisher's terms (1985) from stories,
and we learn about ourselves from them; our "self-concept is a
product of collected stories" (McAdams, 1985; Stone, 1998, as cited
in Browning, 1992).

One of the stories the judge told me taught me something about
him. We were talking about a murder case from several years earlier. A male student in his 40s stalked, raped, and murdered a young
female student at the university in our town. The trial was well pub-
licized and eventually resulted in a conviction and a death penalty

decision by the jury. The judge was talking about the trial and the penalty phase of that case. This is what happened on one of the last days of that phase:

> During the penalty phase of Mr. Kleypas' trial, the jury sent a note to me near the end of one day requesting early dismissal. They were deliberating about whether Mr. Kleypas would be sentenced to death. They were tired; it was the second full day of deliberations and they still hadn't reached a decision. I sent a note back, granting the request. However, this must be done formally as well. Everyone must adjourn to the courtroom with the jury being seated last. I assumed everyone had gathered in court, but when I walked in the courtroom, there were only a couple of deputies, and Mr. Kleypas was sitting alone at the defense table. I sat down at the bench to wait for everyone else to return. I noticed that Mr. Kleypas was crying. I realized that he must think that the jury was coming back to announce their decision. He was no doubt incredibly stressed and fearful. Feeling a little sorry for him, I looked at the defendant and said, "Mr. Kleypas, the jury hasn't reached a decision yet. I'm just going to dismiss them for the day." That was hard to see. (paraphrased)

While I could feel some sympathy for Mr. Kleypas (the judge always referred to him as "Mr."), I was more interested in the judge's response to him. At that moment, he saw the defendant as more than his crime. He saw him as a human being waiting for a decision that might end his life.

The Role of the Judge

There is no black and white in the law . . . only various shades of gray. People think that the law is black and white and then they're exposed to the system, either through being charged with a crime, or serving as a juror . . . and then they see the shades of gray.

Judge Donald Noland

Judges come to the bench as former lawyers, or advocates for their clients or for the state. Now, as judges, they must learn to be impartial and detached. This may be a difficult adjustment for some. In addition, most have practiced a specialized area within the law; their knowledge is narrowly focused. When they come to the bench, they must develop a much broader knowledge and understanding of the law in order to do their jobs.

The procedural role of the judge is to hear and decide legal dis-
putes, preside over trials, and monitor the conduct of cases presented to the court. The judge must ensure that the rights of the
accused are protected. Being a judge is more than the sum of its
parts. The judge sets the tone and demeanor for the court, for the
attorneys who argue their cases, and for the defendants and members of the public who sit in the courtroom. And this demeanor is as
unique as each individual judge.

During the winter and spring of 2003, I observed dozens of first
appearances and hearings. Eventually, I watched a trial. Many of the
accused had been in front of this judge several times before. The
attorneys referred to the repeat offenders as "frequent guests of
the criminal justice system." Sarcasm aside, what I saw was a level of
compassion and respect for people who came before this judge by all
involved in the process. Judge Noland sets this tone—and the attorneys, deputies, and clerks follow suit. He is responsible for how the
people who work in the system interact with one another and with
defendants and victims while in the courtroom.

Noland has been a district court judge since 1991, and was a
practicing attorney fifteen years prior to that. He talks about his
goals in the job. He simply wants "to be fair, to be prepared, and to
make the right decision." He makes it sound easy, though I know
that is not always the case. He wants to "make a difference," though
he admits to a certain amount of cynicism regarding this goal. He
gets frustrated because of the public's general perception of the
legal system. He says most people, when referring to the system or
the courts, ". . . don't know what they're talking about."

The challenges to the judge extend to what happens outside his
courtroom. The caseload has been tremendous on district courts
nationwide, and it continues to increase. Murphy et al. (2002)
explain that "the nation's ninety-four district courts process more
than 270,000 civil and 50,000 criminal cases each year—with more
than 20,000 resulting in trials" (p. 86). In the three counties served
by the 11th District, 12,000 cases are filed each year. Of those, 1,200
are criminal cases, 5,000 are civil, and 800 juvenile. Judge Noland is
one of six district judges, and he hears criminal and juvenile cases
almost exclusively. He told me "if five percent of the criminal cases
went to trial [nationwide] it would break the criminal justice system." When I first started my observations, the judge and attorneys
scheduled their dockets for Mondays, Tuesdays, Thursdays, and
Fridays. Wednesdays were designated as "no docket days"—essen-

tially "catch-up days." Several times those days were filled with first appearances and hearings. In a recent conversation, one of the attorneys told me that now they rarely have "no docket days."

The Role of the Prosecution

The most important thing is job satisfaction. You feel like you are doing good public service. I like trials. It's fun to win and sucks to lose, and I have lost before.

John Gutierrez, county attorney

I am sitting in the County Attorney's conference room, having lunch with County Attorney John Gutierrez and Deputy County Attorney Angie Trimble. We decide to spend this time talking about their work.

> Gutierrez talks about the primary job of the prosecutor: "Our job is to make sure that people's constitutional rights are not violated. I won't file a case if I think a person's rights have been violated and it's going to get suppressed anyway." He talks about how little the average citizen understands the plea bargaining process. "[The] general public needs to understand the guidelines for sentencing. The majority of guidelines result in probation; not everyone goes to prison."
>
> Trimble joins the conversation: "A prosecutor's job should be about justice; it shouldn't be about how many people can I put in jail."
>
> I try to summarize: "Your job is to ensure justice and protect the people."
>
> Gutierrez says in response, "Try to protect the people. We can't [do] anything to ensure a victim's safety. They [the public] have a misconception that we will [physically] protect them." He continues by saying that the public thinks "everybody should be penalized to the upper end of the law. The public doesn't understand that it doesn't work that way. We have a plea bargaining system and it [the legal system] would fall apart it we didn't have [it]. So you [have] to give up a lot to get that. It is about holding people accountable for their actions."

Plea bargaining is a necessary "evil." According to Judge Noland, the United States has a higher incarceration rate than any other nation and Kansas is in the top 15 percent in prison crowding. He says that if this trend continues, by the year 2072 there will be more people incarcerated than free in this country.

More than 90 percent of criminal cases in the United States are decided by plea bargaining. Heumann (1978) conducted a study of the new prosecutor views of plea bargaining, comparing it to the views of veteran prosecutors. He found that new prosecutors are unprepared for the process of plea bargaining; they do not know much about the criminal justice system because law school does not prepare them for the realities they will face. They see plea bargaining as a "necessary evil dictated by case volume . . . [and] trials as what the system is really about" (p. 204).

Experienced prosecutors have a very different view. They take an active role in the process, recognizing that if plea bargaining were eliminated (a fake issue, since it will never happen), the potential backlog of cases would clog the system. This is not, Heumann argues, the primary reason that prosecutors participate in plea bargaining. In reality, "the prosecutor seems almost to drift into plea bargaining" (p. 215). In the beginning he observes that his colleagues routinely do so, and he finds that defense attorneys expect him to do the same. As time passes, the prosecutor realizes that a big part of his job is to distinguish between the "serious" and the "nonserious" cases. His daily obligation to the disposition of cases means that he eventually sees little point in the "more formal adversarial process" (p. 216) that a trial represents.

One afternoon I sit down with Gutierrez for a lengthier conversation than I'd had over lunch with him and Trimble earlier in the year. We talk about the idea of justice. He tells me:

> After dealing with cases, plea bargaining, and knowing what you are working with you get an idea of what justice is in Crawford County. The definition of justice starts with Judge Noland. If you ask for more than what he's going to do, he's only going to do what he's going to do. You get an idea of what to ask for. To a certain degree justice is defined by the judge and his understanding and interpretation of the law.

We spend the majority of the conversation talking about the importance of the Fourth Amendment. This amendment protects the people against "unreasonable searches and seizures."

> We [prosecutors] are officers of the court. We are just as duty bound as a judge to make sure people [have not] had their rights violated by the police, by the government . . . Your house is your kingdom . . . This is where you have your highest expectation of privacy and that's what the Constitution protects. . . . For a police

officer to get into your house, they have to have a great deal of probable cause.

Near the end of the discussion, Gutierrez says,

> When you go to court you are rolling the dice. You can have the best case in the world and not get the outcome you want [or] expect. It can be a clear-cut, well-explained case and the jury can rule much differently than expected. You have to look at the strength of your case, what you can prove . . . you have to weigh and balance that.

"You're only as good as your last trial," he concludes.

The Role of the Defense Attorney

There have been only a handful of people that I've dealt with [defended] that either haven't realized that there are consequences to their actions or have not been remorseful at all. Those are the ones that scare me because it's human nature to feel some guilt [for wrong-doings].

Michael Gayoso, defense attorney

After the final hearing for the day, I am sitting in the jury box and the judge walks over to talk with me (to debrief) as he often does when I have been observing. I ask him about the defense attorney's responsibilities to a guilty client. I assume that the attorney might want to know in order to build a better defense. Suddenly some defense attorneys who overhear our conversation surround us joining the conversation. They make it clear that they do not want to know about a client's guilt. One says that he tells clients during the first meeting, "Don't even tell me if you're guilty; I don't want to know." They explain that a defense attorney's job is to protect the client's rights, not to find the truth. If the client admits guilt, then it is still the attorney's job to defend his rights, not to reveal the guilt. However, if a client admits guilt and insists on testifying, the attorney must inform him that he cannot lie about his guilt on the stand. He will advise him NOT to testify. If the client insists, and claims that he will lie about his guilt on the stand, the attorney cannot ethically participate in suborning known perjured testimony. In other words, the defense attorney will not participate in the process of questioning his client. The judge and prosecutor are apprised of the situation and the attorney has explained the consequences to the defendant before he testifies. At this point, the defendant is on his or her own.

McIntyre (1987) discusses the defense attorney's attitude about client guilt in her book *The Public Defender*, written about the criminal justice system in Cook County, Illinois. She explains that lawyers are trained to cope with complex issues, and to focus on legal rather than moral questions. This is difficult for the non-lawyer to understand. For example, ". . . the factual guilt or innocence of the client is *supposed* to be irrelevant. A lawyer is expected to take a point of view and argue it; a criminal defense lawyer is expected to put on a vigorous defense even when the client is known to be guilty" (p. 140).

One afternoon, the judge, Shane Adamson (defense attorney), and I are standing near the court clerk's desk talking. The atmosphere is amiable and light. I've been talking to Shane about my research and he says, "You make a lot of enemies in this job."

"So why do you do it?" I ask.

He makes some comment about being an adrenalin junkie, referring specifically to being in the courtroom. "It's all about winning," he explains. "Winning is everything. Losing is the pits."

McIntyre (1987) talks about the consequences for lawyers of losing and winning.

> Lawyers hate to lose because, although reason tells them a case is a loser, sentiment says that justice favors not the stronger case but the better lawyer. What makes losing any case, even a loser, so bad is their belief that, in the hands of a good attorney, there is really no such thing as a dead-bang loser case (p. 160).

Most of the attorneys she interviewed seemed to feel this way. For some defense attorneys, winning may have unpleasant consequences. She argues that one fear that public defenders have (though rarely talk about) is that an acquitted murderer may someday kill again. If it did happen, one lawyer admitted that he "probably would move into another branch of law" (p. 167). Success is a paradox for defense attorneys. If they lose, the client loses but society wins. If they win, the client wins but society loses if that client is guilty.

‖ ‖ ‖

One morning in February 2003 I meet with Ed Dosh. I have met him once before, so I am more or less prepared for his communication style, which leans toward loud and aggressive. I once heard someone describe him as "the Howard Stern of lawyers." It fits.

Ed is on the phone when I walk into his office and he motions me to a seat in front of his desk. His normal level of conversation sounds like shouting, so when he puts down the phone, he begins the conversation by shouting at me. I tell him about the research, why I want to talk with him, and he says, "Is that thing on?" (referring to my tape recorder).

"Yes," I answer, "is that okay?"

"Sure." Then he asks to read my research proposal. He asks a few questions while reading through it, and I try to answer. When he finishes, he says, "That sounds like some erudite ivory tower bullshit!"*

Trying to match his style so I won't feel intimidated, I say, "Erudite! Anyone who can wade through legal opinions and court documents deals with erudite every day!" We move on.

I ask him to tell me about being a defense attorney. He says, "That thing still on?"

I nod. "Okay, I got a statement for you! I'm a firm believer in spaying and neutering of human beings. . . ." He laughs, insisting he's serious. He explains that he's conservative economically and politically, and more liberal about social issues. That doesn't seem to fit with his pronouncement about sterilization, but I nod.

Then I ask him, "So why do you do this, if you feel that way?"

"'Cause I was too damn stupid, and I had the bright idea, some fantasy, that I was going to go to law school to help people!" He shakes his head, looking disgusted with himself.

"What's wrong with that?" I ask. "You do."

"Well, that's bullshit. Most of these people I represent don't—they'll say they want your help, but they'll turn around and do something five minutes later that basically tells you . . . they don't give a shit. . . . You know you really can't help most of these people—they're screwed up! You know, you're trying to change 30 years of—whatever!"

"But you help some of them. You must or you wouldn't keep doing this."

"Well, sure. Every now and then you get that rare case where you've got a person that really takes the system seriously, learns from his or her mistakes, and. . . ."

*Given the scientific character of the research presented in this book, Baylor University Press has made the decision not to censure any of the expletives included in the interviews.

I interrupt. "Well, isn't that one person every now and then worth it?" I know the question is a cliché, but I can't help myself.

"No. Not when you do thousands a year, or hundreds a year where you just butt your head against the wall."

The conversation continues in a similar vein. I learn that he's been doing the job for more than twenty-five years. He does admit that the job is never boring. I finally ask what is no doubt an obvious question: "Do you believe that everyone deserves a competent defense?"

"Yes . . . that's the oath you take in front of the bar," he says more quietly. Given his reputation for being an excellent litigator, I suspect he is telling the truth. I believe has been truthful throughout the interview. He may be a cynic, though it clearly does not prevent him from doing his job.

After my meeting with Ed, his partner Shane Adamson and I decide to talk over lunch. So, armed with my notebook and tape recorder, we head over to a bar and grill called Crissy D's. It reminds me of the kind of places I frequented as an undergraduate. It is a large, open room with old tables and chairs, a huge bar facing the center of the room, and wooden floors I suppose you could throw peanut shells on if you wanted to. There is an old-style jukebox next to the bar. It is hard to resist plugging in some quarters, so I remind myself why I am here.

Shane is easy to talk to. He is bright, has a gregarious nature and a great sense of humor. We talk about his background, how he got into law. He has been practicing since 1988 and has always done defense work. Defending people who are probably guilty is hard, he explains. "I think to some degree it destroys part of your humanity and you can't avoid it," he says. "[But] the concept is greater than any one person. And you believe that—at least initially you believe that. Hopefully you still believe it or you better get a new job." In the background, the juke is playing "You Can't Always Get What You Want" by the Rolling Stones. He explains:

> Somewhere around '93 or so I started to have a real crisis of conscience about what I was doing. It bothered me. I'd go out and get drunk all the time and commiserate to myself and to anyone who would listen to me how I was doing good things for bad people. And . . . and having a hard time adjusting to it and rationalizing it. And I suppose any lawyer with a conscience goes through that. And you just reach a point where you either get over it, or you get out of it. I came through that. There's a difference between intellectualizing it and seeing it. And once you see it, and you compare

it to the intellectualization, and your own moral code, you're gonna have a crisis at some point.

Ultimately there are times when you probably do some pretty good work for some pretty bad people. I've also seen enough abuse of power on the other side to realize that there are innocent people in jail as well. And therefore, fighting for someone who may be as guilty as the day is long is just as noble as fighting for the person who might not be or who maybe isn't. And you can't make a decision on that. If you start making decisions about people's guilt or innocence, you better get a different job.

McIntyre (1987) explains that the first eight amendments to the Constitution guarantee citizens protection from tyranny and prosecution by the government. "These rights, as they have come to be accepted in the law of the land, can be expressed in shorthand: no matter how serious the accusation, no matter who voices it, the accused is entitled to be innocent until proved guilty beyond a reasonable doubt" (p. 17). The Sixth Amendment guarantees counsel for the accused, and the Fourteenth Amendment specifically guarantees due process. The defense attorney's primary role is to protect these rights for his or her clients. "Although defense lawyers make it more difficult to convict defendants, in this country their role is justified by the idea that protecting the rights of innocent people is as important as punishing the guilty" (p. 28). In doing so, they help to "preserve the legitimacy of the courts" (p. 29).

‖ ‖ ‖

In mid-June I meet for lunch with Kathleen Cerne, an attorney on rotation to serve as a public defender. Once we get settled and place our order, we begin talking. Kathleen is a very direct person, and I worry a little about patrons seated close to us, thinking that our conversation might disturb, or at least distract them. In other words, I know she will not hesitate to express her opinions or to get to the "down and dirty" aspects of her job.

Interested since childhood in politics, she nonetheless had not planned to go to law school. She majored in business communication then studied pre-law at Pittsburg State University. Finally, she went to law school at the University of Missouri at Kansas City. She passed the bar in 1992 and set up practice in Pittsburg. After meeting Judge Noland in 1993 at a bar association banquet, she got on a felony appointment list and has served in that capacity ever since. She also serves as the misdemeanor defense attorney for the county.

Now she runs her office "on a shoestring budget." She has a personal assistant but she still does much of her own secretarial work. She explains that it is hard to keep up with all the legal work. The bottom line is, she does not like the job. In fact, she insists that she hates it. She would prefer teaching law or practicing something besides criminal law.

I asked her if there was anything about the job that she enjoyed:

> "When you win, it's exciting . . . when you do get an acquittal, especially when the state's case is based on witnesses that are unreliable . . . [that's good]." She thinks for a second. "I caught a cop in a lie . . . that was fun."

She talks about how cynical she's become because of the kind of people she deals with every day:

> I never knew that this 'subculture' existed. I grew up Catholic, got good grades, [and was] not exposed to that subculture. All these little towns are full of meth labs. I'm so sick of methamphetamines. [I] don't even want to hear that fucking word! [It leads] to theft, forgery, batteries, neglect, and abuse of children. It makes you want to puke!

I am reminded of the character Meg in the 1981 film *The Big Chill*. Meg is a demoralized and jaded defense attorney who tells her friends that she did not realize that her clients would be "so guilty."

Most of the people who walk through the court are low-income, uneducated, have physical and/or mental health issues, or all of the above. In short, they are greatly disadvantaged before they walk through the doors.

Substance abuse was a common theme in the cases I observed. Approximately 90 percent were drug or alcohol related. This is not surprising when I learned that the National Institute on Drug Abuse (NIDA) listed Kansas as third in the nation for the number of meth lab incidents (763) in 2002. In 2003 Kansas ranked fifth in the nation in number of meth labs seized, and first in seizures per capita ("Book Explores Kansas Meth Industry," 2003). Since then, the numbers have fallen (564 in 2004), but it is still a huge problem in this region. This is in part because there are more rural areas, and that makes it easier to hide the labs. Poverty is an issue as well. Meth is often referred to as the "poor man's cocaine," so it is not surprising that it is the drug of choice in this area of the country.

Closing Arguments

The people I observed working in the criminal justice system in southeast Kansas share a strong occupational identity and culture that allows them to manage the taints associated with their occupations. In most cases, they are proud of the work they do, though they all expressed some cynicism about the people they serve and their abilities as attorneys to make a positive difference. They maintain a positive work culture and individualize their identities through courtroom performances onstage as well as daily interactions offstage with co-workers. They share common meanings for the work, as evidenced in the stories and jokes that fly among them during breaks in court or before and after work in the court's inner offices. Embedded in the stories and humor are the values and beliefs these people share about the world outside the courthouse walls, a world that has only a surface understanding of what they do, how they do it, and who they are. These offstage interactions insulate (though not isolate) them against criticism from outsiders.

Afterword

It has been four years since I completed my observations of this criminal justice community. I am still not sure I can answer the question about *why* I am interested in this topic. The performances, both onstage in the form of legal rituals, and offstage, in the jokes and stories they exchange, interest me. But it is more than that. It is about the people I tried to represent here, about who they are, not just what they do. I have heard novelists say that the question from readers they dislike the most is, "Where do you get your ideas?" It is hard to answer, because they do not always know. They just get them. So, I guess I'm saying I don't know why I'm interested in these occupations, I just am.

Some parts of this were difficult in ways I had not anticipated. For example, at the beginning of the study, I spent time observing criminal and juvenile cases. After three or four days of observing juvenile court, I decided to limit my study to the criminal cases. At the time I told myself it would narrow my parameters and make my data more manageable. Soon after that I admitted to myself and to the judge that I just could not deal with the "kid cases." They were painful to watch. The abuse cases were hard, of course, though what really broke my heart were the cases of neglect; so many of these children are simply *ignored* by their parents. They are not properly fed or clothed, they do not attend school on any regular basis, and their parents seem to have forgotten that they exist.

At the beginning of my observations, I drove the twelve miles home each day excited about what I had learned, anxious to get my field notes typed. After several weeks I noticed that I felt my view of the world narrowing into two groups of people: "guilty and probably guilty of something." My world seemed to be full of drug users, child abusers, rapists, and wife beaters. My cynical attitude became apparent to me again when I drove to the university where I work on a sunny February afternoon to pick up something from the library. I had not been on campus in several weeks because I was on sabbatical. I drove slowly through campus, watching students walk to class, smiling and talking to one another. I had two clear thoughts. The first one was, "Every one of them . . . potential felons." It was clear I had adopted the viewpoints of the legal professionals. I not only saw the world from their viewpoint, I began to think it was *my* viewpoint. While I had some sympathy for the offenders, I had no real understanding of their experiences. As a white, middle-class female who never had more than a speeding ticket (okay, several speeding tickets) I was ill-prepared to see the world as they saw it. The second thought was that I would be coming back to this world soon. Not a world of "potential felons" (not all of them at least), but to a world of every-age college students, most of them wanting to be successful in life. For many, their biggest problem was how to pay their cell phone bills or how well they did on their last exam. And as much as I had enjoyed my time in the courtroom and with the people I had met, I was anxious to come back to this world.

Despite the difficulties I experienced, the judge and the lawyers whose stories I tell here are always on my mind to some extent. From my point of view, that is reason enough to continue to ask the questions about who they are and how they do what they do every day.

2

Dirty Work and Discipline behind Bars

Sarah J. Tracy & Clifton Scott

Over quesadillas at a local mexican restaurant, Nouveau Jail Correctional Officer Rick Neod described the most disgusting incident of his first six months working behind bars.

> I was working in disciplinary, and I had an unprocessed person. . . . Big guy, probably about 250 pounds, maybe 5'8", kind of short, stocky. . . . The guy, who was breaking me for lunch, comes back and says, "Our guy in 12 is smearing shit all over the wall." And I've heard stories about people with excrement issues, but this was the first time I had dealt with it . . . I almost had a reflex. I almost threw up, just seeing it. . . . He was actually writing on the wall names of girls that he had dated in the past. So me and Derrick went to get him out of his cell to move him up to isolation where he could be seen by crisis management, since he wasn't all there.
>
> We started talking to him, real laid back, like, "Whose are those names up there? Are those your girlfriends?" And he said, "Yeah." And Derrick was really good about it. . . . And the guy inserted his fingers into his mouth. And sucked on them. And that was just like, oh my gosh! It was a shock, but it's . . . kind of like a baptism for me, being exposed to that. He ended up, I mean, he was not combative with us. Derrick just opened up the door and the guy kept on licking his fingers. You can't stop him from licking his fingers.

Working as a correctional officer—the euphemistic and worker-preferred label for a "prison guard"—is a dirty job. Past research has classified the profession as a type of "dirty work" (Ashforth & Kreiner, 1999), and officers' activities are dirty physically, socially, and morally (Hughes, 1951). Officers have to work in a dreary environment imbued with the constant threat of violence and must engage in materially dirty activities such as cleaning up after inmates and conducting strip searches. They also deal with a socially stigmatized segment of the population (Davis, 1998), and therefore deflect the taint that rubs off from their inmate clients (Brodsky, 1982). Last, because officers feel disdain and moral questioning from the larger public, as well as from other criminal justice employees, officers continually have to make sense of, manage, and deflect moral taint associated with their job.

In this chapter, we provide a descriptive picture of the various types of dirty work correctional officers face and repeatedly combat. Examining dirty work among correctional officers is a particularly important issue, given the profession's high level of burnout, emotional stress, employee shortages, and turnover (Tracy, 2004b; 2005). Many of these problems are directly related to difficulties officers have in managing a preferred identity in the face of work duties and societal perceptions that suggest correctional officers are no more than "professional babysitters" and "the scum of law enforcement" (Tracy & Scott, 2006). In providing a description of officers' dirty work, we highlight the organizational practices and communicative interactions that continually reconstruct the filth associated with correctional work and the ways officers engage in "taint management" techniques to negotiate and temper the threatening "stain" of their work. Taint management occurs through day-to-day practices such as reframing dirty tasks as valuable and focusing upon positive aspects of the job.

Examining Dirty Work behind Bars

This analysis is based upon participant observation and interview data gathered over the course of eleven months (May 1999–March 2000) with officers at two correctional facilities, Women's Minimum Prison (WM), and Nouveau Jail (NJ), both located in the western United States. WM held about 400 convicted inmates, most classified as minimum security who walked the prison "campus" at will. NJ held about 385 inmates, with about 92 percent male and 8 percent female. About 60 percent of NJ's inmates were convicted and sentenced (generally for two years or less), while about 40 percent were awaiting court appearances. Depending on their security level, some NJ inmates were locked down in their cell, while others could wander into their pod's "dayroom."

Data Sources

The first source of data was field notes from 80 hours of shadowing 68 different correctional officers, taking down notes and engaging in "ethnographic interviews" (Lindlof & Taylor, 2002). Observations were focused on officers who interact directly with inmates, and barring the hours of 3 a.m. to 5:30 a.m., observations spanned all hours of the day. Second, 33 hours of training sessions were observed and numerous training documents were examined. These data included information on the inmate mentality, emergency protocols, professionalism, effective communications, inmate mental health and management, court procedures, stress management, and physical defensive tactics. Last, 22 in-depth recorded interviews were conducted with correctional employees: 10 with NJ officers, nine with WM officers, and three with organizational supervisors, including the WM warden, NJ captain, and NJ sheriff. Interviews ranged from 45 minutes to two hours.

Methods of Analysis

We viewed the qualitative data, not as a "mirror" of reality, but as a potentially promising way of opening up the scene (Denzin, 1997). We used an iterative, grounded theory approach (Glaser & Strauss, 1967; Lindlof & Taylor, 2002), analyzing the data for recurring patterns. This approach calls for researchers to classify data texts into categories, write analytic memos about the meaning of these categories, and add new incidents to categories until they become "theoretically saturated." Categories for this analysis were inspired by Ashforth and Kreiner's (1999) dirty work model and various types of taint management. Furthermore, other themes, such as "distancing," "differentiating," and "blaming the inmate" also emerged as salient taint management techniques.

The Physical, Social, and Moral Dirty Work of Corrections

A preponderance of prison and jail work is routine and executed in order to *avoid* problems. Officers continually engage in service and security routines, such as watching inmates, contractors, and visitors;

conducting inmate "count"; and searching cells and bodies for contraband. As one officer said, "A good day at work would be a day where nothing happens." Of course, given the nature of the job, "nothing" is not always achieved. The routines of correctional work are punctuated with disgust, depression, and danger, and officers must continually navigate the taint associated with the social and moral stigmas of the job.

Physical Dirty Work: Disgust and Danger

Correctional officers often deal with behavior that most people would consider physically disgusting. For instance during inmate visitation (with friends and family), officers chaperone inmates to the bathroom (to ensure inmates do not hide contraband on/in their body), and conduct inmate "strip outs" after the visitation session. During strip-outs, officers (of the same sex as the inmate) check inmates' every body cavity, including inside their mouth, between their toes, and around their genital area. Female inmates are required to "squat and cough" while male inmates are required to "squat, cough, and lift." Officers described strip-outs as stomach-turning at worst and embarrassing at best (Tracy, 2004a). After strip searches officers said things like, "I've just returned from the depths of hell" and "Lord, save me!" NJ Officer Michael Martinez explained, "I've actually had to take a bar of soap and say *use* this." Another officer said, "Some of the strip searches I have done would totally amaze you. The things that I have seen and the attachments people put on their bodies. . . . A ring attached to the guy's penis, tongue things and earrings and stuff, nipple things, you name it. I've seen it in almost every place you can imagine."

As vividly illustrated in the opening of the chapter, officers also have to deal with "excrement issues." During the span of the research officers told stories about inmates who ate their feces and one who was well known for "making M&Ms out of her poop" to throw at officers. Officers also spoke of having to deal with inmates who, for instance, would destroy property, try to hurt themselves, engage in exhibitionism, rape or assault other inmates, flood their cells, urinate out their cell doors, and throw soft drinks, juice, or urine at officers. While these types of incidents were not common, discussion about them was, and correctional officers were responsible for cleaning up the messes that such occasions left behind.

The routines of correctional work are physically dirty not only because of close contact with material dirt and disgust, but also because of the job's danger—a key factor in professions that are considered to be physically dirty (Ashforth & Kreiner, 1999). One officer cracked, "You're dealing with people that would rather slice you up than talk to you." While violence in the two facilities was rare, a preponderance of employee training involved preparing correctional officers for physically dangerous scenarios. During a particular "defensive tactics" session of NJ's in-service training, the trainees put into practice all of the physical defensive tactics they had learned throughout the week. The trainers, who were dressed in bright, padded suits, played the "bad guys" and a group of three or four officers had to react. The training group was quite relaxed and somewhat excited to have the opportunity to "beat up" their trainers. However, in one scenario, one of the "bad guy" trainers pulled a (plastic) knife and proceeded to "stab" one of the officers. The stabbed trainee officer stopped in his tracks, nervously laughed and announced to the other officers, "I'm dead!" The other trainees also halted their defensive tactics activities, seemingly embarrassed. Then one of the trainers yelled sternly, "You're still going—just because one of you is dead doesn't mean you stop!" The atmosphere instantly changed from playful to somber. In the flash of a plastic knife, the high stakes of defensive tactics became apparent. The training was not just a game. If officers did not correctly handle these incidents, they could die.

However salient, the attack during defense tactics training was pretend. Several months later, one of the officers involved in the preceding training recalled an *actual* assault that occurred during his shift. NJ Officer Fish Tyler said:

> I was working in DSM [disciplinary/special management] one night, and there was this one guy that was having troubles, so I waited until later in the evening to let him out for his hour. Well, I opened up the guy's cell and he looked scared to come out of his cell, so I kind of had to coax him out. . . . Meanwhile, another inmate started yelling and throwing water out of his cell so I went over to talk to him and calm him down.
>
> Then, I heard this awful scream. It was the most awful scream I had ever heard in my whole life and it just rung out through the pod. It was the other officer—a female—I was working with, and it was so awful I felt just sure that she was being stabbed. I can't even describe how awful it was . . . I saw this guy with his hands around [the other officer's] neck, strangling and punching her. I tackled him and he hit the ground hard enough that it knocked him out.

But that sound of the screaming—that was the most awful thing I
had ever heard—it scared me so bad.

When Officer Tyler told this story during his interview, his face
became increasingly red, and several times he formed his hands into
fists. It appeared as though the poignant memory of his partner's
"awful scream" was going to stay with him for a long time.

While several officers claimed they "very infrequently" or
"never" felt scared by inmates in their job, officers nevertheless
constantly dealt with the *threat* of inmate violence. Almost all officers said they had received some sort of inmate threat—some death
threats, others somewhat tamer such as "You're going down."
Officers said, "You're constantly on the lookout . . . you're constantly
wondering whether the inmates are going to have a bad day and
react and jump on you." As NJ Officer Rusty Malloy said, "If somebody's in a fight, you may get hurt, somebody else may get hurt. . . .
We found shanks [homemade knives] in the jail recently . . . so it's
possible that somebody could really get deliberately hurt."

Social Dirty Work: Serving as "Glorified Maids" to Criminals

In addition to physical taint, correctional officers face social taint
because their work requires a servile relationship to clients who are
already stigmatized. According to trainers, more than 30 percent of
inmates are mentally ill, up to 85 percent are classified as anti-
social, and 85–90 percent of female inmates have a background of
physical and/or sexual abuse. In addition to these material realities
of inmates, the public has "washed their hands" of criminals (Tracy
& Scott, 2006). Correctional institutions represent a failure in social
functioning and are thus hidden, isolated, invisible, and silent
(Brodsky, 1982; Foucault, 1977). Referred to as a "contagion effect"
(Brodsky, 1982), criminal stigma rubs onto workers, and officers
sometimes are regarded by outsiders to be not so different from the
population they control. This contagion effect is worsened because
officers must not only interact with inmates, but often must serve as
inmates' "glorified maids."

Indeed, officers often remarked with chagrin that, in many
ways, they served not only as "glorified maids," but also as "babysitters," "airline stewards/stewardesses," or "camp counselors." WM
Officer Jack Clafin said, "I [feel] like an airline steward, really, walk
around with a cart, 'What do you want now? Okay, here's your food.
. . . Do you want juice or Coke? No you can't have both. You can only
have one.' " WM Officer Dave LaBell said, "It's stressful to listen to

the inmates give you lip service every day and just want to tell them to shut up, but you can't." The service part of the job is so prominent that Nouveau Jail quit requiring college degrees for its officers. As NJ Captain Henry McMaster explained, a preponderance of the correctional job is not about inmate counseling, but rather is about "getting people toilet paper."

Training sessions and officer comments also indicate that inmates are considered emotional, verbal, whiny, untrustworthy, and disrespectful. One officer said, "You can go into law . . . if you can handle the emotional stress of everybody cursing you out or trying to spit on you." Another said the hardest part of the job was "listening to inmates run their mouth to you all the time. . . . You tell them to do something and they give you lip service for ten minutes." WM Officer Jack Clafin said, "Women [inmates] are 'me, me, me' and each thinks their problem is the worst."

Inmates can also be stigmatizing because of their level of perceived insanity and intoxication. As illustrated in the following field note, inmates can be noncooperative and scream endless abuse at officers.

> When I arrive at Nouveau's booking room, a man is strapped to a restraint chair in the back room. He is screaming, "Cancer upon you! Cancer upon your anus." He pauses for a moment as I retreat from his line of vision. Imitating an officer, he says, "What is your name?" Then, responding as himself, "My name is I didn't kill [a girl who had recently been murdered in Nouveau City]. The Nouveau PD did!" Five minutes later he yells, "You don't have enough fucking dick to fight a man . . . you kill little girls with billy clubs." Ten minutes go by and he screams out, "Thank you, murderous pedophiles! Thank you, pedophile murderers! I'm glad you are pedophile murderers. Thank you for ruining my life." In response to this, one officer says to another, "I think he's had too much to drink." The other says sarcastically, "Do you think? No, I think it's his personality." The guy in restraints continues screaming at the top of his lungs, "Satanic fucking pedophile. . . ." The officers are totally ignoring this, going about their work. Sgt. Tom Enriques walks by and says, "I think he's talking to me, but I tuned him out about an hour ago. I have auditory exclusion that hits after 2 a.m."

Despite the volatility of the inmate, Tom did attempt to counsel him. The sergeant explained to the man that it was his continuous screaming that was keeping him in the restraints, saying, "You be cool with us and we'll be cool with you. Listen, you just be quiet for

fifteen minutes or so. Show us that you can, and then you can lay
down and go to sleep." Eventually, after an hour of screaming, the
man kept quiet for the next twenty minutes. As promised, Tom let
the man out of restraints. The inmate promptly flopped down to the
cell-floor mat and passed out. There was never an apology or damage repair. A primary part of correctional officers' duties is to deal
with and absorb this type of verbal abuse as endemic to the job.

Social taint also emanated from the sadness and guilt associated
with working with imprisoned people. On a daily basis, officers handle situations that many people would view as depressing or sad.
Officers accompany inmates to the doctor when they get sick, and
write detailed reports when inmates die—whether they pass away
from natural causes, drug overdoses, or suicide. NJ Officer Derrick
Garcia said he had witnessed a number of inmates try to hurt themselves, including a male inmate who committed suicide by "taking a
nose dive" off the second tier of a pod, and another who burned his
stomach lining by gulping down bleach that was out for cleaning.
When these things happen, officers often feel guilty as well as fear-
ful that they might be sued by family members, internally investi-
gated by facility administration, or stigmatized by coworkers.

More so than these shocking incidents, many of officers' day-to-
day duties are dreary. For instance, a number of officers indicated
that they found monitoring inmate visitation sessions to be heart-
wrenching, because as one officer said, it required seeing inmates as
"parents, mothers, fathers, and children." During visitation, officers' security duties include reprimanding inmates who hug their
visitors for longer than ten seconds, or hold a visiting child in their
lap. Long hugs and lap-sitting children can hide the transfer of contraband, and thus, the activities are prohibited. For inmates
assigned to the segregation unit of WM, visitation logistics are even
stricter. Officers are required to cuff, shackle, and belly-chain
inmates in front of their loved ones and stand watch, for instance,
while bawling inmates kiss their children through the glass parti-
tion. As the WM nurse commented while passing through the visitation area on Christmas Day, "I'm glad I'm a nurse, or I'd sit here
bawling."

Moral Dirty Work: Working as the "Scum" of Law Enforcement

In addition to physical and social dirty work, officers also manage
perceptions that their work is morally dubious. Of course, it is of little surprise that correctional officers regularly face public misper-

ceptions about the morality and importance of their job. As total institutions (Goffman, 1961; Tracy, 2000), prisons and jails are purposefully cut off from most people's life paths. While correctional officers are able to escape the institution during their nonwork hours, even when they do so, people outside of the correctional atmosphere largely denigrate the profession. Officers consistently manage the defensive attitude of facility visitors and members of groups affiliated with prisons. Among other things, one of us participated in an information session in which a Christian prison volunteer group negatively portrayed correctional officers as "non-Christians" who did not care very much about inmates' well-being. Furthermore, facility visitors consistently made sarcastic and rude remarks when they learned that they would be pat searched before entering the facility.

Indeed, officers indicated both spontaneously and in interviews that most outsiders do not understand the correctional environment and are largely confused as to why anyone would want to work behind bars. In response to the interview question, "Do your friends, family, or the public in general have correct perceptions of your job," NJ Officer Max Simpson responded passionately:

> No, no, absolutely not. Not even this much (holding his fingers close together). Not even that much (bringing his fingers within a fraction of an inch of each other). . . . They think of all cops the same—as the guys that pull you over.

Another officer explained how friends and neighbors said things like, "Oh, now you're one of *them*." The officer never explained what "them" meant (nor, presumably, did his neighbors and friends); nevertheless, "them" was certainly not something good, but was rather dirty, stained, weird, and unknown. Unlike some such jobs— say the Marines, FBI, firefighters, or Navy Seals—that are considered mysterious or exotic, correctional officers were considered deviant and strange. Officer comments illustrate how the public viewed officers as lax and lazy, brutal, sexually deviant, or silly and stupid.

First, a number of officers indicated frustration in public perceptions that the prison system was too easy. One officer said that after providing a tour of the facility for the public, some of the visitors made comments about how it was ridiculous that inmates could watch television, engage in arts and crafts, or work out in a recreation center. He expressed confusion saying, "We're supposed to be rehabilitating them and then the public gets mad because we're helping them stay connected to the world and learn a few skills? I don't get it." While officers faced criticism for making inmates' lives too easy, they simultaneously faced perceptions that they were too hard on inmates. The idea that officers are brutal is largely perpetuated in sensationalized mass media portrayals of officers. Indeed a new officer said that, based on movies that portrayed "terrible flashing, perverted talk, all that stuff," he thought the job was going to be much worse than it was. WM Officer Dave LaBell said, "They think that officers have sex with the inmates, the drugs are rampant, you have no control." WM Officer Luke Gollett said, "In movies, they depict us as brutal, disrespectful to them. We hurt them, we beat them up. You know, like *Shawshank Redemption*. One guy was going to throw a guy off the roof. . . . It makes us look like we're all brutal."

Questions about the moral worth of the job do not just emanate from nameless, faceless media outlets. Officers said they also had to deal with disdainful medical personnel. One explained, "A lot of the times the nurses and doctors frown at us and make comments about us, like, 'That's cruel,' because we'll come in with women who are hand-cuffed, belly-chained, their ankles cuffed together." NJ Officer Fish Tyler explained,

> We had a nurse who was working here and taking some classes at [a nearby university] and when one of her classes found out that she was working at the jail, her classmates told her that she was working with a bunch of white male racists!

Male officers at WM also commented on how they had to fight the perception that they were "lucky" to be working among all those "lonely, pretty women in prison."

Others felt as though their friends and family thought their job was easy and stupid. An officer said he wished people realized, "That we're hard-working, not stupid. We do more than watch monitors and babysit inmates." NJ Officer Bobby Jon Herria said, "They think . . . you throw them their food. . . . They really have no clue about the personal communication that we have with people." Likewise, NJ Officer Rusty Malloy said that many of her friends thought her job was about "pushing buttons and doors are sliding and that's all there is to it. . . . I don't think they realize the interaction." Many of these comments sounded as if they were rehearsed, as if officers were quite used to defending and justifying the worth of their job to others.

Even though a number of officers said they hung out with cops, they ironically also had to deal with being disparaged by fellow law enforcement officers. WM Officer Nick Axel explained that at a recent neighborhood barbecue, cops who were guests commented that there was "no way" they could work corrections. He explained, "Corrections is like the crappiest job in the criminal justice system. Some agencies don't consider DOC a law enforcement agency." Other officers also complained about their subordinate positions in the law enforcement hierarchy, saying things including, "Police officers don't consider us to even be in their same category." They said that police officers usually labeled correctional officers in one of two metaphorical categories—either as *scum* or as *babysitters*. For instance, officers said "we're the scum of law enforcement" and "we are considered the dregs of the police department." The scum metaphor is interesting in that officers also often referred to inmates using the same label. In this way, officers and inmates were in the same pond of scum, so to speak.

At least ten correctional officers also spontaneously indicated that other police officers referred to them as babysitters—a label that connotes low-status women's work. Comments included, "Police officers just think we're glorified babysitters"; "They consider us professional babysitters, and on occasion, you start to wonder, well maybe I am"; "I've heard police officers . . . call us professional babysitters. That bothers me 'cause we're locked up and these police officers, they put them in jail and we're with them all day long." When officers are labeled as babysitters, they are put in a category of unimportant, low-status, female workers. So, how do officers manage the identity threats associated with work that is dirty physically, socially, and morally?

Managing the Taint of Dirty Work

Correctional officers may face a very dirty job, but they also engage in a number of creative taint-management strategies that help them manage their identity in the face of this identity threatening work. Such taint-management techniques enable dirty workers to achieve an acceptable collective identity and individual sense of self at work. The following discussion reviews the various ways correctional officers go about managing taint via Ashforth and Kreiner's (1999) three specified methods of taint management: reframing, recalibrating, and refocusing. We follow these with several strategies not specified by Ashforth and Kreiner (1999); taint-management practices of distancing, differentiation, and blaming the client also emerged as salient for helping correctional officers navigate their dirty work.

Reframing: Serving as Societal Saviors and Just Being Part of the System

A primary way correctional officers do taint management is through reframing—that is, "transforming the meaning attached to a stigmatized occupation" (Ashforth & Kreiner 1999, p. 421). Reframing is accomplished through *infusing* or imbuing the stigma with a positive value or a "badge of honor," and through *neutralization*, wherein the negative value of the stigma is negated, denied, or rationalized. As illustrated in the following comment, correctional officers *infuse* the job by discussing the unique abilities required for this difficult work. When I asked NJ Officer Dan Vernon the question, "What are some things that you think would be the hardest thing for me to understand or know [about your job]?" Officer Vernon responded,

> The department psychiatrist probably has answered that. She says, "*Why on earth* would you people want to deal with the people of society that society doesn't want to deal with?" I can't answer that question totally.

While Officer Vernon said he was unable to answer the question, he did go on to explain how an important part of the job was feeling as if he helped out where others could not.

Indeed, some officers chose to view their work role as serving as a type of societal savior—as people who would take on a difficult and disliked job that most people could not handle. WM Officer Chris Verner boasted, for instance, about how he convinced a particularly difficult inmate to fill out paperwork and that no one else had been able to accomplish this. Furthermore, he was quite proud of being one of the few segregation officers at whom this inmate had not thrown soft drinks or urine. NJ Officer Dan Robbins told an in-depth story about helping an inmate whom he had first met fifty years earlier. Through the story, Dan framed himself as helping out in a way that other officers could not, and in this way, he saw himself as a "savior" to his friend. In similar vein, NJ Officer Max Simpson said, "I want to make this world a better place for [my children] and that's my ultimate goal in life. . . . I like to teach some of the young [inmates] that." Officers also talked to each other about the vital importance of their job, allowing them to feel good about work that many would consider dirty and distasteful.

In addition to infusing, officers also used the tactic of *neutralizing* wherein they tried to negate, deny, or rationalize their role in the "dirty" parts of their job. For instance, officers would occasionally discuss their disillusionment with a justice system that they agreed did not work very well. An officer at WM said, "It's amazing to me that these women get 25 years for killing their husbands and the husbands that kill their wives get five years. It just makes no sense." WM Officer Lara Huanes also seemed sad and resigned as she discussed how she believed that certain programs should be set up in the prison. Huanes seemed to feel guilty that these programs did not exist and appeared to be confused about how she might play a role in making these things happen. Likewise, NJ Officer Kyle Johnson seemed disillusioned with the system. As he looked at the special management pod on Thanksgiving Day, he mused to no one in particular, "I'm not sure our judicial system is doing justice to any of these people." Another officer was upset that a mentally ill inmate kept getting recycled through the system. When I asked about this inmate, he shook his head as he said,

> There are lots of people here that shouldn't be. The thing is, mental health programs are meant for rehabilitation, not warehousing. So they put 'em through a few classes and they get a tiny bit better and then they let 'em out again. Also, if you're not rehabilitatable, then they won't keep you. So they end up here.

Even the Nouveau sheriff, who had much more power than did officers, seemed somewhat cynical about the system, commenting that "the way we do probation is largely ineffective, because we're trying to make silk purses out of sow's ears."

Officers managed this disillusionment by reminding themselves that they were only one small part of the system, and had very little power to change the policies and procedures that they saw as being problematic. They were resigned to just "following the rules" and "doing their job." By distinguishing their work of *carrying out* policies and procedures as different from the work of constructing them, correctional officers distanced themselves from the features of their work they viewed as ineffective and attempted to neutralize some of the moral dirt of the job.

Recalibrating: Danger and Toughness as the Best Parts of the Job

Ashforth and Kreiner (1999) describe a second family of taint-management strategies as *recalibrating*, wherein employees adjust their criteria of what equals a valued attribute of dirty work and magnify the non-stigmatized parts of the job. Correctional officers engaged in recalibrating by emphasizing the most "dangerous" parts of the job as most desirable. For instance, at Nouveau County Jail, only the most tenured and experienced officers were allowed to work the "disciplinary pod" where the more problematic inmates were placed. In contrast, the duty of overseeing "visitation," which required officers to be servile and polite as well as conduct physically disgusting "strip-ins" and "strip-outs" was largely devalued.

Recalibration is also evident in officers' self-deprecating humor. For instance, one said to another, "Hey, did you hear our life expectancy has gone up to 57?" This comment may be particularly significant since the number quoted by the officer in this particular joking session—57—is actually two years below the 59-year life expectancy of officers (Cheek, 1984). In other words, the officers exaggerated their early deaths, and *laughed about it*. This type of joking allowed officers to portray themselves as tough, different, and exotic.

Some officers also seemed proud, or at least resigned, to being framed as mean or unlikable. For instance, WM Dave LaBell described himself as an "asshole every day." During a walk-through of the WM facility, Officer Stephanie Jones introduced two officers by immediately highlighting their negative personas; both the officers seemed fine with it. First, she introduced an officer saying, "You're probably the most hated officer right now, huh?" He smiled in return and said, "Yeah, probably, but some of them are starting to stick up for me." Jones introduced another officer saying, "This is McDonald—he's been written up by officers and inmates eight different times." Officer McDonald laughed and agreed, unaffected by the insinuation that he was a bad officer. Some officers seemed comfortable and proud of framing themselves as mean. They turned a potential stigma into a sign of toughness.

Refocusing: "I Do It for the Money"

When a third type of taint management called *refocusing* is employed, discourse shifts attention away from stigmatized job features to valued employment aspects. Refocusing is different from recalibrating and reframing because it does not involve transforming meaning or valuation of task features. Instead, it enables members to overlook specific job dimensions entirely. Thus, refocusing requires members to "willfully disattend to features of work that are socially problematic" (Ashforth & Kreiner, 1999, p. 423) and focus upon features that are not inherent to the work itself.

Correctional officers *refocused* by playing up the nurturing and altruistic job features rather than the drudgery and disciplinary tasks. Many officers discussed how their job allowed them to help and interact with others and deal with difficult situations that others could not handle. As NJ Officer Rusty Malloy said, "I like talking with inmates and helping them solve their problems." NJ Officer Derrick Garcia expressed self-satisfaction from being known among inmates as a "straight-shooter," while Officer Sam Rule explained to me that he liked working along with inmates in order to give them a positive role model. These portrayals draw attention to those tasks and challenges that others would be unable to accommodate, and in doing so, the officers distinguish themselves in terms of their rare skills.

In addition to officers focusing on these "happier" parts of the job, many officers refocused on the tangential perks that the job provided for them. For instance, WM Officer Nick Axel explained that he stayed in the job because, "I make a lot of money." The salary (more than $30,000 in 1999) allowed Axel to focus on his "real interests"—running an outside business, spending time with his family and going to graduate school part-time. Another well-respected WM Officer, Dean Everlast, also refocused, saying, "I've got a lot of outside interests. . . . I own my own business with collectible art, designing athletic equipment, and then my karate." NJ Officer Bob Traxler spontaneously asked, "Why do you think anyone in their right mind would stay in a job like this?" Traxler said he did the job, at this point in his life, only because it was good money and he was too close to retirement to stop now. Even the officers, like Traxler, who complained bitterly and appeared extremely burned out in the job still offered up the motivation that "only a fool would leave," because of the good money and enviable retirement benefits.

As illustrated, officers engaged in a number of taint management techniques that fall into Ashforth and Kreiner's (1999) conceptualizations of reframing, recalibrating, and refocusing. However, the data analysis suggests several other taint management strategies that have not typically been identified by dirty work theorists.

Distancing, Depersonalizing, and Blaming the Stigmatized Party

One of the ways officers managed the stigma of their work was through the techniques of distancing, depersonalizing, and sometimes actively blaming the stigmatized party—which in this case is the inmate. By engaging in such tactics, officers were able to maintain feelings of control over the unwieldy, sometimes materially filthy, bodies of their work, and achieve (an often superior) distance from the socially stigmatized criminal element of their jobs.

First, employees did a lot of work to distance themselves physically from inmates. Officers tried to avoid standing within six feet of or turning their backs on inmates, and most kept their correctional officer booths locked so that inmates could not enter without permission. While some of these tactics were used for security reasons, they also allowed officers to maintain distance from the "whiney, verbal" inmates with whom they preferred not to interact. Some officers maintained distance through refusing eye contact with inmates or by wearing sunglasses. Further, even though officers were technically allowed to shake hands with inmates, some officers avoided any type of physical contact. For instance, NJ Officer Rick Neod discussed an incident in which he had counseled a potentially suicidal inmate. Apparently, after the interaction, the inmate had been really thankful. Holding out his hand to Neod, the inmate had said, "I really appreciate what you did for me." Telling me about the incident later, Neod said, "I was like, uhhh, and I shook his hand, which I really shouldn't do, but I was comfortable with him at the time." I asked about his reticence in shaking the inmate's hand, and the officer explained,

> Oh, it just gives something to grab. A guy's just in off the street, he could be just scamming you. You give someone a hand they can grab your hands and break your fingers. I personally just don't like the health aspects of it all. You don't know where they've been, what they do. You see some of the things at the jail, what people do; you don't want to touch them.

So, part of Neod's reticence was due to his suspicion of getting tricked, while part of it was his wariness of where the inmate's hands had been. Given this officer's experience with the inmate who ate his own feces (described in the opening of the chapter), it is understandable that he might attempt to avoid touching inmates in a variety of situations. Doing so serves to maintain physical distance from the social and physical dirt associated with imprisoned criminals.

To complement the technique of maintaining physical distance from inmates, correctional officers also evidenced an awesome ability for depersonalizing inmates and tuning out their abuse and complaints. Sgt. Tom Enriques (described above as the Nouveau sergeant who dealt with the screaming male inmate in restraints) boasted of "auditory exclusion that hits after 2 a.m." Officers "tuned out" and ignored inmates through closing the little window in their officer booths, essentially discouraging inmate questions, complaints, or requests. For instance, NJ Officer Bobby Jo Herria gave an example of an inmate in special management who was really difficult. She said,

> He'll come and talk to you fifteen times in a night. He just demands a lot of attention and for the most part, that's fine, but there are definitely certain nights when a lot of things are going on when you just want to say, "Stay away from my window, don't talk to me for an hour" or "don't come back."

Indeed, officers shut inmates out a number of times. For instance, inmates would come to the correctional officer window and ask for something and officers would say, "Yeah, yeah, okay," without doing anything.

Ignoring inmates was also a way of avoiding direct confrontation with inmate verbal abuse or unwanted sexual attention. Some officers indicated that when inmates were rude, they would just smile or ignore it. Female officers explained how they ignored catcalls and lewd gestures. Sarah personally found herself avoiding eye contact with male inmates. In one instance, when a male inmate came to the correctional officer booth and offered Sarah "scotch and cookies," she laughed, but also made sure she did not look toward that particular inmate for the rest of the observation. Doing so achieved a feeling of distance from the potentially threatening inmate, and effectively discouraged further interaction.

Sometimes correctional officers went beyond physical distancing and social depersonalization to blaming the inmate client actively. Employees engaged in such blame, in part, in order to neutralize their role in the stigmatized work. For instance, correctional officers consistently reminded themselves that inmates deserved their lot, and that they, themselves, were not responsible for inmates' complaints. For instance, when shadowing WM Officer Mindy Allen, an inmate decided to start complaining to Sarah about the prison and its programs. Sarah just sat, listened, and nodded her head as the inmate complained about issues ranging from "crappy public defenders" and "awful drug programs that don't rehabilitate you" to "unfair patrol officers" and "expensive meds." Officer Allen completely ignored the inmate during the complaint session. After the inmate finally left (about fifteen minutes later), Sarah said to Officer Allen, "I didn't know what to do with that woman so I just kind of nodded and smiled." Allen said, "Yeah, that's what I do. Just nod and smile and think to myself, 'Yeah what got 'ya in here, huh?' Like we say, they have to work *really hard* to get in here."

Through turning the blame back onto the inmate, Allen was able to deny responsibility for the inmates' complaints and make sense of the dirty work in a way that did less to threaten the viability and value of the correctional officer position. While Allen did this through self-talk, other officers verbally reminded inmates that it was their own fault for being where they were. In an interview, WM Officer Nick Axel explained:

> An inmate says something to you, "Well, I don't think my rights are being met because of this." I tell them, "Well, let's talk about the rights of your victim. You remember your victim, that's the reason you're here, because you have a victim. . . . Oh, you're not getting your hygiene, well, how about your victim? When you broke into your victim's house and stole their TV, did you think later . . . that they couldn't watch TV? But now you're worried about soap?"

Through this comment, Axel negates his role in the problems faced by the inmate. Axel suggests that it is not his fault that the inmate is not getting his soap. Rather, it is the inmate's fault for being incarcerated in the first place.

The technique of blaming the stigmatized party goes beyond the practice of negating one's role in the stigmatized work. It also strategically suggests superiority over a dirty party. This is why blaming the stigmatized party is different than the neutralization category proposed by Ashforth and Kreiner (1999). Correctional officers would often refer to inmates as the "scum of the earth," and make fun of them, calling them "stupid" and "lazy." As one NJ officer said in defending his job, "The thing that makes it easy is that they're all stupid. Their thinking process just isn't there." Some officers also engaged in practices where they would "inadvertently" punish inmates, for instance, by pretending they could not hear their requests, or loudly banging cell doors when delivering food or laundry (Tracy, Myers, & Scott, 2005). Especially in these servile endeavors, when officers were forced to act like "flight attendants," they engaged in work to distance themselves from the role of the stigmatized party, and in doing so, engaged in taint management.

Conclusion

In this chapter, we have illustrated the everyday practices that make correctional work dirty, and the ways that officers manage taint. Not only must correctional officers deal with situations that are disgusting, dangerous, and depressing; but they work in an environment imbued with the social stigma of criminality; and must manage their identity in light of suspicion from outsiders that their job is immoral, brutal, deviant, and easy. Despite these difficulties, officers find a number of creative ways to manage the taint of their work. They reframe stigmatized tasks as badges of honor, refocus on tangential perks of the job and engage in a variety of activities that create physical and social distance (and superiority over) their inmate clients. These activities suggest that officers are quite resilient and creative in their taint management skills, and that a lot of effort goes into making sense of their job in preferred ways.

However, the analysis also suggests that correctional officers may face challenges in taint management due to their work environment. Unlike firefighters for instance, who can engage in sexual horseplay and fraternity-type antics (Tracy & Scott, 2006), or flight attendants who can gather in the galley and reframe a problem passenger as a spoiled child (Hochschild, 1983), correctional officers primarily work alone. While many dirty occupations foster cohesive work groups that in turn facilitate "esteem-enhancing social identities" (Ashforth & Kreiner, 1999, p. 419), correctional officers may serve as an exception. Because officers do not work in groups with their peers, they have fewer opportunities to reframe dirty work collectively. Indeed, the lack of camaraderie and social support in the correctional scene has been found to aggravate officers' efforts at providing effective service (Tracy, 2005). Working alone also restricts opportunities to communicatively coconstruct a preferred occupational identity (Heinsler, Kleinman, & Stenross, 1990).

Working alone is exacerbated by the total institution (Goffman, 1961; Tracy, 2000) aspect of correctional organizations. Extra-organizational factors—such as the views of family, neighbors, and the community at large—are no less important than intra-organizational factors in determining people's attitudes to their jobs (Drory & Shamir, 1988). As illustrated, correctional officers face moral questioning from a variety of individuals inside and outside of the criminal justice profession. Unfortunately, the total institution aspect of their work makes it difficult for officers to receive social support and reassurance even from their friends and family. Correctional officers mention that the routine and pace of prison life is so different from the "outside" that family members would not understand their problems, and even if they did, stories would only serve as cause for worry (Blau, Light, & Chamlin, 1986). Indeed, "what are generally viable social support systems for individuals do not serve that purpose for personnel who work in isolated total institutions . . . apparently, the regimen and isolation of prison work weakens the significance of marital support and community-based ties" (Blau et al., 1986, p. 139). Added to these challenges, correctional officers face an emotionally trying job and exhibit extremely high levels of organizational burnout (Tracy, 2005). Given this high burnout and the problems associated with working alone in a total institution setting, correctional administrators could engage in several practices that might help employees to deal better with the tainted and emotionally demanding parts of their job.

First, correctional facilities would function less "totally" for members if families and the larger communities that surround them were treated as stakeholders. While the prison industrial complex is booming (Schlosser, 1998), many communities take a "not in my backyard" attitude toward prisons and jails. As Brodsky (1982) explains, "the belief that crime should not exist, and the reality that it does, contribute to a strong desire to keep prisons, prisoners, and facts about prison life invisible and silent" (p. 83). As such, correctional officers are left to try to manage a very difficult and tainted job on their own and in spite of disdainful attitudes that paint prison guards as brutal, stupid, and lazy. Officer burnout and turnover may be reduced if correctional administrators better involved families, communities, media, and government leaders in the correctional environment.

Furthermore, even if facilities do not have full control over outsiders' understanding of the correctional officer job, they do have control over everyday organizational practices and programs. As indicated, officers largely work alone among groups of inmates without regular interaction with colleagues. Given the importance of peer interaction for social support (Shinn, Leymann, & Wong, 1984) and making sense of threatening work in identity-affirming ways (Tracy et al., 2005), facilities should consider doing more to provide opportunities for interaction among correctional officers. The institution of post-shift (or post-critical incident) debriefing meetings, for instance, would provide opportunities during which correctional officers could provide social support and help collectively make sense of their (often very dirty) work in ways that affirm their involvement in the profession.

In conclusion, despite the varied challenges correctional officers face in doing taint management, the data suggests that dirty work can simultaneously serve as work enhancement when it serves to break up boring and monotonous job duties. Service and security routines make up the bulk of the correctional officer job. As one officer said, "Each day is pretty much the same. You let the inmates out and get them to where they need to go." However, when officers strip search a filthy inmate, manage a dangerous situation, or defend themselves against an unfair media report, doing so can also be fun and productive. From this viewpoint, dirty work provides the opportunity to tell stories, joke and talk with coemployees, and manage boredom. Therefore, while doing taint management is a difficult and never-ending job activity behind bars, the dirty work of discipline also provides the opportunity for intermittent excitement, and proof that officers' security routines are indeed justified and necessary.

3

Riding Fire Trucks & Ambulances with America's Heroes

Clifton Scott and Sarah J. Tracy

The results are in, and the people have spoken. Once again, firefighter is at the top of the list in the annual AOL/Salary.com sexiest jobs survey. Our brave firefighters had some tough competition for the spot this year though, sharing the honors with the silver-spooned CEO, whose median salary of more than $600,000 seems to be compounding interest not only in the bank, but also with the ladies. In the two male-dominated fields (more than 97 percent of firefighters and 96 percent of CEOs nationally are men), the fact that number one was a tie between the altruistic, brawny fireman and the bring-home-the-bacon CEO speaks volumes about what we find sexiest in men. But are these jobs really sexy? (Pappassun, 2006).

The survey described above recently named firefighting the sexiest occupation, but when asked to comment on this finding in a media interview, one firefighter retorted, "It's a very rewarding job, but it's not sexy, not unless you think dealing with blood, germs and bodily functions is sexy." Another firefighter agreed, "Firefighting—no, it's not a sexy job." And yet, other firefighters interviewed for the same article (Pappassun, 2006) claimed that firefighting is the essence of sexy work. "Chivalry isn't dead. It is a chance to sometimes be a hero, to ride in like a knight in shining armor," said one. Another said, "It's true that when we arrive on the scene, we are all about helping them. If that makes us sexy, so be it."

Indeed, in terms of how the public generally views the relevance of one's work, firefighting is arguably one of the best jobs to be had. In the post-9/11 U.S., it is difficult to imagine an occupation endowed with more public trust and esteem than firefighting. During uncertain times, the heroism, strength, and manliness attributed to this work by popular culture seem to be a source of comfort for many.

Yet, as reflected in some of the quotations above, the everyday experience of actually doing the work of firefighting often seems far removed from the "sexiest occupation" surveys, beefcake calendars, and dramatic television shows that people might imagine when they witness the dramatic spectacle of the fire truck on the street. In spite of their prestige, firefighters regularly deal with tasks, clients, and situations that are physically, socially, and morally dirty. As we demonstrate in this chapter, the considerable validation given this occupation in spite of its dirtiness is in part a consequence of the "identity work" (Tracy & Naughton, 1994) that firefighters do to manage the tainted tasks, clients, and material filth that mark their everyday experience of this work. Managing the symbolic meaning of the truck and its surrounding activities is not only about "getting the job done" but also maintaining a positive, satisfying sense of self-identity (Ashcraft & Mumby, 2004; Weedon, 1997). Fire trucks are not inherently meaningful except in relationship to those who ride them (e.g., firefighters), the other objects they are intended to save (e.g., victims, burning buildings), and the manner in which this work has been portrayed historically. Thus, for the firefighters, a sense of individual, collective, and occupational self can only be achieved in relation to this truck, its onlookers, the clients its technology is intended to save, and the hazards that inspire its dispatch.

In this chapter, we explore a specific form of identity work, taint management, which includes the communicative efforts of employees to "make work meaningful" by organizing the meanings of stigmatized clients, tasks, and situations. We argue that the situated, local, mundane talk that comprises the everyday discourse of firefighters in this study often appropriates broader, societal discourses in a relatively privileged effort to manage work that might otherwise seem dirty to most outsiders (Tracy & Scott, 2006). While firefighters may seem like an unusual case, we conclude that this taint management is actually central to the identity work that firefighters—indeed that all employees—are trying to accomplish as they attempt, with more or less success, to feel secure about who they are in the work they do.

Riding Along

This study is based on field research conducted by the first author at a major metropolitan fire department. The Bayside Fire Department (BFD) is a large municipal firefighting organization located in a major city on the U.S. West Coast. The first author, Cliff, conducted "ride alongs" with crews at four BFD stations. During each of these periods of participant observation, he helped out with station chores and emergency response activities, observed training exercises, ate meals with the crew, and accompanied engine, truck, and ambulance crews on fire and EMS calls. Along the way, he also conducted ethnographic interviews, informal conversations with participants that were reconstructed in field notes. Restrictions on research access did not allow for formal, structured interviewing. Consequently, his role was that of a "participant-as-observer": since he was known to the subjects as a researcher but participated in everyday work life to the extent that he became familiar with the dilemmas faced by full participants (Gold, 1958; Lindlof & Taylor, 2002, pp. 147-48; Gold, 1958).

Field notes not only reflect what Cliff observed in the field but also early, tentative ideas about potential codes, the relationship between various events being observed, as well as impressions about the entire project (Strauss & Corbin, 1998). Utilizing the constant comparative method (Kvale, 1996), formal data analysis began with open coding (Lindlof & Taylor, 2002), where codes were tentatively assigned to various passages of the field notes that suggested particular categories or themes. Some of these themes were partially inspired by existing theory and others emerged primarily from the data. With an initial coding system in place, the remaining data was coded, and various categories were added, extended, combined, and eliminated where necessary.

The Irony of Firefighting as Dirty Work

So what, then, is so dirty about firefighting? At the start of this chapter, we highlighted contradictions between the espoused image of firefighting known to outsiders and the typical, everyday experience of this work as understood by the occupation's members. Indeed, some readers may be surprised to find a chapter about firefighters in this book, in part because this notion of firefighting as dirty work is in conflict with the dominant, external, preferred image that most firefighters labor to reproduce. If this case is any indication, one reason firefighting rarely seems like dirty work to outsiders is in part because firefighters manage taint so well, in spite of the stigmatized tasks, situations, and people around them.

Firefighting at BFD failed to live up to that espoused ideal, and instead involved a variety of tainted, identity-threatening tasks, clients, and situations. In short, BFD is called a "fire department," and its members travel on fire engines and fire trucks, but the data collected for this study indicate that the vast majority of firefighter calls were EMS dispatches or false alarms—"nuisance" calls that had little to do with fire or serious medical hazards. Most of the calls that were dispatched as fire were either a false alarm (a prankster pulling a street corner call box, or a malfunction in an industrial fire detection system) or were extremely minor (for example, a smoking fluorescent light fixture). Also, on countless occasions, the firefighters were "called off" of fires, ordered to return to the station before arriving on scene because the fire was discovered by another crew to be minor or false. In all, Cliff observed one fire during the course of his fieldwork at BFD, a small grass fire. Most calls involved minor medical concerns of the nuisance variety, and when firefighters were willing and able to attend to these EMS calls, they often complained about the dirtiness of this work by portraying it as incompatible with firefighting.

EMS and Firefighting as "A Bad Marriage"

In spite of the frequency of EMS calls, members rarely spoke of EMS in positive terms. The integration of EMS and fire services under the umbrella of BFD occurred four years prior to this fieldwork, but the tension surrounding this change was immediately evident. Cliff heard stories of paramedics being forced to eat at different tables than firefighters at the stations, and in several separate conversations with firefighters and paramedics, this occupational integration was referred to as "a bad marriage." EMS calls were rarely discussed during station meals, even when members had discussed them with some excitement while returning to the station. Conversely, mealtime conversations and ethnographic interviews often included vivid descriptions of fire suppression and victim rescues that were far removed from the EMS context. When members were willing to acknowledge this conflict between EMS and firefighting, they typically explained that EMS activities lacked the exhilarating experience of heroism. As firefighter and paramedic Will disclosed:

> Well, we don't talk about it because EMS just isn't very fun. It's
> not heroic. . . . Firefighting is like riding down a hill on a bicycle
> really fast, maybe with your hands off the handlebars. The ambu-
> lance service is like fixing that bike. It's okay, but it's not nearly
> as much fun.

Like many others, Will equated fun and heroism with danger and
risk, a tendency he portrayed as just a "natural" part of being a firefighter. Firefighting has long been portrayed as a manly occupation
(Cooper, 1995; Kaprow, 1991; Tebeau, 2003), the performance of
which is thought to be unquestionably heroic (McCarl, 1984).
Firefighters tend to assume that this emphasis on masculinity is a
natural part of who they are, and they are unlikely to become people
who enjoy "fixing that bike." In his view, that is why EMS and firefighting are incompatible.

Beyond their judgment of EMS and firefighting as poorly
matched job activities, BFD members seemed to have tolerated these
changes as structural shifts not to be embraced but rather as identity threats that should be only marginally tolerated. Consider the
following field note from an ethnographic interview with another
firefighter, John:

> John and I end up talking about the Fire/EMS split. He refers to the
> integration of EMS into BFD as a "bad marriage." To him, it doesn't
> really work. They're different jobs for different kinds of people. He
> admits that he has been certified as a paramedic. He says this as he
> leans on the fire engine and averts his eyes, seeming pretty
> embarrassed about this certification. He follows this with, "Yeah,
> I'm certified as a medic, but I prefer to ride on the truck. Who
> wouldn't, right?"

John not only employs the "bad marriage" metaphor but also admits
with rather obvious reluctance that he has actually received the
highest level of EMS training. John's posture, speech, and facial
expressions indicated the shameful, gendered identity threat constituted by his somewhat hidden status as a paramedic. It was as if
John was admitting he occasionally does his own laundry at home—
a necessary evil, something that changing times have made him do,
not work that he wants to.

Within a variety of communicative resources, from formal
structure to occupational symbols and discourse, members worked
to culturally segregate EMS and firefighting. The formal structure of
the organization reflected and maintained these divisions as binary
oppositions. For example, while other fire departments refer to

members as "firefighter/paramedics" or "firefighter/EMT," going so far as to embroider such titles on uniforms, these labels are applied in an either/or (versus both/and) sense at BFD. On one day, a member may be working as a firefighter, and the next shift he is officially a paramedic, as denoted by his dress, yet he will return to being a firefighter with a different uniform on the following shift. When an EMS dispatch was received at the station, someone would quickly check a computer screen and announce over the loudspeakers with a tone of resignation, "EMS, EMS, that's an EMS call."

Though this work was portrayed as boring, if not embarrassing, the supposed lack of excitement and danger in EMS was hardly an objective, unquestionable part of the work. In fact, Cliff perceived many EMS calls as highly unpredictable, risky, and indeed heroic. We believe EMS calls were not interpreted and portrayed in the preferred framework of heroism and excitement, but we argue this was not due to an inherent lack of these ideal qualities in the work but instead because it included stigmatized clients, situations, and tasks that emerged as identity threats.

As BFD firefighters attempted to explain their work, they highlighted the contrast between their preferred, external image and the everyday experience. It is not unusual for members of occupations often portrayed on television (e.g., lawyers) to point to contradictions between public perceptions and lived realities of work. However, in highlighting these contradictions, BFD firefighters typically pointed to job features that were tainted physically, socially, and morally. It seems hardly coincidental that the dirtiest firefighting job features have emerged as a product of the addition of EMS to the department mission.

Physical Taint

Even in their fire suppression activities, firefighters do physically filthy tasks and labor in dangerous conditions (Tracy & Scott, 2006). Particularly in the EMS context, they deal with death, mutilated bodies, and a variety of bodily fluids. Like members of other medical professions (Hafferty, 1988; Smith & Kleinman, 1989), firefighters regularly examine the private areas of client's bodies. Firefighter Bob attested,

"We spend most of our time at this station responding to false alarms and 'shitbums.' We call 'em shitbums because they shit all over themselves and call us. Then we have to take care of them." As such comments exemplify, the threat of this physical taint is highlighted and sustained by pervasive talk of "shit." An ambulance at a BFD station is commonly referred to as "the shitbox" or "the shit carrier." Moreover, there is much talk of the problem of "shitbums." These references to *shit* on the surface appear to revolve around the disgust that both firefighters and paramedics feel about having to deal with *bums*, homeless addicts of one sort or another who pass out and defecate on themselves. Merchants or passers-by call 911, and BFD members have no choice but to pick up the person, attempt to treat him, and take him to the emergency room.

Social Taint

In addition to physical dirt, BFD members also demonstrated a frustration with the social taint of EMS work. In many cases, physical and social taint were derived from the same sources. EMS "shit work," as it was often called, had comparatively less to offer in the way of self-edifying danger because it was perceived as less dangerous and more routine, thus offering fewer opportunities for firefighters to enact the heroic identity that is linked so often with their occupational community. A hero is someone who does things that others cannot, often through the demonstration of some kind of physical or emotional strength. Firefighters have been portrayed (and portray themselves) as heroic servants who primarily fight fires and through their ability to withstand physical and emotional conditions that others cannot (Cooper, 1995). Feats of strength are not heroic unless they are directed toward some apparently benevolent end, so heroes are those who help victims or potential victims, people who are weaker and more helpless than the hero. Thus, work is not objectively heroic; heroism must be (re)accomplished in relation to the comparatively weak and helpless identities of those who are in some way rescued.

This heroism can be more difficult to accomplish when clients come from a low social class. It seems safe to assume that to most outsiders, saving lives and mending the broken through EMS work is hardly the antithesis of heroism. However, within BFD the possibility of heroism in EMS work is more daunting because it is challenged by what Page (1984) called "courtesy stigma." Courtesy stigma is taint associated with working in a servile position for clients perceived as unsavory because of their low class position in society. Since many EMS calls were described as illegitimate, they were a persistent source of frustration for firefighters, particularly since many of these calls seemed to be generated by impoverished citizens who were relying on the fire department and hospital emergency rooms for their medical care. Much of this difficulty could be traced to the social taint these clients represented. For example, consider the following field note:

> On the way back from a car accident, I ask the firefighters, "So what are the top three calls in this neighborhood?" Tim says flatly, "Bums, Bums, and more Bums. Shitbums!" Rhonda adds that there are a lot of elderly people in Little China. Tim adds, "Yeah, and they don't know when to slow down. They'll be having chest pains and still carry six bags of groceries up seven flights of stairs."

Here, the taint is social in the sense that firefighters are potentially threatened by the servile role they must play with clients who should "know when to slow down" or "shitbums" who are not only physically disgusting but represent a lower class in society. Indeed, such clients are the antithesis of the physical and emotional strength, independence, and heroism that make up the public identity of the firefighter (Cooper, 1995; Kaprow, 1991; McCarl, 1984). Heroes are people who personify autonomy and independence. Their superhuman qualities allow them to swiftly intervene, and this intervention is made meaningful when autonomous heroes, icons of control and autonomy, save victims/clients who are in situations that are out of their control. However, the victims BFD firefighters most often encountered during observations conducted for this study were in a dependent, out-of-control situation that firefighters believed was created by the clients themselves. To save someone who is dependent enhanced a firefighter's identity only if the client did not somehow "deserve" the situation that required heroic intervention. In these cases, feigning empathy and subservience was what BFD members found difficult to accomplish. Such clients do little to aid the firefighters in their efforts to secure a sense of heroism in their work.

Moral Taint

In addition to the challenge of performing heroic acts on behalf of low class clients who seem to deserve their plight, the moral questionability of these clients added another layer of taint to the work. While it initially appeared that firefighters were only concerned with the physical and social dimension of EMS taint, their frustration with these clients seemed to take on a moral politic of its own. It was not merely that EMS clients seemed to deserve their situation because they were incompetent. They also were often portrayed as immoral, and some firefighters complained passionately that their work seemed to actually contribute to the depravity of some clients.

For example, many of the calls (fire and EMS) were perceived as illegitimate. These "bullshit calls" were a regular source of frustration for firefighters, particularly those in poor, inner-city neighborhoods in which many citizens rely on the fire department and hospital emergency rooms for their medical care. Here, firefighters often struggled to construct their work in heroic terms when they faced clients who created an unfortunate situation not through incompetence (social taint), but through dishonesty. For example, consider the following field note about a common slogan often uttered sarcastically at BFD: "If you call, we'll haul."

> John associates this with a story about a call they got one time at 2:00 in the morning. The woman was concerned that her kitchen light went out. He asked for a bulb. She gave him one, and he changed it. The light now worked. He just said nothing and walked out. He then follows this with the story of a time when he and another paramedic/FF went on a call to a house where a woman had the flu, but the other paramedic who was actually working on her was sicker than she was.

Each crew told similar stories. These narratives can be considered a means of "letting off steam" or "venting" negative emotion about the challenges of work. However, by choosing such extreme cases, they attribute the actions of these clients (i.e., generating a nuisance call) to moral shortcomings by juxtaposing each call's lack of seriousness against their own merit-worthy behavior (i.e., changing the client's light bulb without comment and serving clients who are less ill than the EMS provider).

Some members also seemed threatened by association with a political system that, in their view, actually rewarded immoral behavior. Here, it seemed that America's heroes were ashamed, perhaps understandably, of their city's official responses to social problems. For example, during an ethnographic interview Bob launched without prompting into a global explanation of these problems—the fireboxes, the bums, the false alarms.

> So what we basically have is a system of handouts for everyone. Right now, we're giving $350 to every person that wants it. If they want it, they get it. Since they claim to be homeless, there's no way to check on any of this, Cliff. If you're homeless, you don't

have to have an address or anything. So we have people from [Middleton] who come over here, get their checks and go back to [Middleton]. Now, Cliff, we've got this councilman here who wants to take all that money and put it into social services for the homeless. That way, they can't just take the money and spend it on whatever their vice is. But, of course, because we've got all these special interest groups, it probably won't happen. So we're stuck. Like I said, Cliff, it's a very political city.

As these comments suggest, members often displayed their frustration at their role in a system that seemed to encourage the very kinds of calls they found most threatening to their preferred identity as heroic professionals that help resolve serious emergencies. Since members were obligated to accommodate shitbums who they believed would not take care of themselves, these firefighters suspected that their labor was perpetuating the very problems they were attempting to resolve and defrauding taxpayers in the process. For example, after providing basic first aid for a homeless drug addict, Timothy, a young firefighter/paramedic stated sarcastically, "Welcome to Bayside EMS!" Firefighter Johnny, his ambulance partner, responded even more sardonically, "Yeah, if you want to do drugs, you can do them, and when you feel sad, when you hurt, we'll take great care of you so you can do more drugs." Because the "system" was corrupted by those who took advantage of handouts they did not deserve and wasted resources on their own vices, firefighters ironically portrayed their work as actively perpetuating a "system of handouts" in service of "special" interest groups with which they disagreed. As we describe next, this disdain for EMS work has been enabled by historical transitions in the fire service.

Historically Situating Taint Management at BFD

This story of taint management at BFD is as much industrial and occupational as it is organizational. Therefore, it cannot be considered separate and apart from the historical conditions that enabled the BFD, indeed the occupation itself, to emerge into its contemporary cultural position (Ashcraft & Mumby, 2004). While there is not space here for a full-blown historical account, it is important to consider the crucial shift in the fire service industry that, itself, can be considered an instance of taint management. As early as the late 1970s, major metropolitan departments of the American fire service began using existing firefighters to deliver emergency medical service (EMS) (Brunacini, 2002). Logistically, this shift made sense because of pre-existing, geographically dispersed fire stations, reliable electronic communications infrastructure, and positive community relations. Economically and politically, the integration of fire and EMS services can also be considered a consequence of wavering political and financial support for expensive municipal fire departments. When mayors and city councils across the country began asking their firefighters to empty parking meters and conduct building inspections, fire department administrators began looking for ways to restructure their revenue stream (Scott & Myers, 2002). The addition of EMS, which in some cases included billable ambulance transport by firefighters in department ambulances, was framed as an economic way of coping with declining financial support from cities in a manner consistent with the implied mission of the fire service more generally.

BFD firefighters were aware of their economic dependence on EMS, a fact that is not well known to the public. The following is from an ethnographic interview with firefighter Jerry:

> "Basically, what it boils down to is that this department costs about $250 million a year to run. You can't justify that kind of money when you only have five great alarm fires per year. That's why they brought [EMS] in. We're the ones running all the calls." I ask him to explain what a great alarm call is, and he basically says it is a "real fire" that requires the dispatch of more than three stations. I said, "So how many small but real fires [does BFD] have per year—say a house that is pretty fully engulfed in flames?" He gives me a sideways, knowing smile, which I interpreted as a reluctance to admit these statistics. He glances around, as if to make sure no one is within earshot. "Oh, I think it was 20 or 30. So that's a huge budget for a few fires. You just can't justify that any more. That's not enough services for all that money. So by bringing in EMS, they have a revenue stream that I think last year covered about two-thirds of the entire budget."

This economic context and the historical conditions that enable it are worth mentioning because we interpret these shifts as instances of taint management at the organizational and occupational level. The wavering political capital and attendant representations of the firefighting occupation that brought about these changes are examples of threats to the occupational identity of firefighting. A common, pre-9/11 perception about firefighters was that they spent most of their time playing cards, drinking coffee, and cooking meals rather than doing "real" work. Resistance to the expansioning scope of emergency services to include EMS, which was not uniformly embraced across the fire service, can be understood as an attempt at taint management, an effort to minimize the threat of encroaching, feminizing stigma. By taking on EMS service, fire departments could not only capitalize on existing resources but also increase their financial backing through labor that remained seemingly consistent with the occupational values of emotional strength, independence, and heroism. In comparison to the less manly alternatives of emptying parking meters and checking construction sites, the addition of EMS was thought to allow firefighters to maintain a high-status occupational role far removed from the subservience of "meter maids" and the bureaucratic restraint of building inspectors (Scott & Myers, 2005). However, as we discuss next, innovation and mission shift was resisted at BFD.

"125 Years of Tradition Unimpeded by Progress"

In spite of this important transition, the U.S. fire service is still often described by its members as "125 years of tradition unimpeded by progress." Innovations in the structure, practices, and technologies of the fire service industry have generally been adopted slowly and with considerable resistance (Tebeau, 2003). There are apparently few major municipal fire departments in which innovations in the fire service have been more stridently resisted than BFD. This opposition remains process and product of taint management practices that emerged within the contested cultural space of the city of Bayside.

Nestled within a west coast city and region renowned (or infamous) for its progressiveness, BFD seems in many ways like a cultural stronghold, an organization clinging tenaciously to the symbols and practices of occupational tradition. Indeed, this resistance at BFD to what most would call innovations in the fire service (e.g., the integration of EMS with fire protection, improved safety equipment, and risk management procedures) has arguably been at the core of what distinguishes this department from others within the larger U.S. fire service. When Cliff mentioned that he had done fieldwork in another large fire department with a reputation for leading reforms in the fire service described above, BFD members were often quick to clarify their value for tradition over change. For example, James described BFD as an "old style, New York wannabe, interior attack department," referencing an aggressive, "old school" style of firefighting that is considered unnecessarily risky by some experts (Brunacini, 2002). Within this context, innovation was often framed as a threat to the preferred meanings of the department's work and the efforts of its members to preserve closely held traditions. Perhaps most visibly, the BFD remains one of the only major fire departments to continue using wooden ladders rather than the lighter and more reliable aluminum counterparts. At considerable expense, the department maintains its own ladder shop that builds and repairs these tools. Moreover, the department had only recently begun requiring that firefighters wear a complete set of turnout pants—the protective gear that safeguards firefighters legs from thermal hazards—decades after most major fire departments adopted this innovation. Not until two years after a BFD firefighter died of severe leg burns did the department institute this requirement, one that apparently was not stringently enforced. Two firefighters at separate stations revealed that "some" firefighters continue to wear "grandpa's turnouts"—protective clothing passed down from previous generations of firefighters that does not meet federal safety standards or the department's own rules.

As we explain next, these symbols of tradition have functioned as discursive resources for ongoing taint management by sustaining privileged notions of what is valued as "real" or authentic firefighting. However, BFD members had available to them a variety of discursive resources that benefited them in their efforts to make their work seem clean to both insiders and outsiders, an issue to which we turn next.

Taint-Management Strategies

Given the everyday experience of work at BFD, members found themselves in an awkward position. They were rewarded externally for the dangerous, heroic nature of their work, yet their typical workday seemed a far cry from the espoused, preferred image for which they are rewarded. Here we describe the communicative strategies and techniques that members of this community employ as part of their efforts to make work meaningful through discursive taint management.

Selective Social Comparisons

One way that firefighters managed taint was to construct selective social comparisons of competing BFD job roles (Ashforth & Kreiner, 1999). These comparisons often hinged on the contested nature of what should count as "real," authentic work. Members' talk often captured and reproduced disputed notions of the comparative value of EMS versus firefighting. For example, paramedics were often quick to note that they handled the vast majority of the calls at each station and that most of the fire calls were just false alarms, suggesting that EMTs and paramedics are the ones doing most of the work. Conversely, as this field note suggests, firefighters who did not perform EMS also used selective social comparisons to define their work:

> The alarm sounds, and for the first time tonight, this is not an EMS call but a call for the fire truck. After hearing the nature of the dispatch, truck captain Ron turns to me and says, "Oh good, Cliff, you're going to get to see some REAL work! We'll show you how it's done!" We are dispatched to a house that has been struck by a car that went out of control. A section of the garage door has been knocked out. The firefighters on our engine pull hammers and nails and pieces of scrap lumber from the truck and repair the door.

What counted as "real" to the truck captain was the rugged manliness associated with working with a physical structure (versus a person, such as an EMS client) using tools pulled from a fire truck. At BFD and other change-resistant departments, a fire truck (as opposed to a fire engine) is basically a large toolbox with wheels. Its riders are given the task of forcibly entering burning buildings, rescuing victims, ventilating roofs, and performing temporary repairs to damaged structures. When asked for tours of the truck, the firefighters did so with great enthusiasm. Their faces lit up as they proudly displayed the heavy steel tools used for breaking down doors, the chainsaws, and Jaws of Life used to extricate victims from collapsed buildings and cars. These symbols of strength and heroism were not just tools in a typical sense (objects used to complete a task); they also functioned as tools of identity work. Discursively, they potentially sustain selective social comparisons of each group's relative worth and authenticity. These are the exclusive tools (only firefighters on trucks used them) that break down barriers between rescuers and the rescuees, and association with these tools seemed to (re)produce a heightened sense of toughness amidst adversity.

Upon hearing descriptions of how these physical tools were used in rescuing victims and breaking into burning buildings and damaged vehicles, the value and relevance of this work seemed unquestionable. The work is real, and you can get hurt or worse if it is not done well (and sometimes even if it is). For example, firefighters at every station enthusiastically described the elaborate process by which fire truck crews must work together to raise the heavy wooden ladders. In nearly every instance, they mentioned the weight of each ladder and described the sort of teamwork necessary to pull off this exercise. Of course, this talk helps to reinforce what makes truck crews different from engine crews and ambulance staff. Through social comparison (Ashforth & Kreiner, 1999), they selectively and strategically highlight one of their more crucial, challenging, and risky tasks. At the same time, they downplays the fact that, in most cases at BFD, truck crews do not directly extinguish fires and that the tools that they often boast about (chain saws, the Jaws of Life, battering rams, etc.) are usually deployed in circumstances lacking the typical self-serving drama (e.g., using battering rams to knock down doors for citizens who have locked themselves out of their own homes rather than to knock down the door of a burning building). People tend to make work meaningful (Heinsler, Kleinman, & Stenross, 1990) by making sense of the objects, tasks, and clients around them in relation to a preferred sense of self. In this example, the identity work of being a firefighter on a truck crew is accomplished when everyday talk is used to selectively portray one's work in relation to these tools (objects) and not others.

Refocusing By Celebrating Manliness

One important way in which BFD firefighters responded to encroaching taint was to accentuate and celebrate their masculine occupational identity. These highly performative gestures were frequent and blatant. As the following field note suggests, these usually took the form of everyday talk that highlighted the emotional and physical toughness for which these members stand and the comparatively feminine weakness embodied by outsiders, particularly those who do not work with their hands or who cannot manage their lives independently.

> Several folks are working in the kitchen, casually getting dinner together. Some are leaning on the counters, just watching and talking. This type of conversation appears routine and includes a lot of joking and teasing. The local evening news is on. The female reporter is describing a traffic accident with some fairly dramatic inflection. Kyle is making fun of the reporter's emotional tone. He starts mimicking her in a high-pitched voice, "Oh my God, three people were injured! Two seriously! Oh my God! Oh my God!"

This ritual of ridiculing outsiders who interpret tragedy or danger in openly emotional terms emerged within all five of the crews observed at BFD. Since clients should not be ridiculed during service calls, firefighters regularly made light of clients outside of their presence (e.g., at the station, in a vehicle while returning to the station). Perhaps most importantly, this mockery was typically aimed at the target's emotional demeanor, and this particular form of ridicule tended to garner the most laughter. For example,

> Sharon is talking about the season finale of *Third Watch* [a show about firefighters, police officers, and paramedics], where the main female character apparently dies in the final moments. She describes how the cameras show her mangled body, her legs practically wrapped around her neck. She describes the emotional response of the character's partner as he watches her die, how he "completely fell apart." Everyone laughs at Sharon's ridicule of this character's emotions, even though most of them do not even watch the show and even fewer saw the episode.

By capitalizing on cultural norms that associate the expression of emotional sadness with weakness and femininity (Mumby & Putnam, 1992), Sharon is able to situate her personal identity positively within this group of men in a traditionally masculine occupation. Sharon's belongingness with this group is accomplished and reflected in everyday station discourse through the way she, along with her peers, characterizes the vulnerability of a fictional first responder as flawed, questionable, and something to be avoided. Once again, the firefighters' discourse encourages a sense that they are of a different class than outsiders.

Refocusing By Celebrating Dominant Sexuality

Dominant sexuality was also employed as a tool for managing identity threats. This identity work could be accomplished in both public and private. The privacy of the fire station's "backstage" often provided a fitting space for male sexual humor. For example:

> Folks are talking, joking, and teasing as they put together dinner. One employee vividly describes how much another likes butter on his biscuits. Another claims that Kyle loves mayonnaise on his biscuits. Another says, "Oh yeah, I bet he does like to squirt a little mayonnaise on his biscuits." He mimics a man stroking his penis and ejaculating. Everybody laughs.

By engaging in sexual banter—highlighting male excess and hyper masculine action (ejaculation)—for an appreciative internal audience of peers, firefighters are able to assert a sense of self that is dominant, carefree, and in control even if the majority of their work time is subject to servile work in tragic, out of control situations. The practices of ridiculing emotional descriptions of tragedy and engaging in "locker room" discussions of sexuality were pervasive in a number of firehouse activities. One firefighter who could ascertain that Cliff was not particularly accustomed to such talk in a workplace explained that "this kind of horsing around" was "typical" at fire stations that have a high call volume.

It is tempting to dismiss this kind of firefighter discourse as common "frat house" behavior. However, in our view, that response would probably categorize such talk as natural, normal, and acceptable—"boys will be boys" (Clair, 1993). Instead, we believe these conversations are significant: if we move beyond a representational view of language and assume that our talk does something more than reflect our attitudes and personalities, we can see this "banter" as more than just bawdy expressions of manliness at work. If the work outside the station renders public and collective perceptions of toughness and heroism insecure, then firefighters in their everyday work may employ such talk as a means of enacting and performing the preferred identity (Collinson, 1992; 2003).

In addition to this backstage talk, the taint of dirty work could be managed through public rituals. Firefighters benefit from an external public that applauds and maintains their status as sex symbols (e.g., "hose" jokes, firefighter beefcake calendars, and ongoing sexual connotations about "fire" and "heat"). However, firefighters cannot rest easy on these meanings; they also work to sustain them. For example, one evening during the second author's observation at BFD, the fire truck was dispatched to a "box call"—a fire call that originates from a street-corner call box and is nearly always a false alarm. Like nearly all box calls at BFD, no fire was visible upon arrival, and the truck headed back to the station. But rather than returning to the station directly, the driver took the exceptionally long ladder-truck though the narrow streets of the upscale North Town district, which consisted mostly of high-end restaurants, bars, and dance clubs. Well-dressed pedestrians, sidewalk diners, and even some patrons inside these establishments waved at the men and women on the truck.

> Women, in particular, wave at us in a way that feels laced with sexual attraction; they smile broadly and seductively and turn their bodies completely to face the truck. The driver rings the brass bell on the front of the truck as we pass several groups of

attractive women, and they motion to do it some more. It certainly feels as though we are, in fact, rock stars.

The crew member who drove the truck that night later disclosed that this trip through North Town was a ritual that typically followed one of the evening box call false alarms on each shift. "Those box calls are a downer, but it's fun to ride through [North Town] and ring the bell. It's like a tradition we have."

This ritual functions as a celebratory performance of manliness, heterosexuality, and occupational identity, which seeks to deflect the taint that might pollute (Douglas, 1966) personal and public meanings of the authenticity of this work. While "box calls" are an opportunity to do the "real" work of fighting fire and rescuing victims and thus highlight the least-stigmatized features of their occupational identity, these calls typically end with disappointing false alarms. By following these "downers" with parade-like journeys through a high-status district, the potential taint of box calls is warded off and counteracted by an activity through which a more preferred identity can be performed. The bell can be rung. The ladders can be shown. The long apparatus of the fire truck can be maneuvered tightly around packed street corners. This practice is the medium and outcome of the glorified sexual status of firefighters, the meanings for which must be employed as a resource in self-objectification. The parade ritual would be much less effective if attempted from within a small ambulance. The truck symbolically reminds the public to treat firefighters in an adoring way, which in turn protects firefighters from the taint of their everyday work and sustains a feeling among the firefighters that outsiders understand their authenticity.

Conclusion

Work is an activity in which we go not only to get the job done and earn a living but also where "we come to understand who we are and who we might become" (Trethewey, 1997, p. 281). Most employees, regardless of occupation, are striving to establish a satisfying sense of self in their work, in spite of job features that would surprise or disappoint outsiders. What's more, how individuals attempt to establish this sense of self-identity in communication with others shapes how the job gets done (or does not get done). While employees all tend to make individual (subjective) sense of their work, these interpretations are developed in interactions with others as they interpret the surrounding events (intersubjectively). There-fore, how individuals make sense of their work has a lot to do with how they collectively interpret their environments (e.g., tasks, clients, and situations). Perhaps most important to this analysis, employees cannot make sense of their environments except in rela-tion to a sense of self (Eisenberg, 2001; Weick, 1995)—as people who do a particular kind of work in a particular kind of organization.

The discourse used as a kind of tool for taint management is important for both scholars and practitioners to consider because, while employees can make choices about how they talk and listen to each other at work, the context in which this happens is not of any-one's own choosing. The systems of meaning through which people speak and make sense of their work are usually evolving long before we enter the scene (Weedon, 1997). Because this limits what sort of talk we can use to speak about and make sense of our work, the cul-tural values of an organization (and in this case, its larger occupa-tion) shape what we see as our options.

And yet, as individuals, organizations, and occupations, we are always in a process of becoming (Ashcraft & Mumby, 2004). Cultures and identities are not fixed; they are always in process—becoming, evolving (Tracy & Trethewey, 2005). They are often reenacted (and occasionally transformed) through our discourse. Therefore, this discourse—talk that is partially enabled and purposeful yet partially constrained and predetermined—influences how we make sense of who we are and the work we are doing. That is, it shapes how we organize.

It is important to note, however, that we are not all equally priv-ileged in our capacity to make work meaningful through our talk. And that is what makes dirty work so interesting. Dirty work is dirty largely because the society that surrounds it has deemed it as such. In other words, "shitbums" are dirty because our society sees them as stigmatized, dirty, and polluted (Douglas, 1966). Therefore the work of firefighters, which includes dealing with "shitbums" regu-larly, is potentially tainted by association (Page, 1984). Firefighters are typically portrayed through communication that associates them with manliness and independence, or what Cooper (1995) called "strength, robustness, boldness, stoutness, bravery, and not being womanish" (pp. 146-47), particularly in the U.S. post 9/11. Therefore, they have relatively easy access to the symbolic tools of taint management that bring to the surface preferred meanings, interpretations, and identities, and sequester those that would taint, stigmatize, or pollute their work (Tracy & Scott, 2006). No wonder the public loves them. No wonder firefighters find a way to love their work.

It seems unrealistic and perhaps unwise to assume that the occupational comparisons discussed in this study are somehow always dysfunctional or preventable. If people in organizations and occupations are to find meaning in their work, they must have a reason to come to work, a relatively satisfying sense of self that can be collaboratively constructed and reproduced through informal talk. The meaning of work is inevitably achieved at least partially through comparison. What it means to do one kind of work has much to do with what it does not mean, with how occupations and organizations may be differentiated from others.

Yet, as this study has demonstrated, clients as well as organizational peers can taint members, and responses to this taint can be dangerous. A key part of identity work for these groups is strategically managing these threats to a satisfying, edifying identity. The broad social values (e.g., attitudes about gender and class) members learn prior to organizational/occupational entry provide plenty of discursive ammunition for self-serving constructions of vocational identity. The risk of poor taint management is the danger that these discursive practices sustain asymmetrical values for various jobs and occupations (Clair, 1996). In the case of BFD, we see an organizational culture that disvalues an activity with flesh and blood consequences that arguably remain no less significant than the preferred structure of firefighting.

These findings suggest that organizational leaders should pay attention to the manner in which organizational and occupational identities are managed. In an age of mergers, acquisitions, and shifting organizational missions and identities, the ability to frame the meaning of change in a manner that is engaged with how members find a satisfying sense of self at work is crucial. Yet, this analysis indicates that it is important that leaders also frame change in a way that allows for a secure sense of self that is differentiated yet not hierarchically valued.

Finally, if this study is suggestive of anything, it is that the thorny search for a satisfying sense of individual and collective identity is a function of everyday talk at work—even among those who are known as "America's heroes." This discourse shapes what work means for people, and so it has important, material consequences for the way work is experienced by members and for the quality of products and services utilized by stakeholders. The communicative nature of taint management, then, is a complex and deeply social process, one that is constitutive of the everyday decisions and practices of members.

4

Without Trucks We'd Be Naked, Hungry & Homeless

Melanie Mills

Introduction

"If you've got it, a trucker brought it. This is the mantra of many people who drive trucks for a living and find themselves misunderstood, unappreciated, and maligned by the general public" (Mills, 2007, p. 127). Even though most of our consumer goods are brought to us by trucks and the prices would skyrocket if subject to other forms of transportation, the occupation does not enjoy high social status. This qualifies as dirty work by Hughes' (1962) definition because it is work that is necessary to our social system, yet stigmatized by its members.

Outside of trade publications, truckers do not get much good press, which is evidence of social stigma. The popular press is likely to reflect the seamier sides of the business (including political bribes for licenses, drugs, and truck stop prostitution), incompetencies (driver errors and accidents), or the damage trucks do to roadways (which causes you peril and is repaired with your tax dollars).

Evidence of the transformation of this "dirt" is found in publications and messages aimed at members of the trucking occupation, which moderate the impact of these outside perceptions of dirtiness. Two bumper stickers truckers like and use include the title and first line of this chapter: "without trucks we'd be naked, hungry & homeless," and "if you've got it, a trucker brought it." Both of these messages serve as a positive identity function for truckers, indicating that, although they are underappreciated, the world would be worse off without truckers.

Truckers manage physical, social, and moral taint (Ashforth & Kreiner, 1999). Physically, the job is associated with dirt, grease, and dangerous conditions. Socially, truckers do servile delivery work that is not accorded high prestige. Morally, they are often suspected of dubious behavior (riding on the edge of the law with regard to driving, drugs, and sometimes prostitution). This chapter encapsulates over twenty years of extended interviews with more than 300 drivers, truck stop observations, content analysis of driver-oriented publications, personal correspondence, and experience on the road. In an effort to demystify the profession and understand taint management, I examine how drivers create occupational identification with their profession and rhetorical communities that provide support, meanings, and communicative norms for them, using ethnographic methods consistent with symbolic convergence theory to enter into the lives of truckers to seek how they make sense of and identify with their work. In particular, how do truck drivers socially construct positive work identities when their jobs are defined as dirty by the larger social system?

Occupational Culture

Since truck drivers are more likely to interact with members of their occupation rather than their organizations, they constitute a unique group to study occupationally. There is considerable utility to examining work through a larger occupational lens instead of the organizational perspective, especially as we try to understand the social nature of work groups (Berger, 1964). As discussed in the introduction to this book, the organizational perspective often accentuates the meaning of work for others (i.e., What is the role of this work or job in the organizational system?), while the occupational perspective concentrates upon the meaning of work for those who do it (i.e., What moves individuals to "be" in this line of work?). Both provide interesting, yet different, frames for the experience of work (Mills, 2007).

Trucking represents "dirty" work, a job whose stigma would seemingly threaten the ability of occupational members to construct an esteem-enhancing social identity (Mills, 2007). Ashforth and Kreiner (1999) found, however, that dirty work instead can foster the development of strong work group cultures. Apparently, there is a strong occupational identification for members of dirty occupations, a sense of we-ness against the stigma of their work in an occupational class system, where they cast themselves as heroes, and those who would disparage them or their work as villains. Symbolic convergence theory provides an explanation of how this we-ness works.

Symbolic Convergence Theory

Culture in the communicative context means the sum ways of living, organizing, and communing for a group of human beings that is conveyed to newcomers and outsiders by verbal and nonverbal communication (Bormann, 1983). Pacanowsky and O'Donnell-Trujillo (1983) describe the notion of culture as meaning, at least in part, reality as it is constructed of "particular jokes, stories, songs, myths, polite exchanges, and so forth . . . that which gives substance to what would otherwise be insensate behavior" (p. 123). They contend that to study culture, you need to try to answer two questions. First, what are the key communication activities, the unfolding of which are occasions when sense-making is accomplished? Second, what is the sense members have made of their experiences? Bormann (1983) gives us an elaborated answer to the first of these questions via symbolic convergence theory (SCT), illustrating how the sharing of group fantasies provides the "key communication episodes that create a common social reality and accomplish sense-making for the participants" (p. 100). The term *fantasy* as used here should not be confused with its colloquial usage as something unreal or made up, but rather, in the context of SCT, as the way communities of people make sense out of their experience and create social reality. To address the second question, Tompkins (1983) suggests that we can gain more explanatory power by tapping the subjective meanings of organizational (or in this case, occupational) members. In other words, ask them.

According to Bormann (1983, 2001), the main task in doing this kind of analysis is to find evidence that symbolic convergence has taken or is taking place. SCT, has several parts, all of which may be applied to the trucking culture (see Bormann, 1983 and 2001, as well as Cragan & Shields, 1995, for extended explanations of SCT; see Mills, 2007, for an extended application to the trucking culture). The first part deals with the natural human tendency to attribute meaning to what people say and do. When a number of people develop portions of their private symbolic worlds that overlap from symbolic convergence, they share a common consciousness and have a basis for interacting together to create community, discuss common experiences, and achieve mutual understandings (Mills, p. 129). The occupation and accompanying lifestyle of the truck driver provides the basis for symbolic convergence, despite the extreme diversity of organizations involved, and also accounting for drivers who work for themselves. The existence of a Citizen's Band (CB) radio language that even has dictionaries available for translations is evidence of a separate understanding of a group language (see *Communication Books*, 1976; and Fensch, 1976).

A second key part describes the dynamic of people sharing group fantasies (narratives with dramatic imagery, wordplay, stories, humor, gestures and so forth). A person dramatizes a message, and others become caught up in it to the point of participation in the drama (responding with laughter, agreement, elaboration, etc.). When members share a fantasy, they achieve symbolic convergence in the development of similar attitudes and emotional responses to the players in the drama. They have interpreted some aspect of their experience in the same way. When I began studying truckers, a question I posed to truck stop personnel was, "Do you know any drivers who tell stories?" The response was overwhelmingly, "Do you know any who don't?" The truck stop, the "yard" (home base), the internet, and CB radio are prime examples of places where truckers meet to tell stories (or share fantasies). Story telling plays a major part in socialization to the occupation. Some examples of work that includes trucking stories include Stevenson (no year recorded), Stern (1975), Ewens and Ellis (1977), McKee (1990), Will (1992), Ouellet (1994), Wise and Di Salvatore (1995), McTavish (2001), and Adams and Ryder (2003), as well as countless blogs on the internet.

A third part of SCT that is relevant to this discussion consists of the factors that explain why and when people share the fantasies they do. When people share group fantasies, they may come to an integrated rhetorical vision, which is a combination of fantasies that gives the participants a broader view of the group, its relationship to the external world, and their place in the scheme of things. While Bormann (1972) first cited rhetorical visions in religious, social, and political movements and campaigns, he acknowledged the same phenomenon in organizational communication (1983). I suggest that, especially in the case of truckers, this idea may be extended even further to include occupations (Mills, 2007). One large-scale example of truckers organizing occupationally is the shutdown strike of 1983, where a large number of truckers acted as a unified body against the Truck Tax Bill of 1982.

Finally, Bormann (2001) uses the term *rhetorical community* to describe people who share a common symbolic ground and respond to messages consistently according to their rhetorical visions. When these groups experience conflict and disagreement, they have a basis for negotiation, compromise, cooperation, and coordination of effort because of their rhetorical visions (or shared values). Truckers have such a community. In the sections that follow, I show how truck drivers socially formulate an occupational culture and collective identity to manage the taint of their dirty work.

A Dirty Job

Trucking has come a long way since its beginnings in the early 1900s. A fully equipped, forty-ton, eighteen wheeler costing well over $100,000 today is a far cry from its early ancestors that did not have windshield wipers or doors, much less a sleeper cab. The physical dirtiness of the job used to come from the primitive driving conditions. Now, at least in part, it is more a matter of personal choice (i.e., it is possible to drive a truck and not be covered in dirt and grease). The taint of physical danger still exists.

Social and moral taint have also evolved with the profession. The servile nature of the work (delivering goods) remains a major source of social taint, but one thing that has changed is the level playing field, or rules of the road. In recent years, many states have enacted speed limit laws that are different for trucks than other vehicles that travel the same roads. In Michigan it is a difference of 15 miles per hour (70 for cars and 55 for trucks). Lawmakers want to slow trucks down to minimize injury and damage from accidents, but the differential speed limits create a new hazard. Truckers often just shake their heads when I ask them to respond to the speed limit changes, as if the world just added another brick to their load. To counter their liability concerns, many companies install electronic speed governors on truck engines to limit their maximum speeds. However, automobile drivers on the same highway have no such restrictors, causing vehicles on the same roadway to travel at speeds that may vary 20 to 40 mph. This makes driving a truck more difficult and more dangerous. Drivers must constantly be aware of the differential speed limits and more carefully observe their speed. Going with the flow of traffic just might earn them a ticket. Not going with the flow of traffic might cause an accident. The double bind of this physical taint (added risk) is compounded by the social injury of not being allowed to travel at the same speed as automobiles. Further, it is not fair (moral taint) to treat professional drivers differently than, as many would say, "any jackass in a car." If you want to get a conversation going at a truck stop diner, bring up the speed limits.

One way truckers deal with these sources of taint is to declare their super competence and ability to persevere despite roadblocks put in their way by the "bastards" who would "get us down." Another way truckers address taint is to note the vital role that transportation has played in the development of our country with a sense of pride. They have been an indispensable part of economic development in the United States. The bumper stickers discussed early in this chapter rhetorically position truckers as economic saviors for Americans. Many drivers I spoke with commented how "most people don't even know enough to appreciate the work we do." Criticizing public ignorance functions to mediate the dirtiness of the job, suggesting that if outsiders only knew what truckers put up with for them or afforded them, they would not assign as much taint to the profession. This is a form of condemning the condemners, a strategy for securing and sustaining a positive social identity (Ashforth & Kreiner, 1999).

The most commonly held stereotype of the American trucker is that of an overbearing, pill-popping, road hogging, womanizing, speed demon (Mills, 2007). To many people on the road in their four wheelers (cars, in trucker parlance), at least parts of this image seem true. At the other end of the spectrum is a romanticized image of drivers as grand adventurers. The trucker mystique is, most broadly, a set of abstract characterizations of types of truckers and trucking situations fueled by a rhetoric and set of images associating power, independence, and excitement (in particular) with the job. Before we can examine how truckers dramatize messages to achieve occupational convergence, it is important to look at the actors themselves as they are defined by both insiders and outsiders of the profession. The next section covers some of these popular images associated with truck drivers, and how truckers view themselves and each other.

Popular Images of Truck Drivers

When trucking became big business with the development of the diesel engine in the 1930s, the job became more complicated for the driver. With increased economic power in industry came governmental regulations in the form of the Motor Carrier Act of 1935, created by Congress to control interstate transport. Truckers now needed official permission to operate in a state and cross state lines. Drivers were angry. Government employees were aggressive. There was much confusion about who could drive what. The government tried to limit the truckers' freedom to move, which is an essential part of their identity, and they fought back with strikes and shutdowns. This was true again in the 1970s with deregulation, the subsequent passage of the Motor Carrier Act of 1980, and the differential speed limits already discussed. Truckers cast themselves as heroes of the working class against big, bad, commonsense-stupid government officials. It is a familiar theme that has long roots in the history of trucking. It is also a theme that has found its way to popular media in such movies as *FIST* starring Sylvester Stallone and *Convoy* with Kris Kristofferson. Breaking the law is redefined as noble, serving a greater good. Ashforth and Kreiner (1999) call this taint management strategy reframing, where "the 'dirty particulars' are wrapped in more abstract and uplifting values associated with the larger purpose" (p. 421).

The CB craze of the 1970s is attributed in part to the popular song "Convoy," along with the *Smokey and the Bandit* movies starring Burt Reynolds, where all kinds of "four wheelers" had "ears on" to play "king of the road" and "ride with the big boys" (Dannefer and Poushinsky, 1977). This fad declined in the 1980s and the drivers got their airwaves back, but there was an increased public awareness of the CB community. There was much academic attention to the CB during the "craze" period. See Runcie (1969), Dannefer and Poushinsky (1977), Powell and Ary (1977), Hendley (1979), Smith (1979, 1981), Smith (1980), and Dannefer and Kasen (1981).

The CB language particular to truckers is an indication of symbolic convergence. You have to be a member, or strongly affiliated, to understand and participate in the conversational exchange. Though most conversations on the radio are cryptic and brief, they serve both a functional purpose (checking road conditions, "bear" reports, getting directions) and a social one (breaking up the trip, talking to stay awake, staying in touch with friends either on the road or on base radios along the road). Some drivers complain that the radio has gotten too "nasty" (foul-mouthed), and many do not keep them on, preferring to listen to music and get directions on cell phones. This has contributed to less participation by some truckers in this aspect of the occupational culture.

Trucker as a rebel with a cause is not the only image of drivers portrayed in popular media. The TV series "BJ and the Bear" had a trucker using his rig to do good deeds for the pure satisfaction of a job done right, frustrating the ill-intended efforts of the bad guys. While these are fictional accounts, they reflect real experiences. Trucker as white knight is a good Samaritan image that some drivers invoke to refocus attention away from the stigmatized features of the work toward the occasional heroic opportunity afforded to those who work on the highways and are often the first responders at an accident scene. The letter columns of trucking magazines regularly feature examples of aid being rendered, frequently at a high cost of time. This allows drivers who haven't had this kind of incident themselves to vicariously experience pride in their profession through the telling of a story about one of them.

In contrast to the trucker as white knight is the image of the trucker as brute monster (Blake, 1974). The movie *Maximum Overdrive* illustrates this image. People are held captive in a truck stop by killer trucks that have mysteriously come to life. Those who have looked in the rearview mirror of their car to see the grill of an oncoming truck closing in on them, particularly one with "teeth" on the grill, will report some anxiety. This image serves the important purpose of providing truckers with a negative example, defining norms by telling them how not to behave. Many drivers are quick to point out that they are not this driver (who is perceived as unsafe), which is taint management by selective social comparison (Ashforth & Kreiner, 1999).

Another image of the trucker is concrete sailor (Belman & Monaco, 2005). This representation combines the ideas of independence and control (Blake, 1974). The trucker has a "girl in every port" (city). It highlights the opportunities married or otherwise committed drivers have to be unfaithful on the road (moral taint). One trucker's wife told me that she knew her husband was not faithful to her, but that it "goes with the job." However, many drivers strongly disavowed this image, telling me I had seen too many movies. They acknowledged this reputation was often a serious concern of or source of insecurity for their partners. It would appear to be the exception rather than the rule. One man told me that he figured guys either "got the energy to do it or talk about it, not both."

Drivers can also identify with the pioneering spirit of stagecoach drivers and wagon masters. The logbook that today's trucker must keep and the old cattleman's diary both describe a journey across hostile territory, whether the writer is at the mercy of bandits or state troopers (Stern, 1975). The term "riding shotgun" is still used by truckers today to refer to the codriver, and there is still a danger of hijackers on the roads in the new millennium. Many cowboy metaphors exist in the language of today's truckers. One driver I rode with often spoke to his truck like a faithful mount, saying, "Whoa there, big truck" as he slowed her down. Many CB handles also reflect a cowboy culture (e.g., Tumbleweed, Colorado Cowboy, Bushwhacker, Highrider). The asphalt cowboy rides all day on the concrete range, and knows his resting place at night will be next to his trusty steed (sleeper cab). His tractor is his "horse" and his trailer load of freight is his herd of "doggies." He sits in the "saddle" wearing a cowboy hat, boots, and belt buckle, as he runs along that "asphalt trail." Drivers who identify with this image may be recasting themselves as Hollywood heroes of the old West in a rebirth of the American cowboy.

The next image is one that is articulated (airbrushed) on the side of many tractor rigs, "King of the Road." There's something about being the biggest vehicle on the road that is powerful (Mills, 2007, p. 135). I think that is why so many Americans are enamored with SUVs. Many drivers feel a sense of power and harmony on the road. One named Thunderball (CB handle) said, "I really enjoy being out on top of my own little world in my big rig. It's a hard life, but a good life. Out there, listenin' to my wheels hummin' down the road, lookin' down on everybody else—I really am king of the road." In this case, isolation from others may be isolation from taint, an avoidance strategy.

A final image that drivers identify with to manage taint is trucker as professional/small businessman (Blake, 1974). It is important for both company drivers and owner operators (who drive for themselves, rather than a company) to be involved in the business end of trucking. While the other images may be found in "songs, magazine columns, truck stop talk, and jokes, the trucker as professional is the image pushed through feature articles in trucking magazines, trade journals, and driving schools" (Mills, p. 136) The driver is performing a job, and is thus a working professional. This involves occupational expertise in loading, maintenance, record keeping, cleanliness and neatness, and even sales as well as driving. Other indications of this image are fax machines at truck stops, and a higher incidence of computers and cell phones in the rigs. Some truck stops on my initial road trips in the 1980s (e.g., White's 76 in Raphine, VA) even had private telephones in the showers! More recently, the Flying J truck stops were among the first to provide Wi-Fi technology at their plazas (Edds, 2004). I remember feeling embarrassed by my surprise when one of my interviewees showed up with a briefcase. This was an image I did not recognize until I saw this business artifact.

Identity Management

Many truckers will report they were born with diesel fuel in their veins. They will describe themselves as hardworking and underpaid, just making an honest living. With the advent of more driving schools, you don't hear of drivers "learning the gears on daddy's knee" quite as much, although there are still many drivers who do. In rural America, the transition from field tractor to highway tractor is not uncommon. There also seems to be a good deal of transitioning from the coal mine to trucking as well (according to interviews in a truck stop in West Virginia). Veterans' benefits are also cited as helpful for starting a career in trucking, providing funds for school, loans for trucks, etc.

Freedom, independence, and control are the most frequently cited reasons for taking to the road (Mills, 2007). Who does it is another story. Although I heard "I only had an eighth-grade education" frequently, I was impressed with the number of college grads on the road. One driver discovered that he had a learning disability when his daughter was diagnosed with one. He believes that is why he did not fare well in school at a time when many learning disabilities were not yet identified or accommodated in education. I suspect he is right. I also suspect that he is not alone. A great deal of value is placed on "common sense," to the point where those with a college education are often tested in that regard to ensure that their "book learnin'" did not erase the "good sense God gave 'em."

A good number of women enter the profession for the same reasons their male counterparts do. Technological advances make it easier for them to physically do the work (e.g., lifting devices, power steering, and power brakes). Companies often encourage wives to join their husbands as codrivers. It is considered good business to keep the couple together (especially considering the high divorce rate in trucking). Eighty percent of women truckers drive double with someone else. Typically, women drive with a husband or boyfriend (96 percent of those who drive double). The experience of women truckers is greatly influenced by male sponsorship, support, and protection (Lembright & Riemer, 1982). In 1950 being a female trucker was odd enough to land air time on the "What's My Line?" television show. She is still a curiosity in many truck stops. While it is difficult to estimate the number of women in trucking, there is evidence that their occupational participation being recognized (e.g., separate showers and other amenities added at truck stops). The industry still maintains a strong male orientation. There is more taint associated with being a feminine male driver than being a masculine or feminine female driver. One female driver threatened to "beat 'em (her critics) with my bra," highlighting her struggle to be taken seriously at times. She contended that in her profession, like many others, "the feminine is only valued for one thing out here, if you know what I mean."

It used to be that you could tell where a driver was from by his "uniform." This distinction is becoming more difficult. The big belt buckle and cowboy hat is often worn by eastern as well as western drivers. Most drivers wear ball caps and jeans. Many have chain-drive wallets attached to their belts. Some southern truckers display the Confederate flag on the grill of the rig, although this is not always a reliable geographic indicator because there are others who display it as a symbol consistent with the rebel image described earlier (reframing the law breaker as hero). The blurring of geographical clothing markers may indicate less need for this identity distinction, because interstate travel has become more accessible for everyone.

One of the first things other drivers notice about one another is what the trucker is hauling. Sometimes it is not necessary to see the load. Pig, bull, or chicken haulers have a distinctive odor that sometimes even a shower cannot remedy. This is also true for leather, paper, and some types of produce. Once I was riding with a load of onions (that we called "funions") and my friends noticed when I returned home, although I, by that time, was no longer aware of the odor. The nature of the load, origin, and destination are all data by which the trucker evaluates his peers. Such in-group social comparisons serve to weight the taint. In other words, there is an intraoccupational taint hierarchy that serves an esteem building function when the driver can identify someone with a dirtier job or load.

Sometimes it is hard to get a straight answer from a driver about what exactly he is hauling. It might make the driver vulnerable to hijacking if the load is valuable. However, another reason for nondisclosure is that the load may be tainted or boring, so the driver may perform identity management and liven conversation by saying the load is "donut holes" or "flies' wings."

The various images of the trucker, from the inside and outside, have been discussed in order to better understand identity management in the social drama of the trucking community. Next we will examine the workplace of the professional driver where the task portion of the occupational drama unfolds: the truck and the road.

On the Road

The Federal Motor Carrier Safety Regulations outline tests drivers must pass in order to determine if they can safely operate the truck (Barrett, 1983; Adams & Ryder, 2003). These include an objective written exam, a medical exam, and a road test. The driver must demonstrate a working knowledge of pre-trip inspections, operating skills, freight handling, rules and regulations, and routes. These categories of evaluation also provide the basis for his stories, his boasts, his songs, and his folklore (Eff, 1978). Drivers learn occupational ideologies that strengthen their identification with the collective while they are "inoculated" against the taint messages they might encounter from the larger social system in these stories and practices.

Another vehicle for work identification and culture development is initiation practices (Ashforth & Kreiner, 1999). Newcomers may be assigned dirty (low status) tasks, be verbally and physically harassed (e.g., derogatory nicknames or titles), or be ignored until they prove themselves. These rites of passage signal acceptance (earned) into the occupational group, and cultivate stronger work-related esteem. Initiating novice drivers is fun for truckers. It is common, for example, to fill the new driver with wild stories of the most dangerous runs, one of which happens to be the one he is leaving on. Other rites include switching the airlines on his truck so that he cannot release his brakes, or unhooking the fifth wheel so that the tractor and trailer separate when he pulls out of the terminal (Mills, p. 138. A codriver might use Armor All to polish the seats of a new companion, which makes it difficult to stay in them. This happened to me. While embarrassing, it also signaled acceptance into the community, which meant a lot to me.

The counter case to initiation and inclusion is termination and exclusion. Just as there are observable initiation behaviors, there are also termination practices. When asked how this happens, one driver, Eight-pack, responded, "They know when they've fucked up [are discourteous in traffic or have otherwise given the profession a bad name] and sooner or later the rest of us do too. Nobody associates with them—nobody wants anything to do with them. They're dangerous." This kind of shunning sends the message that the driver is too tainted for continued membership in the occupational work group. Sometimes a trucker is given an inferior machine in response to inappropriate behavior. Basically, the message is "you are not good enough for a decent truck."

The truck as physical artifact is a status marker in the taint hierarchy of trucking. The trucker develops a special relationship with the truck, often referring to "we" as he describes "their" exploits, usually using the feminine pronoun "she." "She can soothe him with the purring lullaby of her engine, excite him with her strength and power, or anger him when she's uncooperative" (Mills, p. 138). She is his partner. He is her caretaker. How does the truck become so human? One driver named Stewart put it this way: "The truck has a soul. It can be a devil or an angel or just a trusted companion on the long haul. A truck gone wild can be a twisted nightmare, hurling you headlong into the center rail with a front-wheel blowout, or it can be as gentle as a mother's love, rocking you to sleep in its softly padded belly." In occupational dramas, truckers generally have collaborative relationships with their trucks, and more adversarial relationships with the law ("bears") and cars ("four-wheelers").

A majority of truckers believe that the law treats them differently than other drivers, that troopers lie in wait for them, eager to search their trucks for drugs or guns or to catch them going three miles over the speed limit (Mills, p. 138). One time when I was on the road and our "chickens were a little heavy," we took an exit before the weigh station ("chicken coop") to avoid it. A state highway patrolman radioed us that we had to stop, but we replied that we were getting off to visit our favorite sub shop, and proceeded to do so. He got tired of waiting while we took our time with lunch, and he eventually left us alone. Knowing a specific restaurant's name made the story more convincing, and, as the driver noted, "He can't tell us we can't stop to eat, now, can he?" Strategies like this cast the trucker as clever-over-regulated-hero against the letter-of-the-law-no-breaks-villain that is the highway patrol. I heard many hardship stories about fines or delayed loads (which also cost truckers) because of weight problems out of the drivers' control (e.g., accumulated ice on the trailer making it weigh more, or company-assigned overloads that the driver felt powerless to decline). These kinds of situations require the kind of reframing described here in order for the driver to survive. The same was sometimes true for speeding. Drivers are assigned to deliver loads at times they can't make without breaking the law, which puts them in a catch-22 situation. Do they lose the load, or break the law? Do they eat, or speed? It becomes that basic, which contributes to the social and moral taint of the job.

A discussion of life on the road would be incomplete without a comment on the truckers' relationships with four wheelers. Although truck drivers complain about them, especially when they put them at risk by cutting them off or otherwise driving dangerously, cars are also a source of interest and entertainment. Truckers may talk on the radio for miles about what is going on in cars. This is particularly true if there is anything sexual involved (although nose picking is right up there too). Some observations are elevated to legend status. I heard more than once around Highway 270 in Columbus, Ohio about this "lady who drives a Mercedes out here at night with her dome light on and nothin' else, if you know what I mean." Another story I heard repeatedly was about an accident where a guy poked his finger through his brain upon impact and was killed (a lesson about the perils of nose-picking while driving). Drivers discuss accidents very matter-of-factly. Fortunately, not all of them are tragic and some become funny stories (e.g., messy cleanups—ball bearings, chickens, etc.). The setting for the exchange of these stories and the development of much occupational drama is the truck stop (Mills, 2007).

When freed from the rigors of the long haul, laid over in small-town USA, waiting for a return load home, many truckers will take advantage of any available social life. Maybe a good meal. Maybe unwind in front of a TV. Maybe find a beer and some music. Some company. Is this unique to truckers? Probably not. But the place that offers all of this and services for the truck is unique to truckers: the truck stop. Each one has its own character and conveniences. A deluxe model will have live entertainment, motel units, multiple fuel lines, electronic scales, a 24-hour restaurant, a convenience mart, banking services, truck brokers, tire sales and service, laundry, a swimming pool, individual showers, hair stylists, a chiropractor, massage therapy, movies, and a paved, lighted lot with security. At the other end of the spectrum are the ma 'n' pa type stops where the décor, and hopefully the food, are homemade, and if the driver stays overnight, it is in the truck (see Mills, 2007, for additional descriptions of truck stops). It could be argued that creating separate spaces for truckers to layover might constitute letting them know they were tainted (as in not welcome at other locations where members of multiple other occupational work groups meet to socialize). Many places post "no semis" signs, largely because the weight of the truck cracks their asphalt or even concrete parking surfaces.

At whatever kind of truck stop the driver pulls into for a break, you can count on them multitasking. Since most drivers are paid by the mile, time off the road is time off the "feedbag." They will take care of business. Sometimes this is as simple as using the restroom while gassing up the truck. Sometimes it also includes a meal, contact with a dispatcher or customer, or a truck wash (to maintain a "clean" image). Truck stops that cater to this need for efficiency will get more traffic.

Drivers adapt to "shifts" that work for them (driving at night, during the day, straight through all at once, in pieces with breaks, etc.). Whenever they stop to rest at truck stops, it is often a social time to "get together and lie to each other" (Mills, p. 139) Because of the varying work patterns or shifts, it is not difficult to find company at any time of the day or night. This is valuable social time. Some drivers I spoke to elevated story telling to an art form, warming up to a favorite tale, clearly enjoying the responses of a new audience as it came to life with their talents. The story must be marginally believable to be acceptable. If not believable, then it must at least by entertaining (Mills, 2007). Otherwise, the story and the teller were dismissed as "full of shit," which creates a kind of social and moral taint—the line between storyteller and liar is thin.

When I began to collect these stories, I asked a waitress about what they were discussing when I saw drivers gathered in a lounge or restaurant, or even on the parking lot, talking or laughing. She replied, "You can bet they're talking about my ass, your ass, or how fast them trucks can go." Major themes that appear in truckers' stories are the truck, women, the trip, the law, the profession, and the life (Mills, 2007). Sometimes truckers who have been "chasin' each other" in a convoy will stop to eat or lay over together for a weekend. This is a fun time to exchange stories. Boasts and brags usually come after about the third cup of coffee, and some truckers excuse themselves at this point. "After you've been truckin' as long as I have, you've heard it all—you boys have fun pullin' each others' legs and impressin' Sweet Pea here." My CB handle was Sweet Pea, and I frequently encountered "significant exaggeration and flat out lies as a function of (mostly) truckers bragging about their work, and (sometimes) men strutting their stuff" (Mills, 2007). Once when a prostitute came on the CB, asking if any listeners wanted some "lipstick on (their) dipstick," the driver I was with turned off the radio in an effort to shield me from this part of the work environment, so that I would not be tainted or see his occupation "that way." This kind of concealment is a taint management strategy, guiding participants to see (or not see) certain parts of the job.

There are rules for talking over the CB. Very early in my research, an anonymous driver "helped" me with radio road manners. I had asked for a smokey ("bear") report from westbound traffic (as I was eastbound). I got my reply and thanked the driver for it. He waited, and then responded, "now you're supposed to tell me what it looks like behind you. That's the way it works. I tell you, you tell me, I say 'have a safe ride,' and you wish me the same. Got it? If you're gonna use the radio, make sure you mind your manners, four?" The "four" in this quotation refers to the 10-codes, an official set of numerical abbreviations originally developed by the police and other radio mobile services (10-4 means "OK, message received" but, in this case, it was a question about whether or not I understood). I complied. One of the ways of determining rule behavior is observing sanctions for violations and also repairs (Shiminoff, 1980).

Gaining communication competence, or speaking like an insider, contributes to stronger occupational identification. For truckers, this is part of the "diesel in their blood." Some drivers report that they have tried to leave the profession, but that the job is so much a part of who they are that they can't "get into another language," even when they are mortgaged to their ears, and have to drive all day and night to stay ahead of fuel and insurance costs. I saw a T-shirt in one truck stop that read, "My take-home pay won't take me home." The road becomes home and is where drivers return, despite its drawbacks and dangers, to work another day, the scene of their occupational drama.

Conclusions

This essay has provided evidence that indicates that truckers form and identify with an occupational community through a variety of communicative forms. Sharing "war" stories in the truck stop, complete with heroes and villains (us vs. them) illustrates a shared perspective about how things should be interpreted when it comes to the performance of the truck-driving occupation. Through these experiences truckers learn what meanings to attach to common experiences (Mills, 2007). It is also where they learn to manage their identities and minimize taint. The CB and truck stop are prime examples of places where truckers meet to share stories (or fantasies), often in a specialized language unique to truckers. Many of these stories, as typical according to Symbolic Convergence Theory, have interchangeable heroes and villains depending on whose rhetorical vision is framing the drama. For example, many tales revolve around getting past the law. Depending on who is interpreting the story (fellow truckers or police officers), the clever trucker may be the hero or the conniving villain (Mills, 2007). To come to such conclusions requires that the members identify their collective self. Bormann (1983) shows that fantasies that distinguish who "we" are may take the form of "we are not" dramas. Once these boundaries are established through the sharing of fantasies (creating a differentiation between insiders and outsiders), the members create guidelines (usually implicitly) for terminating rituals to force members out and initiating rituals for recruits (Mills, p. 141). Shunning is one method of communicating a separation from the group. Initiating rituals may take the form of good-natured pranks, the weathering of which gives recruits membership status. This examination of the trucking profession illustrates how drivers have a basis, through the experience of their jobs, to perform in rhetorical community, establish collective identity, and communicate taint management strategies.

A trucker sent me the bumper sticker that titles this chapter, "Without trucks we'd all be naked, hungry and homeless." To talk about trucking as a working-class job with statistics about production and accident rates does not tell the entire story (Mills, 2007). Their "dirty work" keeps us in the manner of life to which we have become accustomed, largely mindless of the work of delivering it. Recognizing this minimizes the social tendency to stigmatize the work because it surfaces the taken for granted social needs that truckers meet for us. Truckers form an occupational community that is a fixture on the landscape of our daily living. When we listen to them and validate their taint management strategies, we can acknowledge it truly is because of them that we are clothed, fed, and sheltered.

5

Bitching about Secretarial "Dirty Work"

Patty Sotirin

I begin with a question prompted by the title of this chapter: How is secretarial work "dirty"? After all, secretaries work in the comparative cleanliness of modern offices and rarely get their hands dirty. Nonetheless, there is a paradox involved in secretarial work and occupational identity: on one hand, we sing the praises of secretaries (or "administrative assistants" or "executive assistants"). On the other hand, we dismiss a great deal of their work as trivial and mundane and cast them as (often insubordinate) office servants. In this regard, secretarial work and identity are tainted by perceptions of secretarial tasks as office drudgery, secretarial roles as degrading, and secretarial identity as feminized (Sotirin & Miller, 1994). My focus is on the identity management that secretaries do among themselves to deal with the small injustices and mundane oppressions endemic to such "dirty work" through a particular form of office talk: secretarial bitching. Specifically, I argue that secretarial bitching responds to the physical, social, and moral "taint" that undermines positive social regard for secretarial tasks, roles, and identity. Yet because bitching carries its own social and moral stigma, secretaries cannot effectively reclaim the dignity of secretarial work and identity through bitching. Nonetheless, I caution against disregarding secretarial bitching as simply "women's office talk" or disparaging bitching as a co-opted or damaging form of complaining. Instead, I urge researchers to consider the larger contexts for bitching and to remain sensitive to the political potential for rearticulating such contexts in particular episodes of secretarial bitching.

The chapter proceeds by clarifying what makes secretarial work "dirty" and the social perceptions and moral suspicions that threaten positive regard for secretaries' occupational identity. I offer several examples from my own field research to show how secretaries defend secretarial identity through bitching. The examples support the suggestion offered in Ashforth and Kreiner (1999) that members of occupational cultures engage in stigma-resisting practices in order to sustain a positive occupational identity, but that such practices may have dysfunctional effects.

How is Secretarial Work "Dirty"?

In this section, I detail the perceptions and conditions that render secretarial work "dirty" and that taint the social roles and moral character of secretaries themselves, even though their work is recognized as necessary and they are applauded as the ones who "really run the office."

The Distasteful Drudgery of Secretarial Tasks

Secretaries are tasked with maintaining the professional face of the organization, tidying up the dirty details and managing the mundane duties that are the mainstay of office orderliness: answering phones, managing mail, keeping files, xeroxing, coordinating other people's schedules, making reservations for someone else's trip. Despite the importance of this work, secretarial tasks are stigmatized as necessary but banal. In addition, the short career ladder and low salary ceiling of secretarial work—in 2004, $28,500–$43,000 annually—has historically compromised occupational prestige (Bureau of Labor Statistics, 2006). Instead, secretaries have long looked to interpersonal rewards—the importance of good relationships and the boss's approval—in lieu of material rewards (Kanter, 1977).

However, Ashforth and Kreiner (1999) caution that tediousness and low pay are not sufficient to warrant a "dirty work" classification. Dirty work either deals directly with the polluting elements of social life—garbage, criminals, dirt—or is done under noxious or dangerous conditions. I hold that secretarial work meets both these criteria.

First, secretaries are responsible for disposing of the unwanted elements and disorder that threaten the professionalism and civilized decorum of the office. They must sort out and dispose of office "garbage" from (physical and virtual) junk mail to unwanted visitors. In addition, secretaries are often called on to do personal "dirty work" for their bosses. The classic example is Rosemary Wood, secretary to impeached U.S. President Richard Nixon, who erased a potentially incriminating segment of an audiotape of her boss's comments about the Watergate break-in. To be fair, Wood always denied erasing the tape segment deliberately, maintaining that it happened by mistake while she was transcribing the tapes for a Senate investigation of Nixon's involvement in Watergate. More prosaic examples come from the entries to a contest called "The Good Boss/Bad Boss Contest" conducted annually during the 1980s and early 1990s by 9 to 5, The National Organization for Working Women. The stories about bad bosses that secretaries submitted proved that there is considerable "dirty work" involved in secretarial labor. For example, one secretary reported that she had to sew a button on her boss's trousers while he was wearing them; another reported that she had to deliver her boss's stool sample to his doctor.

Along with dealing with polluting elements, the demands of the secretary's job can be humiliating and onerous. To give just one example, secretaries are bound to their desks and phones so that (more important) others do not have to be. In my fieldwork among a team of executive assistants at an international management consulting firm, this aspect of secretarial work was strikingly evident during an event meant to celebrate organizational culture and promote morale. The company rented a local theme park and gave all employees an afternoon off to enjoy the park at the company's expense except for a group of executive assistants. They had to stay at the office to answer phones because the company's policy was that no caller was ever to be forwarded to an answering machine during business hours.

In response to perceptions of "dirty work," secretaries often espouse what Ashforth and Kreiner (1999) term the "for want of a nail" argument. This involves an ideological recalibration of denigrated tasks, that is, a revaluation of the importance of attending to small details, sorting out the trash, and managing tensions among competing protocols and preferences—the boss's, the organization's, the industry's, and general business standards. If they did not attend to the small details, the larger work could not be accomplished.

Everyday Denigration of Secretarial Roles

National Secretary's Day is a very visible effort to celebrate the importance of secretarial work and roles and to enhance the prestige of the occupation. Yet secretaries are in a servile position in relation to anyone who makes a legitimate demand on their services. For example, the secretaries in my university department must respond to requests from students, faculty, administration staff, and anyone from outside the university who contacts the office. Servility is compounded when secretaries are treated as invisible. It is not unusual for people to have discussions in front of a secretary without including her at all, sometimes even referring to her services as they talk. Being visibly invisible is part of the everyday denigration of the secretarial role that renders secretarial work "dirty work."

Another perception that denigrates the worth of the secretarial role is that secretarial skills and knowledge are fairly mundane. The International Association of Administrative Professionals (IAAP) promotes the professionalization of secretarial work and offers a certification process that promises to enhance not only salaries, promotability, and professional skills but also the esteem granted a "committed professional" (IAAP, http://www.iaap-hq.org/cert/advantage.htm). Yet despite efforts to professionalize the occupation through certifications and specialized training, there remains a suspicion that secretaries do not exercise special skills or knowledge. The popular perception is that anyone can do what secretaries are hired to do. After all, the "ordinary competence and minor initiative" involved in making the pragmatic assessments required for most secretarial tasks is a matter of consistently reproducing pre-established procedural rationalities (Feldman & March, 1981).

The issue, as Pringle (1988) pointed out, is that the competence of secretaries is assessed not only in terms of specialized skills and knowledge but just as much or more so on the basis of the qualities of feminine gentility, including "a well-groomed appearance, a well-modulated voice, maturity, poise and grace and the ability to converse intelligently with managers" (p. 133). The suspicion that secretarial worth is assessed more on the basis of intangible qualities of femininity than on expertise or gender-neutral criteria of professional comportment undermines claims of professionalism.

The link between femininity and secretarial competence draws on the history of women in the office. Secretarial tasks have long been equated with women's domestic routines and feminine traits, like attention to details and willingness to submit to the tedium and restrictions of standardized labor, casting secretarial work as "pink collar" labor. Feminist labor historians including Davies (1984) and Strom (1992) have produced careful historical analyses of the feminization of secretarial work and the complex contradictions and traditions constituting "the secretary" as feminine and predominantly female. Their work documents how complex relations among capitalist, bureaucratic, patriarchal, and technological demands and opportunities along with social, economic, and ideological refigurations of women's "proper place" opened the support infrastructure of the modern office to women workers and eventually locked women into pink-collar clerical occupations. As part of that historical process, secretarial work and roles became indelibly marked as feminine.

The entrenched associations between feminine qualities and traits and secretarial labor and roles inspires what Gutek (1988) identified as "sex role spillover," that is, the assumption that women's social roles as helpmates, sexual partners, or caretakers are incorporated into their roles in the office, casting secretaries as office wives, mothers, girls, and domestics. During the first half of the twentieth century, women's claim on the secretarial role was secured through this conflation of socio-sexual roles and work roles thanks to the popular assumption that women would exert a "civilizing" influence on businessmen and bring a domestic touch to the office (Strom; Davies). However, sex role spillover inflects office relations with the same tensions that characterize gendered relations outside the office, making secretaries vulnerable to harassment and exploitation based on sexual differences and stereotypes. The popular film depiction of secretarial solidarity, *9 to 5* (Higgins, 1980) dramatizes these consequences of sex-role spillover in the characterizations of the three main characters. While Lily Tomlin's character, Violet Newstead, is an "office Mom," Dolly Parton's character, executive secretary Doralee Rhodes, is a sexualized caretaker and Jane Fonda's character, Judy Bernly, is the naïve "new girl." As the film shows, each of these feminized stereotypes is subject to character-typed sexual harassment.

Secretaries reframe and dispute perceptions of servility, gentility, and femininity by asserting their professionalism and emphasizing the importance of the secretarial role to the smooth operation of the office. In addition, the power relations of the office that subject secretaries to mundane oppressions are countered by a modernist image of the secretary as a valued member of the office team, respected by and equal to other team professionals (Pringle, 1988). Despite these ideological defenses, secretarial identity continues to be viewed as feminized, subservient, and morally suspect.

Moral Taint of Secretarial Identity

Discretion, decorum, patience, and loyalty are valued attributes of secretarial character and comportment. Yet these upstanding moral attributes are tarnished by popular suspicions about the dubious virtue of secretarial loyalty and the dangers of feminine sexuality.

Consider the ambivalent status of secretarial loyalty as both an applauded attribute of a good secretary and the basis for the suspicion that secretaries are morally suspect. The problem is this: a loyal secretary must be skillful at prevarication. Secretaries wield considerable behind-the-scenes power in their celebrated roles as "gate-keepers" and "behind the throne" assistants. They are often called upon to help with backstage preparations, to cover up mistakes and ineptitudes, and to keep counsel for those who perform on the front stage of power. In order to perform these functions, prevarication is a necessary professional skill. For example, in the years I worked as a full-time executive secretary, I often had to lie or tell half-truths in order to turn away unwanted visitors, protect my boss's time, cover up for his mistakes, and deflect requests for work he had not finished or information he did not care to share. I knew that those I told these lies to frequently realized that I was not telling the whole story. It is the transparency of such prevarications that makes secretarial character morally suspect.

Along with moral suspicion over secretarial prevarication, secretarial professionalism and occupational worth are undermined by their conflation with feminine gentility. The entrenched perception of secretaries as feminine invites a whole range of taken-for-granted, interconnected gender dichotomies—male/female, masculine/feminine, active/passive, rational/emotional—that structure office relations. More insidiously, perceptions of the feminine nature of secretarial identity invite moral suspicions about female sexuality. Pringle's interviews with secretaries and bosses revealed that despite the asexual veneer of most bureaucratic offices, the relation of secretary/boss was often characterized by oedipal mother/son tensions, the tensions of conjugal relations (popularly connoted in the reference to the secretary as "office wife") or the tensions of implicit sexual attraction.

Such tensions have long been the basis for Hollywood depictions of secretaries as sexual predators or office moms and "war of the sexes" depictions of the female secretary/male boss relation. Likewise, women's competition over men is popularly inscribed in the scenario of the woman whose husband has an affair with or leaves her for his secretary. For example, the 1930s' film *Wife vs Secretary*, starring Clark Gable, Jean Harlow, and Myrna Loye (Brown, 1936), depicts this classic rivalry, while the 1950s' TV sitcom *Private Secretary* (Chertok, 1953–1957) casts the secretary/boss relation as a comedic conjugal "war of the sexes," and a recent film, *The Secretary* (Shainberg, 2003), thematizes the sexuality of secretarial subservience. Similarly, a 1990s' drama, *The Temp* (Holland, 1993), is a cautionary tale about the murderous loyalty of a sexually predatory and ambitious secretary. Across these depictions, cultural suspicion of female sexuality taints the moral character of the secretary. This is not to say that the occupational identity of the secretary is sexual but that sexualized perceptions and attributions are confounding and potentially damaging factors in the social construction of secretarial identity and secretary/boss relations.

Bitching as a Mode of Occupational Identity Defense

The previous section lays out the overlapping perceptions and conditions that constitute secretarial work as "dirty work" and that instigate the occupational defense of secretarial identity. From an occupational standpoint, the formation of a cohesive secretarial culture capable of managing a strong identity defense is weakened by several factors: the discrete nature of the workload, the limited career ladder and reward structures of secretarial work, the ambivalent social perceptions of occupational prestige, and the moral suspicion of secretarial character. Nonetheless, secretaries often seek out other secretaries for instrumental and expressive social support (O'Leary & Ickovics, 1990).

While developing a strong workgroup support network might be seen as a positive move to shore up occupational self-esteem, women's informal office talk is often perceived in terms of negative feminine stereotypes that diminish occupational solidarity and prestige. Specifically, female-identified communication patterns may be strongly affiliative but there is also a popularly perceived culture of gossip and meanness that undermines the development of group cohesiveness. In their study of a female-dominated office, Ashcraft and Pacanowsky (1996) heard women's talk in the office

described as catty, competitive, intensely defensive, petty, moti-
vated by jealousy and full of indirect aggression like back-stabbing
and malicious gossiping, prompting one woman to admit that bitching in the office reinforced her faith in the maxim, "A woman's
worst enemy is another woman" (p. 234). These researchers concluded, "When a [communication] practice is viewed as performance of identity, the two become bound in a reflexive relationship in
which each maintains the legitimacy of the other" (p. 234). In other
words, the denigration of female-identified talk and sociality legiti-
mated the marginalization and denigration of feminine identity,
and promoted a preference for masculinist and managerialist
frameworks to guide actions and socially construct office identities.

   The kind of talk that Ashcraft and Pacanowsky's informants
seem to be describing is popularly designated as bitching. In an
early study of women's informal talk, Jones (1980) defined bitching
as affiliative talk among women that expresses anger and frustration through specific, personal complaints about their lived oppressions as women. She held that while interpersonal bitching is
cathartic—women seek not change but communal solace—bitching
in its political form is "consciousness-raising in the women's movement" (p. 247). Jones's description of bitching remains a useful starting point. It points to two dimensions that are critical to
understanding the micropolitical dynamics of bitching: bitching is
affiliative and a mode of identity defense, that is, through bitching,
women may collaboratively respond to identity threats and promote preferred identity constructions. In this sense, bitching
engages in what Goffman (1974; 1959) described as "self-saving
alignment" or the effort of the speaker to reconstruct a socially
acceptable image of self against the damage of recounted indigni-
ties. Goffman (1974) held that most social talk involves such collaborative efforts at self-saving alignment and that the role of listeners
is to show emotional response and interpersonal support. A third
dimension of bitching that I will return to in the examples below is
implied in the tensions between catharsis, which does not seek
change, and consciousness-raising, which does: the micropolitical
effectivities of bitching are ambivalent.

   Objecting to the emphasis on bitching as affiliative identity
defense, Guendouzi (2001) argued that although bitching brings
women together in a pleasurable flow of conversational cooperation, women bitching together co-produce negative evaluations of
absent third parties, casting bitching as a malicious form of back-

stage gossip "that involves comparative competition for social capital based on hegemonic images of femininity" (p. 34). In other words, when women bitch, they invoke dominant norms of femininity to sanction the actions or character of other women as deviant so that, by comparison, the speaker and her listeners can enhance their own claims to social worth and status.

Guendouzi's specification of bitching emphasizes that bitching is mean talk, that women enjoy this talk and cooperate together in creating a safe conversational space for sharing pejorative evaluations of absent others, and that bitching enacts a competitive, win-lose context in which social capital can be gained at another's expense. However, bitching is also about a speaker's perceptions or experiences of mistreatment or injustice in the context of asymmetrical power relations. This is a critical point that distinguishes malicious gossip and bitching. Without this element, the political import and power of bitching to address the disparagement of gendered occupational identities is diminished. Accordingly, I maintain that bitching entails the collaborative expression of moral indignation over perceived or experienced injustices even as it may enact a competitive bid for social capital at the expense of absent third parties (Sotirin, 1999).

For secretaries, bitching is both a mode of collective identity defense and a risky conversational strategy. Bitching risks invoking negative perceptions of women's nature, as Ashcraft and Pacanowsky (1996) observed. Hence, bitching is conversational "dirty work" that both enacts a collaborative defense of occupational identity and risks perceptions of negative feminine stereotypes that reproduce the gendered stigmatization of secretarial identity and undermine occupational solidarity. Drawing on my fieldwork in a corporate office, I offer examples of bitching as conversational "dirty work" that both responds to and participates in the mundane denigrations of secretarial work, roles, and character.

Site and Data Collection Procedures

I conducted fieldwork in one of the regional U.S. offices of an international management-consulting firm. My project was to study informal communication among the twenty-one secretaries in the office secretarial team. The secretaries themselves were instrumental in organizing my observations. They collectively discussed and granted permission for my visit and my four primary informants were self-selected volunteers. I engaged in both unobtrusive

observations and conversational field interviews (Lofland & Lofland, 1984; Spradley, 1979).

I spent a total of over forty hours on site following my informants through their daily work routines. This intensive immersion
was complimented by two autobiographical factors. First, I had
ongoing contact with this office for over six years prior to my
research. So I was familiar with the company's culture and knew
about many of the issues and events that affected secretarial work
arrangements. Second, I was a career secretary myself for over 10
years, working in corporate settings much like the one I observed. I
shared stories of my own secretarial experiences with the secretaries I shadowed and had little trouble situating myself within the
occupational context and developing rapport with the women I
shadowed. It was this rapport that gave me access to the secretaries'
backstage bitching.

(Gendered) Office Civility

One target for several rounds of bitching among the secretaries was
the sole male secretary. He was a junior secretary, in his early twen-
ties, heterosexual and engaged to be married. Several secretaries
independently related an incident that occurred during a team
meeting in which the male secretary made what was taken as a
crude sexual insult against a senior secretary, one of his office
mates. When she confronted him privately, he reportedly issued
another sexual taunt, saying, "You're all talking about me. I don't
need to be in twenty women's mouths." The reiteration of his crude
allusions suggests that there was a collaborative moral indictment
going on in response to the male secretary's transgression of office
civility. At the same time, this indictment seemed to reinforce the
implicit norm of feminine gentility as a standard for the "proper"
secretary.

A subsequent round of bitching not only denigrated the male
secretary as abrasive and immature but engaged in within-group
comparisons of the female secretaries' responses to this bitching. In
their subsequent bitching, secretaries seemed to engage in the competitive comparisons that cast aspirations on absent third parties in
order to claim social worth for the speaker. In this case, secretarial
bitching negatively characterized others on the basis of age, tenure,
and ambition. Those secretaries not amused by all the bitching over
the male secretary's language were labeled too uptight or too professional. Those who were not dismayed were deemed too young or

too uninvested. This incident is drawn from my work on the ambivalence of secretarial bitching (Sotirin & Gottfried, 1999).

These pejorative evaluations of each others' responses upheld the feminine gentility of secretarial character and comportment and claimed for each speaker a position of superiority over those who just didn't get it, creating lines of divisiveness and struggle over what counts as a properly professional and socially appropriate secretarial attitude. Ironically, this collective bitching episode effectively marginalized the lone male secretary on the basis of hegemonic gender stereotypes coded as a concern for professionalism. Their collective bitching upheld the importance of secretarial professionalism but at the same time created a divisiveness that undermined it.

Bitching about Production

In a second example, the tensions of secretarial work relations were provoked by an e-mail exchange over font choices in the minutes of the daily secretarial team meetings. The secretaries met as a team each morning before the office officially opened. They read company announcements, discussed team issues, allocated the time of the "floating" secretaries (a reserve pool of labor for more efficient response to workload spikes and temporary absences), and assured continuous, comprehensive phone coverage. Responsibility for minutes was rotated and the minutes were disseminated through the secretarial database.

One day the minutes appeared adorned by a graphic of a horse and in a non-standard font, that is, a font style that was not approved for company business. Janine, the secretary I was observing, was reading her database messages as we talked (names have been changed to preserve confidentiality of participants). I had just asked about the antagonism among team members that I had heard about earlier and Janine drew my attention to her computer screen. She said, "Here's one of the things they pick on: the secretarial database. The minutes of the meeting are in a scrolly font. Someone asked for a different font 'cause it's hard to read. There's a whole slew of replies . . ." She offered to print out the minutes and the replies, which at that time, consisted of the following four messages (these are paraphrased):

(1) Please use a standard font for the minutes; this one is too hard to read.

(2) The minutes are the only place we get to use some creativity like choosing a different [i.e., nonstandard] font.
(3) Our minutes are part of the [formal] record for the team and we need to maintain professionalism.
(4) What difference does it make? We're the only ones who see them.

Janine explained to me that these replies came from the same people who were most vocal in team meetings and then she turned to another secretary in her area and asked, "Did you read your database? Did you laugh?" Turning to a second secretary, who had just started—in fact, this was her first day on the job—Janine pointed to her screen and remarked, "Very weird." Later, I asked her about interpersonal tensions among team members and she explained, "There are so many strong aggressive personalities. You either have to be that way or be quiet. I don't fly ideas 'cause I'll be attacked. With fonts—you know it will put someone on the defensive. . . ."

Janine's bitching was not about font styles but about the dynamics of the secretarial team. There were opposed alliances within the team that set older and more tenured secretaries against younger and more recent hires, particularly over the value of the team itself. Against the endorsement of the tenured secretaries, the newer secretaries resisted the idea of a team and prioritized their allegiances to their managers and work groups. All four of the secretaries who had written the messages in the e-mail exchange over the font issue were strong advocates of the secretarial team. Janine was not. Her comments about the e-mail messages trivialized this exchange and those who engaged in it: "Did you laugh?" "Very weird." Her characterization of the exchange as a "whole slew of replies" implied that these responses belabored a trivial issue.

Was font choice a trivial issue? Taken together, the four paraphrased e-mail messages enact a struggle over the possibility of creativity in a professional secretarial culture—in team minutes rather than the boss's reports, in records private to secretaries rather than in a more public format. Does secretarial professionalism require strict adherence to pre-established protocols or is there room for creative license? Does backstage creativity damage the secretaries' vulnerable claim to equal status with other professionals on the office team? Labor theorists might pose the issue in terms of the distinction between mentally challenging, conceptual work and rote labor. If others do the conceptual labor and secretaries are consulted for the proper formats, forms, and filing and retrieval procedures, then secretaries become vulnerable to the perception that their primary responsibilities involve mere rote labor. While these issues were not articulated, bitching over fonts was not trivial—at stake was an occupational claim to professional status and the standards entailed.

Along with mobilizing the occupational ideology of professionalism, Janine's bitching enlisted me and her officemates in trivializing the e-mail exchange. The catharsis of shared laughter at the expense of other team members contributed to the interpersonal antagonisms and alliances that weakened the potential solidarity of the secretarial team. Janine's later comment about being attacked by secretarial team members for stepping out of the norm highlights the contradictory conditions of secretarial work: isolated in cubicles, secretaries work on what appear to be discrete tasks within a discontinuous labor process; yet doing the work requires both task coordination and social cooperation (Strom, 1992; Pringle, 1988). This requisite cooperation was unsettled by the antagonisms of bitching. Further, the e-mail bitching over font choices and Janine's bitching over those responses invited a perception that the secretaries were immersed in a feminized form of office talk tied to negative gender stereotypes of secretarial identity.

The struggle over the role of creativity involved important concerns: the bounds of secretarial professionalism with ramifications for the secretarial team's claims to occupational prestige and status in the consulting firm. Yet these stakes seemed overshadowed by the petty antagonisms and gendered stereotypes of bitching. The incident once again evidences the ambivalence of bitching: the e-mails collectively upheld the importance of secretarial professionalism but inspired backstage sniping and divisiveness that reinforced damaging stereotypes of secretarial talk and identity.

Bitching about Gendered Identity

My third example of bitching as an ambivalent defense of secretarial identity is drawn from a conversation among three secretaries (Ann, Barbara, and Carole) about an upsetting incident between Ann and a manager, Jack, described by Ann as a "high maintenance manager." The incident involved Ann, Jack, and an unnamed client. At the time of the incident, Jack was scheduled to relocate from one of the company's offices in another state. He was in the office with a client waiting for a meeting with Ann's boss. While they waited, Jack asked Ann about a relocation reimbursement request that he had filled out himself and submitted to her boss. The company's policy was to reimburse relocation expenses if the company initiated the transfer but if the transfer was made to accommodate an employee's request to relocate, the employee was expected to pay all costs.

Unbeknownst to Jack, Ann's boss had her change the designation of Jack's transfer from a firm-mandated transfer to an employee-requested transfer, making Jack responsible for his $6,000 moving charges. Ann did not want to show Jack his altered reimbursement request in front of the client. But Jack was insistent and could see that the form was on her desk. So she showed him the change. His reaction was intense and, she felt, inappropriate "in front of the client." Here is how Ann began:

> [This happened] in front of a client—that was the first surprise. [Jack said] "Heard anything else on the transfer?" [I said there were] wording changes on the reimbursement request from firm requested to accommodation transfer. It was not appropriate at the time. He drops his briefcase and says, "Thank *you* for making my day." [My boss's] meeting was on top. This wasn't the time.

Ann represented Jack's actions not only as infractions of the firm's standards for a manager's performance "in front of the client" but also as an injustice against her because he failed to support her efforts to be professional and unjustly took his anger out on her as a subordinate. Ann's comment about a "first surprise" suggests that Jack surprised her not only by acting unprofessionally but by forcing her to interact with him on an issue she thought was inappropriate in front of a client. Further, Ann's bitching framed Jack's actions as an unjust exercise of managerial prerogative. At least in front of a client, secretaries might expect the collegiality of the office team to be maintained.

Here Ann's bitching comes close to laying bare the pretense of office team collegiality. Her narrative both assumes and exposes a social order in which secretaries are disempowered relative to managers and subject to managerial prerogatives. Pringle (1988) argued that the dominant discourses constructing secretarial identity include a front stage discourse of the secretary as a career professional on an office team entailing relations of equality and reciprocity and a persistent backstage discourse casting secretarial work and identity in terms of patriarchal relations of domination/subjugation. While the team was especially visible in this office, Ann's bitching penetrates that discourse to complain about the power relations behind the overt rhetoric of team reciprocity and equality. At the same time, her bitching affirms the subordination of secretaries in the dominant corporate order. This simultaneous complaint against and affirmation of subordination makes Ann's defense of secretarial identity ambivalent.

Ann's opening rendition of her interaction with Jack was followed by a lively exchange among all three secretaries during which the other two reassured Ann that she had acted appropriately and that Jack's reaction had been inappropriate. In discussing the details of the situation, the secretaries drew on attributes of hegemonic masculinity to assess Jack's conduct and character and to both reassert and resist disempowering attributes of femininity.

(Carol)   It's [your boss's] fault.
(Barbara)   It's Jack's own fault. He should get it in writing.
(Ann)   Jack tried to start the process; I give him credit
            for trying to start it.
(Carol)   He's been pushing [your boss]. He's too cocky.
(Barbara)   It's not hard to push too hard before the back-
            lash. Would you do all this without writing?
(Ann)   He called [the secretarial supervisor] about
            what to do. So it's really not my fault.
(Barbara)   It's not your fault. We just type this stuff.

The rhythmic repetition of "fault" opens and closes the sequence. The question of fault carries a moral implication: the secretaries absolved Ann ("it's your boss's *fault*") and found Jack responsible for his own fate ("it's Jack's own *fault*"), but they did this in terms that reproduced hegemonic constraints and gender stereotypes. Jack was held at fault for his own misfortune because he ignored what is common knowledge in a bureaucratic system: you have to "get it in writing." Notably, the secretaries did not consider any alternative basis for evaluation. In this sense, they enacted the hegemonic constraints on moral imagination that MacLeod (1992) argued are characteristic of working-women's struggles against complex oppressions. Hegemonic constraints are evident as well in the way the secretaries constructed Jack's aggressive initiative in terms of masculinity: Jack was at fault because he was overly aggressive—"pushing the boss" and "too cocky." Still, Ann gave Jack credit for his initiative. In these shifts, the secretaries ambivalently applaud and condemn Jack's aggressiveness.

In contrast to the aggressive masculinity in their representations of Jack, the secretaries characterized themselves as unthinking, reactive, and subservient. Most strikingly, Barbara supported Ann by observing, "We just type this stuff." This stark contrast between the aggressive agency of the manager and the subservience of the secretary illustrates how bitching among these secretaries adopted conventional perceptions of masculinity and femininity and reproduced a patriarchal hegemony in office relationships. Despite these constructions, the fact that the secretaries were bitching about the manager can be viewed as an act of backstage resistance and agency (Scott, 1991). Hence, bitching enacted an ambivalent political agency since the three secretaries upheld a subservient image of femininity as essential to secretarial identity even as they objected to the injustice of Ann's subjugation to the ire of the manager.

Summarily, this bitching episode illustrates the contrary injunctions that complicate the defense of secretarial prestige and professionalism: bureaucratic rules are deemed both constraining and enabling; aggressive masculinity is both approved and condemned; and feminized secretarial identity is both countered and embraced. Rather than choosing one option over the other, the secretarial bitching I observed shifted ambivalently. In the end, the secretaries defended Ann's actions and cast aspersions on Jack's character and actions. Yet their bitching remained cathartic and failed to inspire any reflection on the nature of the secretary/boss relation or on the difficulties of living out the dominant ideology of professionalism and team equality.

Bitching as Conversational Dirty Work

Both popular and conventional scholarly views on secretarial bitching uphold the tenacious association of bitching with negative feminine stereotypes. Popular advice to working women is to avoid bitching altogether for the sake of harmonious office relations and mobility aspirations (cf. Duff, 1993). Yet women in feminized occupations like secretaries persist in bitching despite the negative stereotypes and sanctions they incur when their talk is labeled as bitching. One reason is that bitching offers a collaborative mode of defense against occupational identity threats, albeit an ambivalent and potentially dysfunctional mode of defense.

The negative sanctions against bitching in both popular and corporate accounts mean that secretaries who bitch are transgressing the boundaries of "proper conduct" themselves. In this sense, bitching involves secretaries in a marginalized activity that threatens to "spoil" social identity, in Goffman's (1963) sense of moral discredit. Both the class and sexual proprieties of secretarial identity are threatened by bitching (cf. Bergmann, 1993; Penelope, 1990). Hence, bitching threatens to spoil secretarial identity by invoking associations of lower-class sociality and stereotypic femininity. Yet as Coates (2000) pointed out, bitching allows those trapped by feminized stereotypes to "behave badly" in backstage venues as a way of subverting the norms that constrain their front stage professional identities. By collaboratively reconstructing the injustice of a particular incident, secretaries bring to light the relations of power that subject them to hegemonic versions of femininity, patriarchy, and bureaucracy.

As an ambivalent mode of occupational identity defense, secretarial bitching offers a critical case for the model of dirty work and stigma resistance proposed by Ashforth and Kreiner (1999). Bitching is a double-edged response to the physical, social, and moral "taints" of secretarial work, roles, and identity. Given that bitching is a stigmatized mode of talk, secretaries who bitch together often seem to mobilize the stereotypes and social and moral suspicions that provoke their bitching in the first place. As Guendouzi (2001) pointed out, bitching relies on cooperative group dynamics to affect antagonisms that sunder workgroup solidarity and validate oppressive ideological identity constructions. Ultimately, secretaries cannot redeem the prestige of secretarial work and identity through bitching.

Yet while secretarial bitching has dysfunctional effects—undermining both individual secretaries' self-esteem and workgroup solidarity—nonetheless, through bitching secretaries collectively engage the mundane injustices endemic to their work lives. The secretarial bitching that I witnessed during my fieldwork over the meaning and enactment of professionalism, power imbalances endemic to office relations, and the salience of feminine stereotypes was an ongoing and dynamically ambivalent process. This suggests that occupational identity defense is not only reactive and reproductive but ultimately an expression of the collective desire for a just assessment of occupational worth and dignity.

6

Bedpans, Blood, and Bile
Doing the Dirty Work in Nursing

Melanie Mills & Amy Schejbal

Nursing has always been an important health-care task, whether it is performed at home by and for loved ones or professionally as a function of a formal job. It can be understood in a number of ways, and we recognize there are many diverse jobs that qualify to be named "nursing." This chapter seeks to broadly represent multiple nursing professions as a genre of feminized work that qualifies as physically, socially, and (just a tinge) morally tainted. The occupation is physically tainted by virtue of close contact with bodily fluids and functions along with the accompanying stench and possible personal danger. It is socially tainted because of the servile nature of the work, both in service to patients and to doctors and administrators. This servile function is exacerbated in a morally tainted fashion by depictions of nurses in pornographic films. Social expectations of others over the course of the occupation's history have bothered more than a few nurses who found themselves warding off unwanted sexual advances from doctors and patients (leftover social dirt from a time before sexual harassment rules had any teeth). Nurses are still sometimes stigmatized as pink-collar workers (Howe, 1977), although the color has transitioned to more white-collar work for some nursing jobs.

Because of the nurturing aspect of the profession, nursing has traditionally been considered a feminine job. As such, it has also been historically marginalized. Until or unless there were nursing shortages, many nurses report feeling like other people thought they were interchangeable or replaceable. This is consistent with the social definition of work as a mechanistic function (with easily replaceable "parts") that is typical of low status jobs, rather than as an interactional construction.

While there is much evidence that interpersonal issues significantly affect health status (e.g., du Pre, 2005; Thompson, Dorsey, Miller, & Parrott, 2003; Beck, 2001), the social skills of nurses have not always been highly valued or professionally developed. Rather, they have been considered to be a "personality thing" that an administrator might be fortunate enough to "luck into" with a nurse hire. As communication professionals, we recognize the importance of these interpersonal skills, as well as the critical hegemonic implications of such assumptions. As one nurse put it, expressing frustration because her interpersonal skills were devalued, "it should be a big 'duh!'" (that these skills were critical for doing good nursing). We have found that nurses actively and purposefully construct social support systems for themselves to manage these kinds of misunderstandings about their work. This is the subject of our labor here.

One reason that this dirty work is important to understand is that Registered Nurses (RNs) constitute the largest health-care occupation in the United States with 2.4 million workers. Nursing is expected to create the second largest number of new jobs among all occupations through 2014. Nurses work in hospitals (three out of five RNs), physicians' offices, nursing care facilities, home health-care services, employment services, government agencies (including schools and prisons), and out-patient care centers. One in four RNs works part-time and there is currently a nursing shortage in this country (Bureau of Labor Statistics, 2006). Even though there is a dire need for these professionals, their work remains tainted.

Our interest in nursing has slightly different origins. Amy's mother has been in nursing for 45 years, so nursing has always been a part of her life. As part of a graduate-level occupational communication course taught by Melanie, she had the opportunity to explore the history and nature of her mother's work. This involved an extended in-depth interview that helped her appreciate the importance of nursing, not only in her life personally, but also in the larger social system. It was also interesting to understand her mother as a professional. We will present multiple excerpts from this interview as we go along.

In addition to having family members in several health care professions, Melanie has been a coordinator of the interdisciplinary Health Communication Program at Eastern Illinois University since 1990. More recently, the school has launched a nursing-degree program. Over the years, she has had occasion to interact with many nurses, not only in classes and workshops, but also on internship sites (a requirement of the Health Communication program) and socially. She has acquired much occupational culture knowledge in the process of developing these relationships—call it "learning by hanging out," or to hitchhike on the title of a Bill Rawlins's (2000) article, "research as a mode of friendship." Long before this was a research project for us, it was simply a personal interest in an occupation of people we care about. We begin with an abbreviated history of nursing that shows social development of the occupation. This highlights how taint is socially derived and socially managed. General job descriptions highlight the physical taint of nursing. Then we discuss the social impact of technology and changes in public perceptions of personal responsibility related to health management and health care. Next we examine cultural artifacts and their relationship to the everyday performance of nursing work. And finally, we look at the role of professional spaces (physical, psychological, online, and third spaces) in the social construction of what it means to be a nurse.

A Brief History of Nursing: The Evolution of Social Taint

No man, not even a doctor, ever gives any other definition of what a nurse should be than this—"devoted and obedient." This definition would do just as well for a porter. It might even do for a horse.

—Florence Nightingale

Nursing began as nurturing, caring for, and aiding in the recovery of patients. The word stems from the Latin word "nutricia," which literally means to nurture or to nourish (Chiarella, 1995). Nurturing or nourishing back to life was a livelihood before it became a formal occupation, and long before terms like *accredited* or *formally educated* were considered. Nursing as a profession resulted as a demand for nurturing increased beyond the means of individual families. The most obvious sources of such a demand were wartimes and epidemic outbreaks.

During the Middle Ages, monks and barber surgeons (men) provided health care outside the home. Women were not perceived to have the constitution to deal with health problems outside of their immediate homes. This myth of female frailty was especially evident in the upper classes (Ehrenreich & English, 1973). The modern red-and-white barber pole is said to come from a time when more stoic male barbers performed surgeries, blood letting, and teeth extractions, hanging bloody bandages out to spin in the wind as they dried outside their shops (Douglas, 1994). These constitutions of the job minimize the social and maximize the physical taint of the work, almost as a badge of honor. While nurses still "wear" (sometimes literally) their occupational dirt (the physical taint of blood, feces, urine, vomit, phlegm) as a badge of honor, it is no longer a masculine prerogative. It is, instead, a reframing process to manage social taint (Ashforth & Kreiner, 1999).

Despite a lack of accreditation or the standards of nursing we have currently, nurses of any sort were usually high status socially, despite the physical taint of the job, likely because they were so critical to the survival of the social system. Historically, examples of such high-status nurses were Irish midwives and the deaconesses of the Christian church. At the same time, from a very primitive perspective, nurses also were stereotyped as witches, using magic to heal (Chiarella, 1995). Medicine ranged from the scholarly to the superstitious. It was alternately praised and condemned. It was, in turn, a secular and a spiritual practice. This influence (and tension) persists in church-funded hospitals and other institutions that provide compassionate care to the public.

The Crusades sparked a need for a formalized, militaristic subset of nurses. At this time men performed nursing as a subset of military duties. Later, nursing and midwifery were among the first recognized jobs outside of the home for women in colonial America. Because of the physical hardships of the time period, this "women's work" was essential and socially as visible as men's (Matthaei, 1983). The Civil War, World War I, and World War II perpetuated the need for formalized or occupational nursing in the United States (Chiarella, 1995); however, the prevailing assumption was still that most women were too delicate and uneducated (or uneducable) to be in certified health care (du Pre, 2005).

Some people say Florence Nightingale is single-handedly responsible for reinventing hospitals and the nursing profession. She was instrumental in formalizing educational programs for nurses (Junion-Metz, 2006). What is amazing was that she was highly educated during Victorian times, and able to pioneer the idea that social phenomena could be objectively measured and subjected to mathematical analysis. She was an innovator in descriptive statistics, dramatizing needless deaths caused by unsanitary conditions, and spearheading social reform. In honor of her impact on the nursing occupation, the International Council for Nurses created "Nurses' Day" on May 12, her birthday (Anionwu, 2006). She definitely put a feminine face on nursing as a "helping profession." Helping professionals are expected to be caring, fair, wise, pragmatic, and self-sacrificing. Powerful social norms suggest that the helping role take precedence over other roles (e.g., nurses must stop at accident scenes even if they are off duty). Grossman and Stewart (1990) suggest the goal of nurses as helping professionals becomes the "renunciation of their power over any given individual client, patient, or student, as a result of their effective performance" (p. 13). This view emphasizes the servile nature of the work over the physical taint, a change that comes with the feminization of the occupation.

Beginning in the later decades of the nineteenth century, the "better" classes waged a moral war on the "lower" working classes (largely immigrants). The distinction between "dirt" and "sin" was unclear, but there was a clear relationship between disease and immorality, which led to prayer as a solution to epidemics rather than sanitation (Ehrenreich & English, 1973). Large numbers of nuns performed nursing services under the auspices of the Roman Catholic Church. Prior to this time, hospitals were generally defined as places for the poor and indigent. Anyone who could afford it was cared for at home. Nursing in hospitals was, therefore, an act of charity, serving the needs of patients who were usually dirty and illiterate as well as sick. This made nursing less of a health-care profession and more of a religious calling (Cockerham, 1995). Morality issues significantly affected social perceptions of the job. Florence Nightingale was influential in turning medical attention (and blame for outbreaks) from "sin" to "dirt" with the "science" of sanitation.

In the first decades of the 1900s, Margaret Sanger was leading a birth control movement suggesting that the world's problems (war, poverty, prostitution, famine, feeblemindedness) were caused by overpopulation. There was resistance from those who saw birth control as a scheme to "take the penalty out of vice," and "degrade the wife to the level of the prostitute" (Ehrenreich & English, 1973). Public health movements of the time focused on women's roles in hygiene, which drew reformers to become social workers who became nurses in many cases. It was one of a few professions accessible for women in the early parts of this century. Professional legitimacy (a social evaluation) was a long time coming. Achterberg

(1991) describes women in the healing arts as alternately revered as earth mothers, vilified as witches, diminished for a lack of scientific knowledge, or condemned as the embodiment of original sin (and therefore unqualified to practice healing). That is some serious social taint.

Social taint all but decimated the midwifery profession. Midwives are women who assist a mother during childbirth. It was one of the earliest forms of care available for women and is often associated with nursing. In colonial America, they attended most births. By 1900, only about half of all births in the United States were attended by midwives. By 1950, midwifery was only practiced in remote areas (Cockerham, 1995). Obstetrics as a medical specialty all but drove them out of business, lobbying to make their practices illegal. These physicians redefined home births as unsanitary and dangerous, as well as primitive—who would want to take such risks or forego pain-killing drugs during delivery? While midwifery has enjoyed a resurgence of credibility among those who value natural childbirth, it is still illegal in many states.

There were nationwide nursing shortages in the 1980s and 1990s that still have not been resolved. In an effort to attract nurses to health-care institutions, salaries have been increased significantly (along with signing bonuses), working conditions have been improved, and professional development opportunities have been created. Reasons for shortages include expanding job opportunities for women (including medicine), population growth, an increase in the average age of Americans, and an exodus from the field because of poor working conditions. Nearly half a million registered nurses in the United States were not employed as nurses in 2002 (U.S. Department of Health & Human Services, 2002). In 2003 the federal government made millions of dollars available for people from underprivileged backgrounds to attend nursing school (du Pre, 2005). This creates a taint tension in the nursing field. On one hand, increased need elevates the status of the job. On the other hand, encouraging marginalized people to enter the profession creates some measure of social stigma for it.

Ideally, this kind of strain would move us to socially minimize occupational taint, which would be a step toward a more egalitarian social system that values its dirty workers. The magnitude of the physical taint associated with the job inhibits this kind of progress. And while the social taint has evolved, the servile nature of the work, especially coupled with the gross-out factor of the physical taint, makes it still quite evident.

Physical Taint

Nursing school definitely did not prepare me for all the poop I cleaned up in my first hundred days as a nurse.

—ICU nurse in Arnoldussen, 2004

Poop, piss, perspiration, projectile puke, prolapsed parts, and putrid pustules are routine job "hazards" for most nurses. They see people at their worst. Patients are some combination of diseased, drunk, demented, dying, disturbed, and sometimes decomposing (really). They smell bad for various reasons—infection, hygiene, inability or unwillingness to control bodily functions (diarrhea, vomiting, bleeding, urinating, various discharges, spitting, and even ejaculating). They leak. They hurt. They are angry. They are frightened. And they need care. Care that may require a nurse to invade their most private personal places. To cause pain. To take control. This is not someone people look forward to seeing. One nurse said, "In public, patients see their doctor, point him out and explain how he bypassed two blocked arteries—they see their nurse, and turn tail hoping she doesn't remember how they got confused after surgery, stripped naked, and peed in the hallway."

On the other hand, good nurses listen. They take time with patients (when the medical system allows it). They provide care in multiple senses of the word. One orthopedic nurse put it this way, "It doesn't really matter how well you can give a shot or do a dressing change. Usually, the best medicine is a good conversation" (Arnoldussen, 2004). One T-shirt we have seen around the local hospital reads "Nurses are angels in comfortable shoes." Angel of death or angel of mercy? The job has different definitions from different perspectives. One thing most people can agree on is that nurses deal with some difficult (gross) stuff, and we are drawn to the stories they tell about their work. They reveal ". . . in a sometimes shocking and sometimes comical fashion what the caring profession is really like" (Kirkus Reviews in Heron, 1998).

Themes of nursing stories include messy physical experiences, "gag me" gross things, objects inserted in assorted orifices, fat people, unusual body ornamentations, and stupid human tricks. There are, of course, other topics that are more specific to particular nursing specialties, but we include these general ones for your amusement, education, and most importantly, the development of empathy for these health care practitioners.

Messy physical experiences usually involve forceful spewing or splattering of various body fluids. Whether it is impacted bowels or diarrhea, vomiting or drooling, or some combination thereof (did you know that people can vomit fecal matter?), the digestive system is a subject of much nurse talk. Patients eat turds, leave them in strange places (like drawers), ingest odd things and pass them (like an apron) or sometimes obstruct their bowels. Sometimes in the process, nurses get in the way and end up with blood, poop, spit, vomit, or pus on their clothes, in their hair, on their skin, in their shoes, on their glasses, or if they are not careful, in their mouths. Ewwwwwww, right? It gets better.

Every nurse has a "gag me" gross-out story. Different professionals have different tolerance levels for bodily fluids and assorted behaviors. For many it is phlegm. "I can deal with blood, vomit (although I might have to mouth-breathe), shit, or pus . . . but when they hack up loogies, I'm gagging" (Sharon, personal interview). We got a lot of agreement in a focus group that ear wax and irrigating ears in general, is disgusting. Many of the things that gag nurses are related to foul odors (poop, vomit, infection, rotting flesh) or icky behaviors (patients who eat scabs, play with turds, or suck pus). One nurse advised us to NEVER eat anything offered by one of her residents (in a long-term care facility). It might be chocolate. It might not be. One patient offered to share his beer with a nurse. He had made it himself because he was thirsty. He made it from his own urine. A nursing home resident vomited and then sucked his dentures clean afterward. Another nurse lanced a patient's boil and it shot into her eye. Are you still with us? Many of these routine "hazards" are not only repulsive, but also dangerous—the epitome of physical taint.

Let's move on to things inserted in various orifices. Emergency room nurses have huge collections of stories about odd items found in vaginas, penises, and rectums. These include money (hope it never made it back into circulation, but suspect it did), teeth, the armrest of a wheel chair, clothes, lipstick, batteries, a peanut butter sandwich, Q-tips, a hairbrush, a light bulb, a child's sippy cup, a TV remote (we don't even want to know), live (and dead) animals (don't ask), and a glass jar of pickle relish. We learned that if you puncture the lid (assuming it was inserted lid end out) that it is easier to remove. One nurse found five pieces of fried chicken that a patient on a diet was smuggling in vaginally (appetizing).

Which brings us to fat people. While the nurses we spoke with qualified that not all fat people are filthy, many are. They agreed that if you can't reach it, you can't wash it, and if you can't wash it, it's going to stink. Often doctors will not examine patients until a nurse "cleans them up." For morbidly obese patients, this may involve as many as three nurses to hold skin apart so the folds may be washed. We heard a number of stories about things nurses found in fat folds including maggots, spoiling food (liquefied), eye glasses, pencils, teeth, a rotten popsicle stick (that the flesh had rotted around, too), and clothes that had to be peeled off. There were also stories we suspect are urban legends about nurses (friends of a friend) who found a dead kitten under a breast, or a decomposing dead fetus in the leg folds of a woman who hadn't known she was pregnant. Tragic, if true.

More entertaining stories involve body ornamentation (piercings and tattoos). While many of the piercing stories involved infections, some were simply descriptions of how people ornament themselves, and further, how they connect their ornaments (nipples to penis, for example). We will never listen to the hymn "Love lifted me" quite the same way after hearing about those words being tattooed in a man's groin area. A number of women apparently date men who need directions because they have them tattooed on their bodies.

A discussion of nurses' stories would not be complete without mention of some of the stupid human tricks that bring people to hospitals in the first place. Emergency room nurses often see them first. Some of them they see often (frequent fliers). In addition to the insertion stories we have already discussed, there are a number of GDFD (got drunk fell down) ones every weekend (and many weeknights). Some are funny. Some are sad. Sex is always good for a laugh—for example, the wife who nearly "bobbited" her husband who wrecked the car while she was performing fellatio, or another who super-glued her husband's penis to his thigh upon hearing he was unfaithful. Some involve extended erections from drug use. Some involve patients who masturbate in creative fashions or get sex toys stuck in unfortunate places. The nurses we know laugh at our common human foibles, not at individual people. Sometimes they laugh to keep from crying.

Nurses are known for their dark sense of humor. In fact, many will defend it as a survival mechanism against the extreme physical taint of their work. In Jeff Foxworthy tradition, a lot of nursing humor takes the form of "you might be a nurse if," followed by an assortment of identifying characteristics. One of our favorites is "if, in the process of cleaning up a patient who has had an enormous liquid stool, you are reminded that you need to pick up brownie mix at the store tonight." Disgusting, right? Others are: "if you feel you can diagnose passersby at the mall based on physical presentation," or "if you firmly believe that 'too stupid to live' should be a diagnosis," or "if you believe there is no body cavity that cannot be reached with a #14 needle and a good strong arm." All of these highlight disgusting aspects of the work and give occupational members a lighter frame for talking about them.

While people outside of the profession will not understand the humor in a lot of nurse talk, it is an important part of taint management. One nurse told us how she and some friends were asked to leave a café because their dinner conversation was disturbing the other patrons. She had not fully realized the effects of their work talk and felt socially ostracized. The following post on a public cyber-nursing-community site (www.allnurses.com) where nurses unwind by swapping gross stories illustrates this idea: "Lots of people would gag, pass out, or be revolted at the stuff we deal with on a daily basis. . . . Thanks for posting a reply to my message. I think it's therapy for the soul to post and to read humorous experiences in nursing. It keeps us going, don't you think?" (Fran, retrieved August 14, 2006). Another notes, "God knows how much we need sick humor, and he provides it for us marvelously" (Christie, retrieved August 14, 2006).

As is true for many occupational groups, nurses develop professional jargon and shortcuts to talk or write about their work. "LOL" might mean "laughing out loud" in colloquial use, but for nurses it might also mean "little old lady." "SOB" might be used to refer to a jerk, but it also means "shortness of breath." We sometimes had to ask for translations in written correspondence with nurses, not because they were showing off or trying to exclude us, but because this kind of expression is so taken for granted in their everyday communication. Specialized language may be used to protect outsiders from the physical taint of the job, or to create humor in difficult situations. "Booty dust" refers to dried fecal flakes that a nurse might find either on bed sheets or airborne in the "wind" after a patient passes gas. A "Code brown" refers to patients, recently expired, whose muscles have relaxed and released the contents of their bowels. Nurses are usually the ones who clean them up before their families say good-bye.

Moral Taint

After two days in the hospital, I took a turn for the nurse.

—WC Fields

We found over 500 nurse porn movies at one site in a less than 30-second Internet search. Titles are very explicit about how the nurse is "used" in the films. "Slave Nurses," "Busty Nurses," "Nurse Me," and "The Sensuous Nurse" are some of the tamer titles in this collection. The sheer number of these productions and ease of access contributes to an occupational moral taint. Nurses do not have to be in the profession long before they run into "dirty old men that have seen too many movies" (Mona, personal interview). They are groped, grabbed, flashed, and sometimes even ejaculated upon by patients and other visitors to their work space. Unwanted sexual behavior is targeted toward both female and male nurses, whose masculinity may be questioned if they rebuff advances. Further, while it does not happen with the frequency (or openness) of earlier years, many nurses also report sexual harassment by other employees. Moral taint adds another layer to the stigma of nursing work.

Other Occupational Changes

The nursing occupation has changed in the sense that now it is more of a business than a care facility.

—B. Schejbal, personal communication, June 4, 2006

A business approach, or metaphor, has taken over hospitals and care facilities, turning the art and occupation of care giving into money making. No longer are nurses expected just to provide quality care, they are expected to provide quality care to a large number of patients and limit time with each patient. Nurturing and nourishing have turned into pill-pushing and administrative work for many nurses. Such a shift in occupational goals socially taints the profession internally and externally.

Another change in the occupation is the integration of men back into nursing. As stated earlier, in historical times military men formalized and constituted a subset of soldiering that was labeled "nurses." However, as the occupation evolved, the most common stereotypical gender expectation of nurses is that they are women. As of 2005, Nursing Management reports that in order to minimize such a gender-specific stereotype, the proportion of men in nursing would have to increase "by more than nine times from the current 5.4% to 49.1% which matches the proportion [of men] in the U.S. population" (Sherrod, Sherrod, & Rasch, 2005).

The shift from the occupation being strictly female (or feminized) to gender neutral has not been completely accomplished. Mainstream media have portrayed men as nurses. Media icons like Gaylord Focker in *Meet the Parents* and Jack McFarland in *Will and Grace* have helped Americans visualize men in the occupation. But such stereotypes do not exactly encourage men to enter into the profession themselves (Romano, 2006). After all, the name "Gaylord Focker" was used to create a spineless character scared of his father-in-law, and Jack McFarland is an out-of-the-closet homosexual who encapsulates every negative gay stereotype there is.

The success of the United States medical system after World War II has also been its downside. The emphasis on individuality and the value of human life fostered the expectation of equal treatment for all (not just those who could afford it) and extreme measures and expenditures for single individuals. Research and technology advanced, which also added more expense to medicine. Managed care emerged as a response to cost containment needs (du Pre, 2005), and with it came enormous amounts of paperwork. Nursing moved from a nurturing job to a mechanized one, with a primary goal of meeting production goals, sometimes at the expense of patients' needs. One nearly universal gripe among nurses is the time that "business" takes from patient care.

Technology and Change

Technology has also made some of the work easier. With computers, filing and paperwork can be done much faster and it is easier to access. In addition, technological advancements with medical equipment have been amazing.

—B. Schejbal, personal communication, June 4, 2006

The computer age has revolutionized the way Americans store, process, and use information. For nurses this means a number of things, but most prominently it means increased attention to record keeping, one of the more tedious (and therefore dirty) parts of their work. Many nurses will explain that they do not have extra time to file or fill out paperwork leisurely. For most nurses, any extra time to spend on making rounds or assisting patients is more useful than sitting behind a desk. While technology as a way to access and disperse information has made the health-care industry more time efficient, it has also contributed to the dirtiness of nursing jobs. Somebody has got to do it. As with many dirty jobs, the social system requires it (especially with our more litigious cultural mindset these days), but does not esteem it.

While increased record keeping has added a burden to the job, new forms of technology have allowed nurses to utilize multiple resources and create organizational efficiency (Lawler, 1998). Portable documentation or mobile clinical charting located throughout facilities allows nurses quick and real-time communication, which ultimately increases quality of care and decreases negative outcomes (DeLaHunt, 2005).

Social Definitions and Change

People stereotype nurses as hospital nurses and there are so many different types of nurses and specialized branches of nursing. People always think it is like "ER" and television shows instead of thinking about the everyday school nurse.

—B. Schejbal, personal communication, June 4, 2006

We have already discussed some of the social images associated with nurses over time, from high-status people who wanted to nurture and nourish the sick back to life to witches using magic to cure the sick in primitive times (Chiarella, 1995). Social definitions of the job range from heroic efforts to make life optimal for patients to being nothing more than a secretary or assistant. Nurses work in the service of patients and also their loved ones. They are liaisons between families and medicine. They get to know patients and their families in an emotionally draining way. They experience the everyday trials families go through with terminal illnesses. They watch children die, they watch the elderly deteriorate, and they care because that is what nurses do. Like other medical professions, there is much specialization in the field. It has become more difficult for lay people to understand the finer differences among nursing occupations, and the wide range of contexts for nursing.

To be a nurse you must be a people person. Caring for people, helping others, and making a difference in your patients' lives is what being a nurse means. It cannot just be learned, it must be practiced.

—B. Schejbal, personal communication, June 4, 2006

Practicing conscientious health care has shifted from a professional responsibility to a personal one as well. Of the top ten current causes of death, virtually all are lifestyle related. One hundred years ago, this was not true. Many were infectious diseases like influenza and pneumonia, which are now under better control with advances in medicine and prevention. This change has created less tolerance for self-induced health problems and affects social expectations for care. It has also mandated that nurses become lifestyle coaches to help other people make healthy choices.

It is widely believed that we have a direct responsibility for the contraction, progression, and resolution of our own health crises, and we should choose to behave according to that responsibility. We expect the alcoholics to seek treatment, the obese to lose weight, the smokers to quit, and the sexually active to be "safe." This has two major effects on nursing. One, nurses are expected to meet healthy standards (practice good health and look like it), and two, nurses expect others to do so as well. Noncompliance is the number one professional frustration nurses have with patients. There is no pill for some health conditions. Failure to comply with lifestyle modifications means health status will not improve.

> *Nurses really do care and they want good outcomes for their patients. Nursing is constantly changing patients and still worrying about the past patients you have had. It is all work and responsibility, no play or time to let your guard down.*

> —B. Schejbal, personal communication, June 4, 2006

Nurses are with patients consistently, whereas doctors stop by for visits. They take care of and nurture patients; they fluff the pillows, clean the bed pans, and are often there when patients pass away. Interactions with caregivers and dirty workers are the subject of most of the everyday stories within a health-care facility (e.g., nursing homes in Farmer [1996]). They clean up after their patients, they grow to care about them, and it does affect them when they lose a patient. A nurse is truly the people-person that patients and their families grow to rely on. Nurses are a ready source of information and often the first professionals approached with medical questions.

Material Artifacts of Nursing

Material culture contributes to both insider and outsider perceptions of what it means to be a nurse. Studying objects (e.g., tools of the trade, dress, and texts) can make invisible aspects of the culture visible. Material artifacts of the nursing occupation range from texts on name tags to buildings. Physical objects convey meanings subtly and can readily be studied over time. There has been a recent call to examine the role of material culture in identity construction more closely (Leeds-Hurwitz, 2006). We make no claims of being comprehensive in this chapter, but do note that there are some interesting nursing artifacts that signify occupational meanings.

An obvious artifact is the texts from which nurses learn their practice. Undergraduate nursing texts are "tools in the socialization process of nursing students" (Huntington & Gilmour, 2001). These texts teach the people studying them how to be nurses. To function productively in the profession, one must know the language. Textbooks and other course materials are instructive. For example, much of the information included in texts from courses we surveyed online has a strong scientific orientation, which signals to students that anecdotal evidence is not as credible as quantitatively gathered data. This is consistent with other messages about research discussed in a later chapter of this book (ethnography as dirty work). Interestingly, however, nurses report learning most vividly from either experience or "storied" data, so while credibility may be derived from scientifically reported information, practical understandings often come from stories. Similarly, while they are professionally evaluated on their technical expertise, often their preferred part of the job is interpersonal in nature.

Titles and their display is another interesting area of material culture. There are multiple designations for nurses, largely based on levels of education achieved. Nurses assume different status identities based on their degrees or certifications, including those who are or have a bachelor of science in nursing (BSNs), registered nurses (RNs), licensed practical nurses (LPNs), and certified nursing assistants (CNAs). There is also a range of other specialized certifications. The nurses with BSNs are the highest in the nursing staff hierarchy, followed by other RNs, LPNs, and then CNAs. While there is some joking about what these acronyms stand for (e.g., LPN as "low-paid nurse" or "let's play nurse" to RN as "real nurse"), health care is a very role-conscious culture and professional credibility is strongly related to title. Hospital employees routinely wear their credentials on their name tags in the form of abbreviations after their names. In some contexts, nurses also add decorations (stickers and pins) to their name tags to make them more personalized and friendly. This is consistent with their nurturing image, and also sometimes intentionally designed to minimize the status role distances that the institutionalized name tags create.

> *CNAs are not always motivated because their salaries are so low and these nurses have numerous patients to care for without any help; usually it is one nurse per floor.*

—B. Schejbal, personal communication, June 4, 2006

Although CNAs are highly needed in nursing facilities, particularly in long-term care places, they are usually low-paid workers that are accordingly unmotivated to provide other nurses with help they really need. Identity roles shift within this subset of nursing workers alone. Long-standing CNAs believe that new hires come from a whole different experience. Experienced CNAs feel that newer CNAs exhibit a "lack of compassion, dedication, work ethic, and sense of teamwork" (Hoban, 2006). When such competition and inconsistent identities arise within this subset of nursing workers, it is obvious how many tasks may go overlooked and why the registered nurses' demands for help may go unsatisfied. The material culture (name tags) draws attention to role differences and may impede collaborative work. On the other hand, they are a convenient way to quickly determine who has what training.

Gloves, safety glasses, and masks are critical tools of the nurses' trade. They explicitly are designed to protect them from physical taint. These are not personalized because they are disposed of after taint exposure. Other common professional paraphernalia carried on their person includes a stethoscope (which can be personalized) and a watch with a second hand. Past these, there is a wide variety of things nurses might need to do their jobs, depending on their individual expertise.

An interesting aspect of material culture is studying what counts as trash and is discarded (Goodall, 1989). For instance, many medical instruments that used to be sanitized after use are now created for one time use and tossed. The treatment and expense of these material artifacts reflects the larger social fear of being sued in our litigious social system, as well as the physical fear of contamination. Further, the protective "gear" described above that is the norm for the field now was not standard a relatively short time ago (historically speaking). Evolving social definitions create material cultures (red bags and hazardous disposal receptacles). They also create language. For example, "biohazard" is a word that entered the national everyday vocabulary about the same time as latex gloves. These all affect how we expect nurses to behave.

Cruise the employee parking lot of a hospital and you will note clever bumper stickers with messages about who nurses are and how they should be treated. You will also note who has assigned (guaranteed) parking, which is covered in the upcoming space section of this chapter. Some of these sayings are also found on other material artifacts like T-shirts, tote bags, key chains, and notepads. Take these messages, for example, "Nurses are IV leaguers," "Nurses are patient people," and "Always be nice to your nurse" (along with its elaboration "your butt is in her hands"). Since nurses choose to adorn their work spaces, vehicles, and selves with these messages, we assume an intentional identity (and taint) management motivation for these artifacts.

Occupational Space

How space affects social interaction and the construction of social identities is a final point of discussion in this chapter. Like material artifacts, space is a rather concrete concept (especially in parking lots!), generally accessible, and helpful in understanding abstract ideas about how occupations are organized. How groups construct a feeling of community using space is a less concrete, but interesting, endeavor. We consider both approaches to space by examining physical spaces, psychological spaces, cyber spaces, and third spaces. Again, we make no claims of comprehensive coverage of nursing spaces, but rather cover the ones that emerged as relevant in our studies. Finally, we speculate about what these various spaces provide nurses in their efforts to engage in taint management.

Physical Spaces

As already alluded to, the organizational patterns of parking lots convey messages about who is important in the institution providing the parking. Generally, you will see assigned spaces for administrators, doctors, emergency vehicles, and disabled people. Some will have special drop-off points (valuing consumers' convenience and comfort) or even valet parking.

To understand power distribution, look at work spaces. Most nurses do not have individual offices, but rather may have a desk (or even just a drawer or locker for personal and professional belongings). They rarely have windows. Space studies overlap with material culture studies as we consider what is in the work space. Is there a separate cafeteria or eating place for different employees? Is there a different menu? What is adorning the walls of the space? Who has the solid-wood desk and who shares a metal one? What is the noise level in the space? Spaces with carpet are rarely found where nurses work (more difficult to clean than linoleum or tile). All of these messages from what you find in whose space, and how it is organized for privacy, comfort, and flow of traffic, construct meanings about the status of people who work in the space (both in and of themselves and also by comparison to the space of others).

Psychological Spaces

People expect way too much from nurses. Nurses do not have the help they need.

—B. Schejbal, personal communication, June 4, 2006

As dirty workers, nurses do jobs that most Americans would rather not do, and they give assistance and hope to patients who may have no one else. Families do not "do" dirt like they used to. Health-care reform has negatively impacted the working conditions of nurses, requiring people in the system to handle a larger volume of patients. Unions offer nurses a number of things including, but not limited to: increased quality of work conditions, increased productivity, increased employee loyalty, increased employee benefits, and job stability. All of these factors are designed to aid nurses in their work and protect nurses from burnout or a lack of job security (Bruder, 1999). Unions provide a psychologically safe place for nurses to go when they feel beat up by the dirt of their jobs.

The list of nurses unions and organizations is very extensive. We found a list of over thirty support organizations on one Web site (*History of Nursing Resources*, retrieved June 5, 2006). These lists provide only a bit of insight into how many nursing organizations and unions there currently are. As stigmatized workers, nurses need social support to deal with the burnout, stress, and health issues that arise from engaging in dirty work (see Thompson et al., 2003, for discussions of the importance of social support). Taking care of their mental health is crucial to surviving in the profession. Many health-care organizations recognize this need for psychological space and provide employee assistance programs to deal with dirty aspects of the work. Some nurses point out that this recognition is rather recent and largely a response to nursing shortages, suggesting that it might be forced rather than emergent from value for their work. The same is true for professional development space. Being recognized as professionals with support to attend conferences, meetings, and training seems likely to improve the morale of workers who need space to interact with others who manage the same taint.

Cyberspace

For those nurses whose employers are not inclined to provide a high level of support space physically or psychologically (and even for those who have these things), cyberspace is full of nurses who will chat at any hour and commiserate about lousy work conditions. Nurses can find commonality, friendship, advice, encouragement, empathy, and an ear online. They can also find certification programs there. Nurses can enter cyberspace with multiple taint management needs and find support there.

Third Spaces

Third spaces are public places where people gather to interact face-to-face in social communities away from their homes and work (Stripling, 2004; Oldenburg, 1999). They may be bars, corner stores, coffee shops, barber shops, or cafés. What they give people is a place to gather and work out the complexities of life in their other two spaces (home and work), or maybe just take a break from them. Either one of these social activities provides taint management opportunities with others who share occupational taint.

Ashforth and Kreiner (1999) conclude that dirty workers have stronger occupational communities than other workers. We believe that having supportive physical, psychological, online, and third spaces encourages this for nurses. Nursing is hard and often thankless, but when you ask the men and women who vocationally choose it, you learn they find extreme fulfillment in their work. With successful taint management strategies and good social support, they enjoy strong occupational communities. They find a way to do work many of us could not do.

7

Crack Pipes and T Cells

Use of Taint Management by HIV/AIDS/Addiction Caregivers

Stephanie Poole Martinez

God of our hope, make us one as we challenge poverty, ignorance and fear, prejudice and discrimination, particularly those living with HIV/AIDS and substance abuse.

—Alexian Brothers Welcoming Ritual

The success rate here is very low.

—Donald, Resident/Employee
Alexian Brothers Salus Place

Residential transitional environments for people living with HIV or AIDS (HIV/AIDS) and addiction play an important role in building a strong community for those facing these challenges, but like many organizations, these communities face issues such as budgeting, workforce turnover, scheduling, and a myriad of other issues. These issues are stressful enough, but workers must also deal with daily concerns regarding communal living, illness, substance abuse, depression, and, in some cases, other forms of mental illness. Perhaps because of these precise concerns, members of this occupation have been classified as "dirty workers" (Ashforth & Kreiner, 1999). And as such, members of this occupation may actively perform "taint management" in order to reframe their work in a more positive light (Ashforth & Kreiner).

The purpose of this study is to examine communication processes that serve to promote a positive occupational identity and offer social support for those working within a residential community for people with HIV/AIDS and addiction. More specifically, I draw primarily on Ashforth and Kreiner's (1999) research on dirty occupations and their model of taint management to examine how identity and stigma are managed. To accomplish this goal, I divide this chapter into four sections. First, I propose to study those working within an HIV/AIDS and addiction population as an occupational culture of dirty workers. Second, I consider the messages that Alexian Brothers Salus Place (a residential community for those living with HIV/AIDS/addiction in St. Louis, Missouri) employees receive about the dirtiness or value of their work. Third, using "thick description" (Geertz, 1973; 1976), I describe and analyze emergent themes of taint management in Alexian Brothers Salus Place. Finally, I conclude with a summary and discussion of my analysis and its implications for the study of occupational communication.

A Dirty Work Perspective for the Study of Communication in HIV/AIDS and Addiction Residential Communities

In their historical review of dirty work and occupational culture, Ashforth and Kreiner (1999) suggest that an "AIDS worker" is an example of a "dirty worker." "Dirty work" refers to tasks and occupations that society is likely to perceive as disagreeable on a physical (working with dirt or bodily fluids), moral (doing a task that is considered "sinful"), and/or social (in relationships with a stigmatized population) scale (Hughes, 1951; Anderson, 2000; Ashforth & Kreiner, 1999; Perry, 1998). In addition, Ashforth and Kreiner point out that occupations may have more than one type of taint. For instance, prostitutes could have both physical and moral taint. Furthermore, they explain that taint and dirtiness are social constructions and are not "inherent" in the work. People decide what work is dirty or tainted and what work is considered prestigious. Although people may praise those who work in a residential community for people with HIV/AIDS and addiction, they are glad that someone else is doing it. Thus, the physical, moral, and social taint of dirty work often affects those who work in this area even though they are often admired for doing this work (i.e., "You have to be a really good person to do this type of work because I couldn't do it").

This study utilized over a year of participant observation (an average of twenty hours per week), twenty-five hours of audio-taped conversation (meetings and dinner conversation where both residents and staff attended), and fourteen open-ended ethnographic interviews. This fieldwork was conducted from October 2001 through January 2003 at Salus Place. Initially, data were not collected to study taint management. Instead, they were part of a larger study (Martinez, 2003). However, analysis of data suggested that taint management techniques were actively performed in the community during the months I spent there.

In their essay, Ashforth and Kreiner (1999) provide a thorough review of the different types of dirty work and a useful model of taint management. The goal of this chapter is to use their framework to extend my analysis of workplace communication. Thus, the first research question is how do employees of Alexian Brothers Salus Place qualify as "dirty workers"?

Salus Place: A Residential Community for Those Living with HIV/AIDS and Addiction

It is estimated that more than a million people are living with HIV/AIDS in the United States (Avert, 2006). Internationally, it is estimated that between 38.6 and 46 million people are living with HIV/AIDS (Avert). In the United States, the epidemic is disproportionately infecting the African American and Hispanic communities (Avert). Of those who are infected, some live in poverty without proper health care, food, and housing. A few of these people have turned to residential transitional living environments such as Salus Place.

Salus Place is a residential community for homeless people living with HIV/AIDS and addiction. At the time of this research, all of the residents at Salus Place are dealing with crack addiction. This community is governed by the Alexian Brothers, who are the same order of Catholic brothers who work with Bonaventure House in Chicago where Adleman and Frey (1997) conducted research for their book, *The Fragile Community: Living Together with AIDS.*

In an HIV/AIDS/addiction residential community such as Salus Place, workers face multiple types of taint and qualify as dirty workers. First, employees of Salus Place face physical taint because of their work with addicts and those living with HIV/AIDS. For example, during my observation, residents became sick due to opportunistic infections. Residents show up high and/or drunk after they have relapsed. Employees of Salus Place clean dirty rooms, send residents out for drops (drug tests), and deal with late night relapses (high, drunk, crying, physically ill, physically and verbally violent residents).

Second, workers at Salus Place negotiate social taint. As previously mentioned, social taint comes from having relationships (in this case working) with a stigmatized population. The residents of Salus Place are stigmatized on multiple levels. They are stigmatized for living with HIV/AIDS, for being addicts (specifically crack addicts), for being homeless (many also dealt with some type of mental illness), and for living in poverty. Thus, the workers of Salus Place are socially tainted on multiple levels for working with HIV/AIDS homeless crack addicts.

While Ashforth and Kreiner argued that AIDS workers faced physical and social taint, I would argue from my participant observation that employees at Salus Place are subject to some degree of moral taint as well. While employees are not engaging in tasks considered "sinful," they are working with a population that confronts moral taint due to societal moral judgments about those living with HIV/AIDS and crack addiction ("The first question is always 'How did you get the disease?'" a resident named Leon told me. "Does it really matter?"). People living with HIV/AIDS (and those working within a HIV/AIDS population) are challenged with the moral stigma that is associated with this virus because of fear of the contagion and its history within the gay community (Adelman & Frey, 1997; Hooper, 1999). When I asked one resident what it was like to be HIV positive, he stated, "Oh my God! In St. Louis! You might as well put a scarlet letter on your chest and be cast out on an island." So, while knowledge of HIV and AIDS has been in the public forum for over two decades, the moral taint that is associated with the virus still exists.

Addicts are also subjected to moral judgments regarding their substance abuse issues. Since several of the employees at Salus Place are former addicts themselves, the moral taint of addiction is important to note. Thus, workers at Salus Place negotiate a social/moral taint due to working with a morally judged, stigmatized population.

After spending over a year at Alexian Brothers Salus Place, I would argue that workers qualify as dirty workers due to physical, social, and social/moral taint. To better understand the messages that employees at Salus Place receive, the next research question is what messages do Salus Place employees receive about the dirtiness or value of their work within this community?

Messages about Self-Identity and Occupational Identity at Salus Place

The Alexian Brothers are a religious congregation of Catholic men who joined together in Germany over 700 years ago to serve the sick and poor (Alexian Brothers, n.d.). According to the Alexian Brothers, their HIV/AIDS residential communities were built in order to "enhance the quality of life for people with HIV/AIDS within a supportive community." Salus Place was built to create a safe environment that allows residents to regain control over their lives and improve their quality of life. For the many residents, this meant accessing consistent medical care, obtaining public benefits, and establishing individualized plans that addressed chemical dependency and/or psychological health care. The main objective of Salus Place was to help residents achieve mental and physical health and independence so that they no longer needed the residential community. So, rather than being a place to come to die, Salus Place was a transitional community that people came to in order to live better (Martinez, 2003).

In order to be a resident of Salus Place, a person had to be a man or woman who was over the age of 18 living with HIV/AIDS. All of the residents were also dealing with some form of addiction, either drugs and/or alcohol. According to Steven, the director of Salus Place, all residents interviewed for this study were addicted to alcohol and 75 percent of those who had ever lived in the house were crack cocaine addicts. During the time of this research, all of the residents were crack addicts. Considering the use of crack cocaine, it was not surprising to hear that almost all residents had had legal problems associated with drug use. In interviews, several residents discussed having "done time" for various offenses such as assault, robbery, and/or dealing drugs.

From the inception of Salus Place, sixty residents have lived there. Two residents left the community and returned at another time. One resident had been in and out of Salus Place three times. Out of the sixty residents, four of the residents have been female. One reason for the large sex discrepancy could be that there are more men living with HIV/AIDS in Missouri than women (Center for Disease Control, 2002). Also, according to Steven, at the time of this study, there were more support services for women who were living with HIV/AIDS and addiction in St. Louis than there were for men (Martinez, 2003).

While residents could live at Salus Place for up to two years, the average length of stay was seven to eight months. Residents paid 30 percent of their income for room, board, and services. Many did not, however, have any income, so they did not pay anything or paid little to stay there. Out of the sixty residents who lived there, approximately fifteen of them were asked to leave. According to Steven, only six residents successfully left the house to lead sober, healthy lives. A resident who worked at Salus Place stated that only one person had left the house and been successful in staying sober (Martinez, 2003).

Applicants had to be homeless at the time of entry in order to live at Salus Place. Staff members conducted a full-day assessment and a mini-mental assessment with the applicants to assess their physical and mental condition. They had chest X-rays and a test for tuberculosis. There was always a waiting list for spaces at Salus Place. People living with HIV/AIDS who were too sick to take care of themselves could not live there, because the house did not have hospice rooms or a full-time medical staff. In some cases, residents transferred to a hospice because they became too sick to stay in the house (Martinez, 2003).

For this research, I volunteered at Salus Place. Before I began my volunteer work, I had a physical and a tuberculosis test to make sure I was healthy enough to work with people who have weakened immune systems. All of the paid workers and unpaid volunteers had to have these tests before working with residents. My volunteer work ranged from working a Cardinals baseball game with residents and staff (cooking hot dogs for donations), to participating in role-playing during an anger workshop. I participated in interviewing one future resident along with a staff member as well as helping out during meetings. Once in a while, I helped clean up rooms when residents left or helped with dinner and clean-up. Observations proved to be a rich resource for discovering the negotiation of occupational identity within this particular community.

During the year I spent at Salus Place, employees included a director, a program manager, a night supervisor, support group facilitators, and an administrative secretary. It is important to note that two of the workers were former addicts themselves, and one of the employees was a current resident living with HIV/AIDS/addiction.

Messages about the value of work within Salus Place differ depending upon the worker and the audience. The Alexian Brothers were very positive and received positive messages about their work in the community. In fact, it was described as a mission—not a job. From my observations within Salus Place and the outside community, the Brothers seemed to be regarded as being holy men who were helping those less fortunate. However, the Brothers were not the ones who worked with the residents on a day-to-day basis. Instead, a program manager and resident/supervisor were the ones who most often were present in the house.

Program managers were especially important to social interaction within Salus Place because they held much of the overt power within the community. When rules were broken, program managers could require residents to make changes or move out. During this study, the original program manager (Chuck), who quit shortly after I began this study, had allegedly furthered the stigmatization of this community due to his issues with homosexuality. During my year of observation, residents and employees often remarked that Chuck had not permitted talk about homosexual relationships and HIV/AIDS in the house (names have been changed to protect anonymity). Residents and one worker said they were often concerned about breaking communicative rules within the house because Chuck could have them removed from the community.

While both workers and residents of the community spoke of being silenced about topics such as homosexuality, personal relationships, and HIV/AIDS, they were silenced in the way they spoke as well. A resident (Frank) told me that he could not be the "queen of the day" in the past because of the atmosphere in the house. When I asked Frank what he meant by "queen of the day," he first placed his hands on his hips, gave me a look, and sighed. Frank then took his hands off of his hips, dramatically threw his arms up in the air, smiled, and said, "you know" in a campy manner. When Frank said he could not communicate the way he wanted to in the past, I realized that many male employees and residents who were homosexual, feminine, and vocal about homosexuality and HIV/AIDS were silenced by Chuck.

Researchers have found that there is a difference between being silenced and being silent (Clair, 1998). Being silenced is one way of marginalizing an individual and taking away power. Being silenced does not mean that someone never speaks. Instead, it means that a person must speak in a prescribed way and may not speak about certain subjects. Hooks (1989) states, "I was never taught absolute silence, I was taught that it was important to speak but to talk a talk that was in itself a silence" (p. 7). In other words, Hooks was taught to speak in a way others thought was appropriate, but not in a way she wanted to speak. The alleged silencing of homosexual residents and employees by the former program manager definitely sent a negative message about both the value of the work being done in the community and the value of homosexual employees/residents themselves.

People who work in residential communities such as Salus Place face a large amount of stress and heartbreak for little money. In light of this work environment, Steven, the current director of Salus Place, told me that there is a great deal of employee turnover in this specialized area. According to Ashforth and Kreiner (1999), while "the stigma of dirty work undermines the status of certain occupations, it simultaneously facilitates the development of strong occupational cultures." One of the exceptions that Ashforth and Kreiner offer is high employee turnover. In light of Chuck's "shame" and high turnover within the house, occupational identity (and residential culture) seemed to be negative when I first began my observations.

Chuck was already working at Salus when the new director, Steven, started work. Steven stated, "Chuck, the previous program manager [and one must assume the previous director], ran the house differently." According to Donald, resident/employee, who had lived in the house for almost two years at the time of his interview, "Chuck ran the house as a drug treatment center." Donald stated, "HIV/AIDS slash substance abuse got us here, but then HIV/AIDS was ignored." Donald noted that rules were stringent, and people were regularly "dropped." If a resident tested positive for drugs he or she was "kicked out." There was no tolerance for relapse.

Chuck enforced two types of rules that residents had to follow. His first rule was that if a resident tested positive for drugs, he or she was kicked out. The second rule was that being homosexual or living with HIV/AIDS was not something that was discussed within the house. Since relapse resulted in being asked to leave the house, relapse was a subject that no one wanted to talk about. Josh, a resident, stated, "There were a lot of pink elephants at Salus Place among the residents—certain subjects we wouldn't approach." When I asked what the pink elephants in the house were, Josh told me that relapse and homosexuality were not discussed. Josh said that since Chuck left, homosexuality was not as big of an issue in the house. Relapse was still not often admitted to because of the ramifications of relapse (i.e., losing residency, outpatient rehab, etc.). Thus, relapse has become the stronger stigma within the community.

In the year after Chuck left, Donna, the new program manager, seemed to have gained the trust of the other staff and residents. In light of this new environment, the residents and employees discussed HIV/AIDS and homosexual relationship issues more openly. For example, at least once a week, I found Frank rubbing Donna's back or shoulder to "steal her estrogen." This was a pattern of play between the two of them. Frank would say he was stealing Donna's estrogen and then Donna would tell Frank to give it back because she needed all the estrogen she could get. With this type of play, Donna promoted acceptance within the community. With this acceptance, a more positive attitude toward work and life was created in everyday communication.

In contrast to people within the Salus Place community, the public had different opinions about the nature of this work. Steven and Donna both showed an awareness of the low prestige of their work in the community. One day, I observed that Donna was upset. She told me that she had read somewhere in a newspaper that a crack addict had been murdered and that the newspaper author had inferred somehow that this addict had deserved it because he was an addict. In other words, the people Donna worked with everyday were described as deserving of violence. On the other hand, the Brothers applauded their work as community service. Academics, such as myself, came to study their organization and considered their work important. They received awards within the community. Therefore, it must be noted that some members of the public did not threaten the positive occupational identity of employees at Salus Place.

The Influence of Taint Management on Positive Occupational Identity

Since there are a number of choices available to manage taint, the third research question asks, How did employees at Salus Place engage in taint management strategies? Ashforth and Kreiner (1999) argue that workers overcome the stigma of their dirty work by renegotiating or managing the idea of dirty work. They created a model for taint management that included the techniques of *reframing*, *recalibrating*, and *refocusing*. The purpose of these techniques "is to transform the meaning of the stigmatized work by simultaneously negating or devaluing negative attributions and creating or revaluing positive ones" (Ashforth & Kreiner, 1999, p. 421). In other words, in order to create a positive occupational identity, workers transform the meanings of their work and cast the work in a more positive light. In this section, I use this model to discuss how employees at Salus Place perform taint management to negotiate and sustain a positive occupational identity.

First, employees at Salus Place engage in *reframing*, which involves "transforming the meaning attached to a stigmatized occupation" (Ashforth & Kreiner, 1999, p. 421). In other words, reframing involves attaching a positive meaning to something that has been stigmatized (also called infusing). For example, Donna is a white, 40-something female who self-identified as a recovering alcoholic. Donna volunteered at Salus Place for several years before becoming a staff member. Donna told me she volunteered as one way to make up for some of the pain she caused when she was abusing alcohol, and to give back to the community. In other words, one of the ways that Donna managed the taint of working within a HIV/AIDS/addiction community was to reframe it as paying back society for things she had done in the past.

A second way employees at Salus Place engaged in reframing was to infuse the job with positive value. At Salus Place, employees often talked about working in the war against AIDS. So, they transformed the stigma of the position into a "badge of honor" (Ashforth & Kreiner, 1999).

Reframing was also helpful in dealing with the uncertainty that came with working with crack addicts. One day at the house a former resident stopped by to visit. The former resident was extremely drunk (possibly on drugs) and was both laughing and crying with Donna on the front stoop. Later that day, Donna told me that this resident was one of her favorites. I asked her if it was hard to see him using again. She said that she was "used to losing people at the house," that it was "just part of the job when working with addicts." She said the house would be here when he was ready to quit again. In this way, Donna transformed the stigma (and the uncertainty) of working with addicts to providing a positive environment for when they were ready to quit using again.

Dirty workers also engage in a technique called *recalibrating* (Ashforth & Kreiner, 1999). Recalibrating refers to "adjusting to implicit standards that are invoked to assess the magnitude (how much) and/or valence (how good) of a given dirty work attribute" (p. 422). At Salus Place, employees do recalibrations when they say that without Salus Place, these residents would have nowhere to go. In other words, employees are saving lives by working at Salus Place.

Employees also manage taint by engaging in *refocusing*. When refocusing, "the center of attention is shifted from the stigmatized features of the work to the non-stigmatized features" (p. 423). At Salus Place, employees focus on the day-to-day business of the house, which often included fundraising. Both employees and residents would work on fundraising efforts for the house. This included working baseball games, dinners, and providing lunches for employees at a nearby hospital. By focusing on fundraising, a positive part of the job, employees could avoid thinking about more stigmatized features of the job. Therefore, they had the opportunity to transform their dirty work into "good work."

A fourth taint management strategy that was used by employees (and residents) within Salus Place that does not fit neatly into Ashforth and Kreiner's (1999) model is the use of humor. Research suggests that humor is prevalent in health-care and health-related situations (du Pre, 1998; Ragan, 1990). Also, humor is an important aspect of good health. According to Koller (1988), physicians have found that humor actually seems to help maintain or improve some processes of the body, such as blood pressure, circulation, and digestion. In addition, humor seems to improve a person's psychological well-being (du Pre, 1998), and it reduces face threat (Ragan, 1990). Within Salus Place, I found that dark and/or silly humor about their work within the community, HIV/AIDS, addicts, and addiction seemed to be another way staff and residents manage taint that did not fit as easily within the model offered by Ashforth and Kreiner (1999). While this humor did not refocus occupational identity in a more positive light, the humor did seem to serve as a way to lighten the more "dirty" aspects of the job.

Conclusion and Implications for the Study of Dirty Work Communication

I like to view this house, the community within here, like a T cell. Sometimes the t-cell ain't doing too good. Sometimes it is really bad. Sometimes it is right in the middle.

—Frank

Frank used the metaphor of a T cell to explain the Salus Place community. The T cell that Frank was referring to is a CD-4 T cell, which the HIV virus attacks. When a person's CD-4 T cell count drops below 400, the person becomes susceptible to all kinds of other viruses, funguses, etc. When a T cell count falls below 400, a person can die from opportunistic infections. For Frank, the Salus Place community was highly valued, just like a good T cell count. However, the nature of recovery and HIV/AIDS made social interaction precarious inside Salus Place, just like a T cell that is being attacked by the HIV virus. In other words, Frank did not say that the community is ever good.

In this chapter, I have attempted to answer the challenge of studying an occupational culture in order to better understand how people negotiate identity as they perform stigmatized jobs as posed by Drew, Gassaway, and Mills within a framework articulated by Ashforth and Kreiner (1999). I demonstrated how those who work in the area of HIV/AIDS and addiction could be considered dirty workers as described by Hughes (1958) and elaborated on by Ashforth and Kreiner (1999). Furthermore, this research illustrated the ways in which employees in Salus Place negotiated their identity with taint management strategies.

At the beginning of this study, I had three research goals. First, I hoped to learn what qualified employees at Salus Place to be classified as dirty workers. My research suggests that those who work with people living with HIV/AIDS and addiction are "dirty workers" through the taint of their work. While Ashforth and Kreiner (1999) argue that "AIDS workers" face physical and social taint, I argued in this chapter that HIV/AIDS and addiction workers must also consider some degree of social/moral taint management.

My second research goal was to come to a better understanding of the messages employees at Salus Place received about the value of their work. I found that employees received both positive and negative (tainted) messages about their work from insiders and outsiders. Within the house, program managers influenced how residents and employees talked about their community and jobs. Outside the house, I found both positive and negative communication about the community and those who lived and worked there.

My third research goal was to identify the taint-management strategies as outlined by Ashforth and Kreiner's (1999) model to understand how employees at Salus Place negotiated their occupational identities. I found that employees engaged in predictable taint management techniques. The employees discussed the lack of success stories in the house, but they also talked about the "good" they were doing in the HIV/AIDS and addiction communities. They took negative aspects of their job (lack of success, relapse, illness) and cast these aspects (*reframed*) in a more positive light. For instance, Donna said she was working to make up for some of the pain she caused when she was abusing alcohol and to give back. Badges of honor were given, for helping in the war on AIDS and drugs and in providing a place for addicts to go. Furthermore, employees took negative parts of their jobs and *recalibrated* by talking about the lives they were saving. In addition, workers *refocused* their attention on tasks such as fundraising, a more positive aspect of the job. Finally, a fourth taint management technique of humor was used by employees to make light of many of the more stigmatized aspects of their jobs.

While I found the use of fieldwork, taped conversation, and interviews to be extremely helpful in understanding some of the ways that taint management gets done in this community, one limitation was that many of the residents were paranoid of the tape recorder for several months. In addition, while I found dark humor to be a taint management technique that does not necessarily turn the negative into a positive, I am curious if humor might be used in other ways to deal with taint. Future research might look at other occupations and see if and how humor is used as a taint management technique.

This study of employees of Alexian Brothers Salus Place provides a glimpse into the important phenomenon of dirty work in an HIV/AIDS/addiction community. Through examining the choices employees make in dealing with the more "dirty" aspects of their job, we gain a better understanding of the ways workers negotiate occupational identity on a day-to-day basis. And ultimately, this research helps organizational scholars gain an understanding of how organizational identities and cultures are created, negotiated, and sustained.

Part II

CASE STUDIES

8

Good Cops, Dirty Crimes

Bob M. Gassaway

Crime scene investigators, who are technically skilled specialists in the modern police department, face a seemingly endless series of encounters with the victims of violent injuries and death. Members of this specially trained work group commonly spend many hours on the scene of a crime, searching for and analyzing evidence that often is socially defined as foul, gross, or objectionable. The evidence these investigators diligently search for includes blood, saliva, perspiration, semen, hair (frequently pubic hair), flakes of skin, bits of flesh and bone, body parts, fingerprints or footprints (often dried in blood), and occasionally urine. And they routinely search the trash at crime scenes to look for evidence.

Despite the working conditions they face, these crime scene specialists commonly confront their work with humor and an almost continuous verbal interaction with their peers at the scene of the crime that helps to divert their attention to less objectionable aspects of their work.

Yet, the reality of their work is never far from them, physically or intellectually. This chapter draws on a two-year ethnographic study of the crime scene investigators in the Criminalistics Unit of the Albuquerque (N.M.) Police Department. During the course of the study, I visited more than two dozen death scenes, watched an autopsy, and spent several hundred hours observing the work of the crime scene investigators at crime scenes, on routine patrol and in the much cleaner environment of offices in the crime lab. Through it all, I found investigators who talk calmly and professionally about death, injury, and crime, investigators who are proud of the work that they say makes a difference in removing violent criminals from society.

My research interests included trying to understand the degree to which these investigators perceived that they were somehow tainted—socially, physically, or morally—by the work they were doing. I sought to understand how they managed their repeated encounters with death and the great bodily harm inflicted on some of the victims they saw.

Background

Crime scene investigation has emerged in the past twenty years as a police subprofession, but many of the technological advancements have come in the past fifteen years (Fisher, 2000). This study considers the work of Field Investigators, who are uniformed police officers, and Field Evidence Technicians, who are civilian technicians, plus the primary and secondary investigators who are specially trained police detectives who guide and direct the investigation of major crimes, and the supervisors for these investigators.

The Field Investigators (referred to in police argot as FIs) and the Field Evidence Technicians (called FETs) usually are the first crime scene specialists dispatched to the scene of a crime. They collect evidence and photograph the scenes at the most common sorts of police calls—domestic disturbances, assaults, burglaries, car thefts, non-violent deaths, damage to a police vehicle, etc. But when FIs and FETs encounter homicides or suspicious deaths, they call out the major crime scene team, which brings the primary and secondary investigators, many of whom have been to hundreds of death scenes.

The police officers and all but one of the civilians who work in the field have experience in other jobs in the police department. The FIs have all worked as patrol officers, or "field services" officers as they are called in the Albuquerque Police Department, and the civilians have worked as police dispatchers, 9-1-1 operators, property clerks or in some other civilian position. So these investigators knew at least to some degree what they were getting into when they transferred to the police crime lab.

The Dirty, Smelly Crime Scene

Crime scene investigators seem to have no illusions about the nature of their work and the environments in which they often find themselves ferreting out the tiniest bits of evidence and the nuances of devastating crimes.

‖ ‖ ‖

One Saturday evening Sgt. Guy Pierce stood on the sidewalk outside a home where an elderly woman had been beaten to death with a claw hammer; he described his reaction to being paged on his day off to help investigate the case. He is a blood spatter specialist, and the supervisor on the case, Sgt. Paul Feist, wanted Pierce's expert analysis of bloodstains at the scene.

Pierce had been in a theater with his wife waiting for the road show cast of *Riverdance* to begin a Saturday afternoon matinee when he received the murder call. He had paid $120 for their tickets six months before the show came to town.

> "I was sitting in my seat when my pager went off," he said. "I got my wife's cell phone and went out and called. Paul Feist told me about it and said he would need me out here about 8 o'clock," Pierce said. The 45-year-old detective tugged at the small black pager hanging from his belt.
>
> "It's a beautiful show, great costumes, good staging and everything. I was aware of everything. But it kind of spoiled the show for me. I was thinking, 'I've wanted to see this show for months, and I'm enjoying the show. And when it's over, I have to go out to a stinking, smelly crime scene, and I really don't want to be here. It's getting time to retire.'"

Later, I asked him how he knew the scene would be stinking and smelly.

> "Just in general," he said, "most of the crime scenes we go to—probably 75 percent of the crime scenes we go to—the homes are filthy dirty, they stink, the lights don't work. They are just places that most of the people who are in my circle of friends wouldn't want to spend the night there, let alone live there. It's always been kind of a running joke with me, at least in my mind, that better than 90 percent of the houses we go to as homicide scenes, either all of the lights or most of the lights never work in these houses."

Pierce, who estimates he has been to a thousand death scenes, said that a normal bodily function at the time of death adds to the disagreeable nature of death scenes. He explained that at the time of death, the ring-like sphincter muscles in the body that constrict the bladder and the rectum commonly relax and the dead often defecate and/or urinate on themselves. "That's one of those unpleasant aspects of the crime scene that you deal with," he said.

|| || ||

Urine contains some cells that can be used for DNA analysis, but urine sometimes tips investigators that a body has been moved or a person's clothing has been rearranged after death. Sgt. Feist (who since has been promoted to lieutenant) recalls a case in which a woman reported she found her husband hanging in their garage; she said she cut him down and tried to resuscitate him.

> "It didn't seem like a suicide," Feist said. "They had tickets for a cruise the next week and were planning a nice trip. Having future plans is unusual with suicides."

An examination of the body helped explain the case. "His pants were fastened and looked normal," Feist said, "but his underwear was wet and was rolled and bunched around his hips. How could his underwear get wet and his pants not get wet?"

When investigators pointed out this discrepancy to the wife, she admitted she had found the man with his pants off and his underwear pulled down.

"It was an autoerotic asphyxia," Feist said. "We found some pornography in the garage where he had hidden it."

Investigators say they see this type of death several times a year. Feist explained that the man apparently had gotten up onto a can or box or some other object, tied a noose around his neck and was masturbating. Psychotherapists and medical researchers report that people who engage in this sexual practice hope to achieve orgasm at almost the same time they lose consciousness, which produces euphoria; they have a plan to release the pressure on their necks before they die (see Cesnik & Coleman, 1989; Williams, Phillips & Ahmed, 2000; O'Halloran & Dietz, 1993). "But this one went wrong," Feist said. "He died. Then he must have urinated on himself; that's what got his underwear wet. Later, his wife pulled up his underwear and she put on his pants, which were not wet."

|| || ||

At a homicide scene, a dead man lay on his back in the hallway of his apartment, his feet extending into the kitchen area, one elbow extending into the bathroom. The dead man was wearing a blue shirt, blue jeans, black-and-white athletic shoes and white cotton socks. His right leg was straight and his left leg was slightly bent at the knee. His head was turned to his left; his left hand was on his abdomen; the left hand was relaxed, his fingers in a loose, fist shape, his knuckles resting on his navel. His relaxed right hand was two inches above the waistband of his pants. Detective Carl Ross said the man had been in a fight with another man.

Ross pointed out blood in the man's mouth and nose; some of the blood was clotted. Ross also pointed out that both the man's eyes were black and some of his teeth had been knocked out, but they were still visible in his mouth. Ross said later that an autopsy showed that the dead man drowned in his own blood, apparently after he fell onto his back and lost consciousness.

As he worked around the body Ross inadvertently bumped one of the man's feet, causing his legs to separate slightly.

Immediately Ross turned his face away from the body and said: "Uh-oh! I've unleashed the monster."

Quickly, two investigators working a few feet away in the kitchen rotated their bodies to put their backs toward the dead man and hunched their shoulders. As the investigators turned away from the body, the stench of intestinal gas flowed over a wide area around the body, including the kitchen and a portion of the living room. The original pose of the man's body had contained the gases, but the slight movement of his leg allowed them to spill into the room.

∎ ∎ ∎

Investigators check everything at a death scene. At the crime scene where a four-year-old boy accidentally killed his 22-month-old playmate, I found the supervisor on that case, Sgt. Paul Feist, searching a garbage can in the kitchen and asked what he was doing. He said police had questioned the four adults in the apartment at the time of the death about what they were doing when the gun was fired. He said he was checking to see whether the physical evidence confirmed what the mother of the dead child said in response to the police question: "She said she was changing the baby's diaper in the other room, and I'm looking for a dirty diaper."

On a homicide scene where he was the primary investigator, I watched Andrew Feist, Sgt. Feist's brother, searching a trash can in which he found bleached towels and rags that indicated the killer had tried to destroy evidence at the scene.

"Always check the trash at a crime scene," Andrew Feist said. "You'd be surprised what people will throw away at a crime scene."

Dead on a Trash Heap

Investigators often cannot avoid the stench of human waste at a crime scene. One Saturday evening Detective Dave Wade was the primary investigator on a case in which he found a murdered man literally on a pile of trash. The man was in the bathroom of a "shooting gallery," the police name for a place where people, especially transients, gather to do drugs. In this case, squatters had repeatedly broken into the vacant, factory-built home and sometimes stayed for weeks, even though the building had no electrical or water utilities.

The dead man was on his back in the bathroom. Wade noted that the body was atop a layer of trash several inches deep on the bathroom floor. The man's head was about at the middle of the doorway from the living room. His body and legs were hidden by the wall to the right of the doorway. His bare feet stretched into the shower stall, which was littered with more trash.

Wade asked, "Do you want to guess where the toilet is? It's not in here." He walked into the kitchen and used his flashlight to illuminate an open five-gallon plastic bucket that contained human feces, toilet tissue, and a yellow liquid, presumably urine. A partial roll of toilet tissue sat on a black box, available to the user's right hand. The stench was strong through the entire building.

The dead man's hands were on his chest. The right hand was in a natural-looking, relaxed position just below his right breast. The left hand, also relaxed, was below the right hand. The man had a neutral look on his face; certainly there was no smile, but his face reflected no anguish, no grimace. His black hair, looking freshly washed, was combed straight back. He was generally handsome.

He was wearing blue jeans pulled down to the hips; the jeans were unbuttoned and unzipped. Curly black pubic hair was visible in the last two inches of his fly, but the jeans covered his penis. Wade saw an abrasion on the man's right hip and observed, "It apparently didn't bleed. It's probably *post mortem*," meaning it happened after the man was dead.

Wade squatted beside the body and used his foot-long, rechargeable flashlight to examine the body. The skin on the man's neck appeared smooth when Wade pointed his flashlight directly at the man. Then Wade moved the barrel of the light up beside the man's head and let the light shine obliquely along the neck. The light made visible barely perceptible ligature marks on the neck; the marks suggested the man's neck had been wrapped twice. Then Wade applied oblique lighting to the man's wrists; the right wrist appeared to have been wrapped twice and the left three times. Wade then pointed out a length of electrical cord that was visible beneath the body under the left arm. A narrow trail of blood, thinner than a pencil, led from the right front of the man's neck toward the back of the neck. The blood had dried.

Wade concluded the man's hands had been tied and then he had been strangled. A confession from a suspect later affirmed his analysis. The blood on the neck apparently had nothing to do with the death.

Trash and litter were scattered in every room of the house. In the living room, dirty blankets and quilts and clothing and several beer cans were strewn over much of the room. As investigators worked in the dirty house, the smell of human waste permeated the air. Wade pretended to look on the lighter side of the situation and offered a joke: "The thing about working in a place like this is if you have gas, nobody will know."

Later, as she moved about in the house taking more photographs to document the scene, FI Lori Grube said: "I'm sick of smelling this shit in here. I'm getting a headache."

Disposing of the Body

Killers occasionally try to get rid of a dead body by throwing it into a trash barrel or a commercial dumpster.

Detective Joe Foster was the primary investigator on a case in which a man and woman were shot to death in the apartment they shared with two homeless men they had taken in and granted free shelter. The homeless men first tried to bury the woman in a shallow grave in the backyard, but decided to dig her up and put her into a trash barrel. A garbage truck with a mechanical arm to handle trash barrels picked up the woman and dumped her into the truck without the driver noticing he had just picked up a body. After police found blood in the trash can, they spent days sorting through tons and tons of trash in the city landfill before they found the body. The murdered man was simply stashed in the trunk of a car.

In a case in which Detective Denise Herrera was the primary investigator, police crews spent thirty-one days picking through thousands of tons of garbage in a large section of the city landfill looking for a body that one of the murderers confessed to dumping into a commercial dumpster. Police finally abandoned the search after officials of the federal Occupational Safety and Health Administration became concerned about the health threat to police officers and FETs working in the garbage.

"This was in August," Herrera said. "This stuff was decaying. OSHA was concerned about us breathing that stuff."

‖   ‖   ‖

Although it happened more than ten years ago, crime scene investigators still talk about the dirtiest case they can remember. Police say the victim had been a very good university student in a pre-law program before she started taking drugs; within months she dropped out of school and turned to prostitution to pay for her drugs. Then she was found murdered.

Herrera was the secondary investigator on that case. She remembers that a man who had been out walking his dog called police to say he had found a human hand sticking out of a manhole cover. "The dog was very curious in taking him over into that area," Herrera remembers. "That's when he went over and found the hand sticking out of the manhole cover."

Herrera remembers the sewer lines well: "It was deep, like fifty feet. It was where two sewer lines come together and feed into a big main line."

The primary investigator, Jeff Arbogast, pulled on plastic coveralls and climbed down a ladder into the hole. "He started finding pieces of the body and pulling them out," Herrera remembers. "Then the fire department dropped some type of metering system down in the hole, and they found there was not enough oxygen in there to sustain life; it was all methane gas."

After that, investigators put on breathing apparatus and used a fire department light to work in the sewer hole.

"At one point Jeff came out of the manhole and he had maggots in his mustache," Herrera said. "Another officer flicked two or three maggots out of his moustache. Jeff got very sick from that and was hospitalized. He had some intestinal type of problem that he sustained from that.

"I think we found nine pieces of the woman's body," Herrera said.

The autopsy report said the body had been sawed into pieces after the woman was killed—a murder that remains unsolved.

Looking through the Camera Lens

Lt. Francisco "Rocky" Nogales retired in 2003 after more than twenty years with the Albuquerque Police Department as a patrol officer, a field investigator, a field investigator sergeant, a sex crimes investigator, a homicide detective, and other jobs. But in an interview, Nogales, who trained new field investigators, remembered one important aspect of his work as a field investigator very clearly.

"One thing I really pay attention to with the detectives is you want to photograph the wound," Nogales said. "You've got a little powder burn around the wound and you've got to photograph the wound at a 90-degree angle with a scale." (The paper scales adhere lightly to the skin; they are marked to illustrate the approximate size of the wound.)

"There is a different view of the world thorough a camera lens," Nogales said. "You have to make sure it's focused, and you're looking at a gaping wound. Maybe it's next to a wrinkle, and you can focus on that wrinkle. You're up close and personal with a trauma, and you've got to spend some time over it. You've got to develop a way of protecting your psyche and still getting that picture. You'll see investigators at times lose their control before they finish their job. Other investigators have to help and finish it for them."

He recalled a case of his own like that early in his work as a field investigator. He said the case involved an older couple who lived in a mobile home.

This man had a British Enfield assault rifle. He got into a fight with his wife and says, "I'm gonna go kill myself." She says, "Why don't you go do it instead of talking about it?" He went off and got his British Enfield assault rifle and put it under his chin. It opened up his whole head. His face and head and brains were on the ceiling; stuff was dripping. When she walks in, it is dripping. She's naked. His body is still doing "The Chicken" [a popular rock 'n' roll dance of the time], the last spasms of the dying nerves.

The officer who was dispatched was nearby. He heard the gunshot and was looking around. He hears the woman screaming. He is already driving that way, and he sees people moving toward the mobile home where the couple lived. When he goes in, here this woman is, sweating. He says the body (of the man) was still moving.

The man was sitting in a chair with the Enfield between his legs when he pressed the trigger. The shot lifted him and he fell in front of the chair. The bullet went through his head and the top of the trailer. It just left some flaps of skin where his head was. The body is still doing "The Chicken," still twitching, when the officer arrives. The woman is trying to pull him (the officer) in so she can show him; he is trying to grab the woman and he just now realizes she is naked. He grabs her (in his arms) and takes her out.

For the next hour and a half, stuff is dripping on me. I didn't realize how much had dripped on me until I got home and took off my jacket.

He was in a sitting position in front of the chair. I was doing an overall, mid-range shot.

As he recalled the scene, Nogales arranged pieces of cardboard that happened to be in his office to demonstrate how the man was sitting, his legs straight in front of him, the rifle still between his legs, near his groin.

I'm trying to focus on the rifle, and I'm looking through the viewfinder, and I find an eyeball staring at me! And I lost it! I walked out of the room, probably white-pale. I called another FI, and he came over. He was a salty old guy with lots of experience. I took him in, and I told him to look, and he said, "That's an eyeball!" But it didn't bother him. He leaned over to look at it, and he said, "Damn, Rocky! That's a glass eyeball!"

He said, "Have you seen this guy's I.D.?" I hadn't, and we went looking for it. This guy was pretty ugly. He had already tried this before, and the whole right side of his face had been restored, and he had a glass eyeball!

We had a good laugh, and went back in and finished up. The humor lightened the tension.

But, Nogales added, "What occurs in that camera is close and personal and it messes with your psyche."

Other investigators agree.

|| || ||

For example, Detective Herrera was the primary detective one Sunday night on the case in which a four-year-old boy accidentally shot and killed a two-year-old playmate. The boy had found his father's .357-magnum revolver hidden beside the bed where the children were playing. Herrera was observing as other investigators photographed the body of the dead child with a digital camera that connected to its flash unit with a swivel joint that allowed a 90-degree pivot.

As Herrera watched investigators using the camera near the body of the child, she acknowledged the virtues of that particular camera's design: "You get a 90-degree angle and you don't have to lean over them, smell them or nothing."

The Nature of the Evidence

The evidence takes different forms and requires different treatment at various crime scenes. For example, Detective Herrera was the primary investigator at a murder-suicide, and without discussion she stepped up and handled the most repulsive job of the evening herself. The victims were a man and woman who had been married fifteen years and then divorced about five years before they were shot to death. Both bodies lay on the floor in the living room, perpendicular to a small home entertainment center. A 21-inch television set was the dominant item in the home entertainment unit, but it also held a PlayStation and a VCR.

> "The woman probably was sitting on the sofa when she was shot," Herrera said. "The man then apparently moved her body to the floor in front of the TV set. Then he shot her in the head. That is a contact wound and star-shaped tearing. Then, he laid down and shot himself in the head."

The single wound in the man's head was above the nose in the middle of his forehead.

When the Office of the Medical Examiner removed the bodies, Herrera found a thick pool of coagulating blood as large as a dinner plate on the floor where it had flowed from a wound in the back of the man's head. Herrera pulled on two pairs of rubber gloves and then knelt so that she could search through the blood with her right hand to find any bullet fragments that might remain in the blood. Dipping her right hand into the blood and tissue, she combed her fingers through it.

"I'm going to puke!" she said. "Ugghh!"

But she did not puke, and she continued her work until she had felt to the farthest edges of the pool of blood. She said later she did not ask anyone else to check the blood because as a primary investigator she does not ask other people to do things she will not do herself.

The television set and the home entertainment center were spattered with blood from the shootings, and the light-colored wall to the right of the victims bore splotches of blood and tissue. "That's goobers, plain old goobers," Herrera observed, using a word that usually is a slang term for *peanuts.*

Later, wearing rubber gloves, Detective Dave Wade collected the dead man's gun as part of the evidence. "There's stuff in the barrel," Wade observed. Then he held the pistol for Sgt. Art Acosta to photograph. Wade used the same term Herrera had used for the blood and tissue on the wall when he observed, "These goobers and whatnot that are on here are starting to rust this gun already."

Herrera, standing nearby as Acosta photographed the gun, told him, "Really, all I want is the goobers." She explained that the bits of flesh and blood on the weapon were evidence that the gun was very close to the victims' heads when it was fired.

Later, Herrera said the term *goobers* is used to describe any human tissue that may be blown away from the body by a gunshot or torn away by other violence, but it is most often used to describe brain tissue. She also used an informal term at that crime scene to describe blood on the floor near where the woman had been shot initially. Herrera said, "She gorked." I asked what that meant, and she said she was noting that a narrow stream of blood on the carpet was the result of "an arterial spurt," a more direct and clinical term.

Working Language

Humor has been recognized as a coping device for physicians (Turnbull, 1998) and nurses (James, 1995), especially those who work in hospital emergency departments (van Wormer & Boes, 1997), and nursing instructors (Talbot, 2000), as well as people in other occupations, particularly in situations involving stress (Bippus, 2000; Ramsey, 1999; Thorson & Powell, 1993; Weiss, 1997; Witkin, 1999). However, the academic literature offers few insights into how police deal with death situations. Much of the humor fits the description offered by communication researcher O. H. Lynch (2002), who says:

> Humor is cognitively based because it is dependent on the individual's perception of an event, individual or symbol in comparison to what is considered typical. If there is a discrepancy, the humorist registers the incongruity between the perceived event and the expected norm to find humor in the relationship (p. 428).

By keeping up an almost constant flow of talk, much of it casual and unimportant, about things other than the crime scene, the crime scene investigators are effectively "layering" their conversation, or a series of conversations, over the reality of the crime scene.

The crime scene still is present and the investigators are aware of it. They continue their work as they talk, performing skills that they have previously learned and are reproducing in a physically different but logically similar circumstance. Much of the talk is humor, some of it quite pointed and direct; one detective calls it "grab-ass" humor and another calls it "dogging." By carrying on a series of casual conversations during much of the investigation, joking with each other, making fun of each other and otherwise creating a level of social interaction that they can attend to and focus on, they can distance themselves emotionally, socially, and intellectually from the homicide, suicide or other deadly event that has befallen another human being, including the often brutal injuries or other cruelty that they are investigating.

Engaging in humorous exchanges or joking does not prevent officers from being aware of the death and carnage in front of them. They have to be aware of the physical details of the injuries to the victims and the technical details of recording these injuries for later use in court. However, by keeping up a running line of conversation and joking, they can avoid focusing all their attention on the scene before them and thus minimize the percentage of time in which the gory details of death and physical destruction of a human being are the primary focus of their attention at the scene.

‖ ‖ ‖

Sometimes the humor fits the job the officers are doing, as it did late one night as Field Investigator Jerry Roach and Detective Glen Walker were collecting hairs from the bed of an elderly woman who had been raped and beaten almost to death.

Roach was picking up hairs with tweezers. I asked about the dull color of the tweezers and Roach explained: "They are disposable, and they are plastic. That helps keep static electricity from building up so quickly."

Walker, who was holding a white paper envelope open for Roach to drop the hairs into, told Roach he was primarily interested in pubic hairs because he was concerned the woman had been raped. After they had put more than a dozen hairs into the envelope, Walker asked: "Who wants to lick the envelope for me?" The two detectives in the room laughed but declined the opportunity.

Later, in the crime van, Walker jokingly complained to L.T. Guenther, the primary detective: "I don't know why no one would lick the envelope for me after we picked up all the hairs we could find."

‖ ‖ ‖

Yet, another time at another crime scene, finding a pubic hair produced an almost euphoric response from an investigator. Detective Carl Ross moved into the tiny, one-room apartment where a 68-year-old woman had been beaten to death and robbed. The body was in a three-foot area between the woman's bed and a large front window. A chair and a nightstand took up part of the space. So Ross stood astraddle of the woman's feet. Ross stood still for several minutes as he surveyed the body with a practiced eye. Suddenly his face seemed to brighten and he bent to examine something near her left hip. Then he asked FET Andrew Feist to get a special container for him. Feist exited the room, opened a kit on the sidewalk outside the dead woman's room and prepared a bindle paper and a small manila envelope.

"He found a hair," Feist said. "It looks like we have a nice, dark pubic hair." Then he returned to the room.

Ross again bent and held a white card near the left leg-hole of the woman's panties to point out the hair and Sgt. Paul Feist photographed it in place. Then the hair was placed into the bindle paper and dropped into an envelope for later DNA testing.

As the investigation continued, Paul Feist lifted fingerprints from one of several metal cookie cans he found in the apartment. He said later he "processed" (looked for fingerprints on) the cans "because they looked out of place. They looked like something the guy had moved." He also lifted fingerprints from a cigarette lighter he found in the tiny apartment. Why did he fingerprint this ordinary object? "There were no ashtrays in the apartment and no signs that she smoked. I figured it probably belonged to the guy," he said.

Police later arrested a 19-year-old man who had a pocketful of change and a record of extorting money from residents in the apartment complex, including his 94-year-old great-grandmother. His fingerprints matched those on the cigarette lighter and cookie tins. When prosecutors outlined the evidence police had collected, the man pleaded guilty to the crime.

Blood-borne Pathogens

Unlike the workers in some occupations (see Jervis, 2001), exposure to pollutants is not limited to lower-level workers at crime scenes. The primary investigator in most instances will want to see where blood was found or where a bloody fingerprint was discovered and may grab a pair of tweezers to personally pick up a hair from the body of a victim, hoping the hair will provide the DNA necessary to link it unequivocally to a killer. Investigators of all ranks are trained to beware of a variety of blood-born pathogens, including hepatitis, HIV, and AIDS.

The first case where I observed the investigators at work involved a man who was shot to death in a hotel room. Investigators worked around the body for almost four hours; then, after it was removed, the investigators carefully stepped around the blood stains on the carpet. However, an hour or so after the body was removed, Detective L. T. Guenther accidentally stepped in the blood.

> "L.T.!" Herrera snapped at him in a chastising tone.
>
> Guenther walked into the bathroom vanity area where Herrera was working, and she said, "Let me see the bottom of your shoe."
>
> When Guenther lifted his shoe, the sole obviously had blood on it.
>
> Herrera voiced her exasperation: "Gaaahh!"
>
> But Guenther quipped: "Why didn't he take his blood with him?"
>
> With a small smile, Herrera responded: "Yeah. Why did he leave it on the carpet?"

Obviously, the two colleagues were joking, but there was no laughter and no real evidence of amusement. But I perceived no real disrespect for the dead man. They simply were using gallows humor to relieve the stress of a half day's work next to a dead man's body. Now that the body was gone and their work was almost done, they could relax a bit and make a grim joke that did not really amuse them.

Later I asked Herrera why investigators so cautiously avoided the blood.

> "If you're in a crime scene, the blood is important," she answered. "You don't want to mix it or smear it or change anything.
>
> "The other aspect, in this case, was the blood was not important. But I don't want to track it out of the scene into my car and from my car into my house. And I touch my shoes every morning when I put them on. It wouldn't be just blood, but it's vomitus, feces and urine and any body fluids you can transfer diseases with. This is because of bio-hazards and blood-borne pathogens."

Investigators routinely use what they call "bleach water," which is a mixture of water and laundry bleach, to kill any germs they may pick up on a crime scene. Sgt. Feist said that when he returns home from work every day, "I rinse my boots in bleach water before I go into the house. You bring these things home. There was one investigator who got something (on her shoes) that got into the carpet. Her dog died." The bleach water dims the shine on cops' shoes, but that doesn't bother Fiest, who says, "I've been on (the police department) 14 years, and I've never gone to work without shining my boots."

Crime Scene Humor

Humor at crime scenes takes various forms, but it is not the static, canned humor reflected in the retelling of a preexisting joke. Rather, the humor is almost always created on the crime scene, drawing from the social interaction or observable facts or incongruities of the particular situation. But sometimes the humor is created as a means of dealing with some other element in the shared occupational lives of the crime scene investigators or as a way of reviewing in a humorous fashion some event that has occurred to someone in the crime lab at an earlier crime scene, or perhaps to a violent crimes detective or some other police officer.

Often, the humor seems simple, obviously intended to relieve the strain of working over dead human bodies in an environment that often is dirty and smelly. For example, one night Detective Glen Walker was the secondary investigator on a case where two men had died in a small, cheap, filthy apartment. One man had been dead at least 24 hours, and the other may have been dead two or three days; both bodies were beginning to smell of decomposing flesh. When he first pulled on rubber gloves and picked up equipment in the custom-built Mobile Crime Laboratory in preparation for entering the scene, Walker was serious as he observed, "This is a stinky one."

Later, after he had worked close to the bodies for an hour or more, Walker returned to the Mobile Crime Lab, took a chair near his partner on this case, visibly relaxed into the chair, and made another announcement: "I've got one thing to say." Then, screwing his face into a look of disgust, he uttered a sound I would much more have expected from a teenage girl than a 45-year-old veteran detective: "Eeuwwww!" He enjoyed his pronouncement and smiled broadly at his own humor. His partner also smiled.

Paul Feist described how the humor sometimes seems necessary. During his years as an FI supervisor, he commonly grabbed a camera at a crime scene and helped shoot the pictures, even though his rank would have allowed him to assign other investigators to do the work. But Feist readily described how shooting pictures thrust him into frequent close contact with the victims of violence.

> "When you look through a lens at a dead body, and when you have to zoom in on a bullet hole or injuries where the car bumper hit the face, you're at the real nitty-gritty," Feist said. "If you see it through the lens, you are more focused in on it. Humor helps. It has nothing to do with disrespecting the dead guy."

Sometimes the humor seems to come from nowhere; it is just a brief break in the work pattern. One night at a murder-suicide, Sgt. Art Acosta was sitting in a straight-back chair at the kitchen table less than a dozen feet from the two bodies. He had been coughing, sneezing and blowing his nose throughout the hours on the call.

> Herrera said, "Stop faking the cough." But she tickled his ribs lightly to signal she was joking.
> Detective Wade added, with a smile, "You sound like you're coughing up a hairball, Art!"
> "It feels like a hairball, too," Acosta answered.
> Then, a minute later, Wade coughed. Quickly, Acosta pounced him, asking, "Got a hairball? What's going on there?"

Wade later resorted to a wry form of humor to salvage the situation when he inadvertently touched one of the bodies. Wade had been videotaping the scene, and at one point, he was between the bodies and the south wall of the apartment. As he stepped over the bodies to move over near where Herrera was working at the table to develop a diagram of the scene, Wade's shoe sole accidentally brushed the female victim's bare foot. Wade clearly was surprised; he had intended to step over the foot. As he put his foot on the floor, he turned around to look directly into the dead woman's staring dark eyes and say, "Sorry, Lady."

Later, Wade was sitting at the table when he observed, "This place is nice and clean. It's refreshing to go to a clean crime scene." Then, after a short laugh, he added, "Most of the crime scenes we go to, you don't want to sit down."

Voices of the Dead

Crime scene investigators commonly point to the importance of their work by saying it is their job to speak for the victims of crime, especially in death investigations.

But Chris Rubi, a nationally certified fingerprint examiner who works only in the crime lab, not at crime scenes, thinks about both the dead and the living victims of crime. She is clear about why she likes the job she found by accident shortly after she finished her criminal justice degree.

> "I found out about this job through a friend who saw the listing," Rubi said. "I was working for the city in the recreation department scheduling softball games for the parks and recreation department, and bid on it. I figured the worst they could tell me was no. And if nothing else, it is good interview experience. Eleven years later, here I am. I love doing what I do. It is fun. In some ways it feels like you are giving back to the community, doing something to help better the community, being that final voice for a victim.
>
> "You feel very violated when your house is broken into or when your car is broken into," she said. "Sometimes just being able to explain to the victim how the system works helps, or in a homicide you are that final voice for the victim. Being able to identify that offender is a good feeling."

Acosta said it is important to get everything right in every investigation, but especially in death investigations where a homicide may resemble a suicide. "As I heard Sgt. Guy Pierce say once, 'In a homicide, you're the voice of that victim.' That victim no longer has a voice."

Sgt. Pierce said he picked up the concept at a training program years ago. "We are essentially a voice for the dead," he explained. "By looking at the evidence and crime scene reconstruction, we can tell people what happened when nobody else can."

Diminishing the Taint

Crime scene investigators find ways to reduce their exposure to distasteful aspects of their job by putting on rubber gloves before handling dirty objects or even dressing in protective clothing that establishes a whole-body barrier against physical taint. Sometimes they signal through verbal comments or facial expressions and body language that they consider certain aspects of their jobs disgusting. The act of recognizing the unpleasant nature of the job is in itself a form of social protection because it allows the investigators to indicate to themselves and to others that they have not relaxed their personal standards despite the pressures of often encountering foul or dirty objects. By signaling that they understand certain aspects of their job should be considered repulsive, they establish their links with the other members of society who would find the tasks unpleasant. Yet these police officers have developed the ability to adopt a grin-and-bear-it approach, signaling that they are willing to undertake the repugnant tasks because that is necessary to the job. They see their jobs as essential to the successful investigation of crimes. Their work helps establish the evidence necessary to prosecute criminals so that they will be taken off the streets and thus protect the good and honest citizens of the community.

Despite the nature of their work, however, the crime scene investigators do not seem to feel much personal taint. They appear to share the view that they are beyond taint because they are on the side of righteousness. However, several crime scene investigators indicated in interviews that they often are unable or unwilling to talk with their spouses or significant others about many of the events they encounter at work because of the violence or foul nature of their work. Instead, if they feel the need to talk about what they have encountered, they talk with their peers at work.

Of course, all police officers have experience in dealing with taint. For example, a uniformed officer working in a patrol unit routinely comes into contact with people who are drunk or high on drugs. Some of these people are so inebriated that they may have urinated on themselves, vomited on themselves or even defecated on themselves. Still the police officer must search the person for weapons, alcohol, and drugs and needles, and put the person into the officer's usually pristine police car—which is the street cop's office—for the ride to jail. The odors readily permeate the vehicle and may even be strong enough to make the officer's uniform smell after the event has ended. The officer may also have to physically subdue the person being arrested, which requires close and often prolonged physical contact with the person.

The Right Language

One way crime scene investigators diminish the impact of a scene is in the way they talk about its elements. By referring to tissue, especially brain tissue, as "goobers" and using other euphemisms, such as "gork" to describe arterial bleeding, the investigators can avoid coming to grips with the situation as directly as they would if they used medical terms. In fact, the crime scene investigators have developed their own jargon to describe crime scenes, to talk about the victims and the people they refer to as "the offenders," the people responsible for the crimes. The crime scene investigators have already mastered the argot of the police department, but they have extended that language by creating their own within-group terminology for their specific work. That extended language is unintelligible to many ordinary cops who have little crime scene experience.

Humor is a persistent form of emotional self-defense. Humor and conversations unrelated to the crime scene were a part of all the crime scene investigations I observed. Detective Glen Walker was blunt when I asked him why the cops often joke at crime scenes: "I think it is just a way of dealing with the scene itself, I guess a coping mechanism."

However, I concluded that casual conversation at crime scenes, even without humor, is also a part of the coping mechanism. By carrying on a running conversation, the investigators create something on which they can focus their attention, thus diverting it from a constant, direct focus on the crime scene. Despite their ability to cope with their work, however, I never heard a crime scene investigator say he or she was eager to get the next call.

9

Cops, Crimes, and Community Policing

Shirley K. Drew & Mendy Hulvey

I hate that part of it—being stigmatized and stereotyped . . . [there's a] perception that we're bad people. . . .

—Sgt. M. Schaper, personal communication,
March 27, 2006

When you're a kid . . . you wanna be the hero.

—Officer J. Noga, personal communication,
July 5, 2006

Introduction

It is a truism that we are judged by the work that we do. For many of us, what we do is a central part of who we are and so it influences how we judge ourselves. Hughes (1958) argues that work is one of the most important parts of our social identity and thus of our lives. When society defines the work we do as dirty, then it is natural that as "dirty workers" we attempt to revise the public's perceptions, as well as our own, in order to construct positive self and occupational esteem. Police work is physical, social, and moral dirty work. It can be physically disgusting. Police officers often have to deal with offenders, or "the bad guys" (as they refer to them), who are physically dirty, smelling of alcohol, vomiting, urinating, defecating, or spitting in their patrol cars or on the officers themselves. The work is socially dirty because officers spend their work lives dealing with stigmatized groups. In a sense it is also socially tainted because it puts police officers in a servile relationship to those same stigmatized groups and to other members of the community as well. In order to maintain some dignity and freedom, police officers construct barriers that create social distance from the bad guys. For instance, at the Pittsburg Kansas Police Department the patrol cars are equipped with cages to separate officers in the front seat from prisoners in the rear seat. Entering into the inner sanctum of the department offices and interrogation rooms requires codes (like a bank PIN) or having someone inside "buzz you in." Finally, policing is morally tainted as well. This occurs ". . . where an occupation is generally regarded as somewhat sinful or of dubious virtue or where the worker is thought to employ methods that are deceptive, intrusive, confrontational, or that otherwise defy norms of civility" (Ashforth & Kreiner, 1999, p. 415). The media provide the public with images of police interrogators or detectives who lie or use trickery to get information or officers who abuse their positions in some way with members of the public, through brutal behavior or expecting free meals at the local coffee shop. While this behavior may be an exception to the norm, these media images contribute to a public perception of cops as morally tainted. It is probably more common, particularly in rural areas where community policing is the norm, that moral taint is attached when officers are perceived as rude or uncaring.

I am curious about real police work, not the fictional representations that the media give the public. My curiosity is due at least in part to the occupation's closed nature, its multiple cultures, including languages, artifacts, and rules. And, I must admit, I'm curious because of the life and death aspect. How do police officers do a job knowing that their lives are often at risk? Obviously others have studied police culture (See, e.g., Van Maanen, 1988; Pogrebin & Poole, 2003; Trujillo & Dionisopoulos 1987; Payne, Berg, & Sun, 2005), but I was interested in how policing is done here—where I live—in Pittsburg, Kansas.

This chapter was cowritten by the two authors. My individual experiences (Shirley's) are represented by the use of the first person. Examples of these experiences include the ride-alongs with officers, informal conversations, and my interaction with the Pittsburg Police Department's (referred to as PPD) First Citizens' Academy. I've tried to provide balanced representations of the accounts of the officers I spent time with. I consulted with Sgt. Roger Rajotte and Deputy Chief Brent Narges regarding who might be most willing to talk with me, as well as on many other issues. I spent time with officers across a range of ages and lengths of service (referred to as LOS from this point on) in the occupation. The remainder of the chapter is a collaboration between Chief of Police Mendy Hulvey and me. Chief Hulvey has been in law enforcement since 1985. She joined the PPD in 2000 and was promoted to Chief of Police in 2005.

In this chapter we first provide a brief cultural and socioeconomic history of southeast Kansas and how it informs the nature of police work in Pittsburg, Kansas. Next, we compare community policing and professional policing in the PPD through examples of conversations during my ride-alongs with eight officers, four women and four men. Both styles of policing influence how officers construct their social identities. Finally, we offer explanations of how members of this occupational group manage the taint of their occupation through private as well as public communication strategies.

‖   ‖   ‖

The Pittsburg Police Department is housed in the Public Safety Building on Pine Street, sharing this space with the Pittsburg Fire Department. The building is shabby and in disrepair. Chief Hulvey describes it as "nasty, grimy, and an electrician's nightmare" and ". . . an awful working environment for all of us; half of our offices are in the garage." Although the city has recently painted the corridors, the lobby and some of the offices, the building still has the feeling of an old steam plant, which was its actual function from the 1930s to the 1960s. The lobby floor is tiled and there are a few plastic chairs and a side table sitting at one end for visitors. On the left, one-way mirrors separate the dispatch room and the public reception area, and to the right of the chairs are doors to the offices that employees open with codes. Visitors can be "buzzed in." Across from the one-way mirrors, on the right, are windows between the lobby and the reception area, with small round openings so that visitors and personnel can pass documents back and forth. The interior has offices for the supervisors and administrators, including the chief of police and the two deputy chiefs. It houses the dispatch room, and two interrogation rooms that are visible by remote camera in dispatch.

I initially gained access to the Pittsburg Police Department (PPD) in 2003 through former Police Chief Mike Hall. I called him and introduced myself as a communication professor from Pittsburg State University. I told him I was interested in doing a study of police work as part of a larger project. We met and talked at length on two occasions, mostly so I could get a sense of how he managed the department, or in police terms, "the agency." When I returned in 2005 to continue the research, Hall had retired and Chief Mendy Hulvey was at the helm. I'd interviewed her in 2003 when she was still deputy chief and knew her to be someone who was open to the project I was doing. I arranged with her to continue the research, first with some graduate students that I supervised, and then on my own. From there, I worked primarily with administrative Sgt. Roger Rajotte. Roger eventually became my chief contact, as well as my mentor in police matters.

My primary sources of information include several semistructured interviews as well as informal interviews. The informal interviews were, in effect, ethnographic conversations during ride-alongs and while hanging out at the PPD. Finally, I attended a ten-week Citizens' Police Academy (the first ever for the PPD) beginning April 4, 2006. Some of the experiences from my academy classes are integrated into this as well.

A Sociohistorical Context

Mining and Bootlegging in the Balkans

To understand better the nature of policing in Pittsburg, Kansas, it is important to have a basic understanding of the multiple sociohistorical contexts of this part of the state. To be direct, lawlessness in Southeast Kansas is an integral part of the region's history. O'Brien and Peak (1991) explain that mining was the major industry in the late nineteenth and early twentieth centuries with immigrant groups as the primary work force. The area was ill-prepared for the cultural clashes that emerged. "Fifty-three languages were once spoken in the mining camps, dance halls, and churches" (p. 1). Loyalties to the region emerged, as if we were our own secret society, a part of, but always separate from, the rest of the state—the "armpit" of Kansas. O'Brien and Peak concur and argue that even now, the Southeast corner of Kansas (particularly Crawford and Cherokee counties) has maintained only "tenuous" ties with the rest of the state.

Bootlegging and violence were common during the turn of the twentieth century. The cultures of the immigrant community differed from their American neighbors; the American part of the community was responsible for prohibition. Prohibition created conflict between the two groups; the immigrant population ensured that the southeast corner of the state remained "wet."

Today we are a society that is still willing to accept a certain amount of lawlessness. Although our drug of choice is now methamphetamine (though alcohol abuse is still prevalent), our behavior patterns are reminiscent of the early twentieth century. We have either been unwilling or unable to break the backbone of our social and crime problems. Cyclical behavior patterns—particularly those related to alcohol, meth, depression, and family violence—remain apparent.

Perhaps when the mining economy dried up, those who were more fortunate were able to either relocate or reestablish themselves into other occupations. Those who were not remained desperate and dependent on alcohol and crime as a way of life. Today those individuals still exist in our region and in our city, desperate, with no hope of any other future. Lawlessness has become a way of life, passed down from generation to generation.

Policing in the Early Days

Thomas (1975) documented the early years of policing in an unpublished manuscript. She points out that alcohol was a problem from the city's early beginnings (the city was incorporated in 1876). Liquor, gambling, and vice were rampant and lawlessness was apparent. In the early days, appointed marshals who served a one-year term led city police officers. It was not until the turn of the twentieth century that the region appointed a police chief as we would think of them today. During this period the chief of police was charged with attempting to manage drunkenness, prostitution, and a growing Red Light District, unprecedented by today's standards.

In the 1905 city directory, twenty-five saloons were listed, although Kansas was a dry state and the consumption of alcohol was illegal. We were, however, a city comprised of immigrants who did not share the same values and regard for the law as did the "Kansas Drys." Murder was quite common during the early years and many slayings remained unsolved. At one time, the southeast corner of Kansas was thought to be one of the most violent spots in America (O'Brien & Peak, 1991).

Policing Today

Although we have entered into the twenty-first century, many of
the practices of the early twentieth century remain reminiscent of
our past. The city of Pittsburg still has some of the highest crime
rates in the State. For example, in 2004 ("Crime in the United
States," 2004) the city of Pittsburg had the second highest Part I
Crime Index in the state of Kansas. This included eight serious
felonies: murder, rape, aggravated assault, robbery, burglary, lar-
ceny-theft, motor vehicle theft and arson—per 1,000 residents in the
state. This is second only to the Kansas City, (Kansas) Police
Department. Many variables influence or drive a crime rate, such as
communities on state lines, university communities with transient
populations, or socioeconomics conditions. We would suggest, however, that the demographic, geographic and cultural (historical)
indicators of the Southeast Kansas region in combination have created an environment "ripe" for crime.

Immigrants Reemerge

The population of the Pittsburg area until recently reflected a
diverse heritage of many countries, primarily white and European.
This region was commonly known as the "Little Balkans" because it
was populated in the late nineteenth century by immigrants from
European Balkan countries who came to provide needed labor for
the coal mines and smelters. The last group of immigrants came to
the region from Italy approximately eighty years ago.

In the last few years of the twentieth century, Pittsburg began to
experience a new wave of immigrants, this one predominately
Hispanic, seeking their own version of the American Dream as they
supply the much-needed labor force for local factories and busi-
nesses. Not unlike the late nineteenth century, this new wave of
immigrants arrived to a community that was again emotionally and
structurally unprepared for the resulting communication issues and
demands it would place on the city's resources. Recognizing the
challenge to notice commonalities and value diversity, as well as
hoping to avoid a future "us versus them" syndrome, a grass roots
organization known as the Pittsburg Area Community Outreach
(PACO) emerged to ensure that the diverse populations within the
community could come together for the common welfare of all residents. PACO is a proactive, community-based organization founded
to help ease immigrants' transitions into the community. The focus

of this "grass roots" organization is integration, not separation. When immigrants live separately, they feel separated. When they live alongside established residents, they learn how to live together and, hopefully, better appreciate each other. The Pittsburg Police Department works in tandem with this organization.

The Pittsburg Police Department

The Pittsburg Police Department is a small, municipal agency comprised of thirty-nine sworn officers and fifteen civilian personnel, with an annual operating budget of approximately $2.9 million dollars. Of the sworn personnel, six are women, who represent 15.8 percent of the department, which is slightly above the national average of 14.3 percent. The gender diversity is a uniqueness of this department.

The chief of police serves as the chief executive officer of the department and is charged with the responsibility of achieving the overall objectives of the agency. The department is separated into two divisions—Operations and Administrative/Support Services, with each division managed by the deputy chief of police.

Organization

The organizational chart of the Pittsburg Police Department is similar in nature to that of a large, urban, centralized bureaucratic organization. The difference, however, is the rural or small town nature of the police department, which is naturally more service oriented. As a result, it operates from a community-policing perspective as a response to the kinds of social problems that create the southeast Kansas culture. The Pittsburg Police Department's simple structure offers a great deal of flexibility, movement, and input at all levels of the organization. In small-town police organizations, structures are not as centralized or hierarchical as those more commonly seen in larger municipal agencies. Instead of the more traditional, authoritative disciplinary model of management, the chief of police encourages a community-policing approach.

Community Policing in Pittsburg

In the early 1990s the Pittsburg Police Department began to "rethink" its traditional style of management, viewing modern community-policing techniques as an avenue to not only improve community relations, but to expand the department's resources. By 1995 the department had "city-wide" administrative support; it was given the financial resources necessary to improve both its technology and its professional image. Internally, the police department reorganized the overall structure by flattening (reducing) its command staff. This organizational shift provided additional resources and manpower where they were needed the most—on the street. The police department also implemented a series of changes designed to improve customer service and to promote a "professional standard" within the department. More importantly, perhaps, police administrators began to forge relationships with outside agencies, which included law enforcement, social services, and private and nonprofit support/advocacy groups. The administrative staff felt that a multifaceted approach to crime and its prevention could best be effected and coordinated with a joint approach.

Community Policing (CP) vs. Professional Policing (PP)

"Community Policing is a philosophy that broadens from a narrow focus on crime to a mandate that encourages the police to explore creative solutions for a host of community concerns, including crime, fear of crime, disorder, and neighborhood conditions," said Sgt. Thomas Roughton during one of the last sessions of the Citizens' Police Academy class on May 30, 2006. He explained that community policing is "something that we try to live, not just do. Some officers will never really accept community policing in this department." He said that some officers adopt the more traditional "professional model" of policing through strict adherence to rules and a focus on enforcement efforts. The professional model is the Joe Friday "just the facts, m'am." And of course it is about arresting the bad guys. Chief of Police Mendy Hulvey continued the mission started by former Chief Mike Hall to make the PPD a community-policing department. Her leadership sets the tone for the officers and staff, and she determines procedures for how her officers do policing in Pittsburg.

> "There's a struggle between the two models in any department that tries to do community policing," Roughton explained. "There are many difficulties in maintaining this approach. First, it is labor intensive; it's time consuming and it requires additional resources. It requires interactive officers who have good communication skills and creative thinking abilities. It also requires flexibility on the part of the officers."

Community policing is a public strategy that strives to develop and enhance a positive image of the police department and officers with the citizens of the town. It is a proactive style of police work focusing on problem solving and order maintenance rather than reactive practices of law enforcement (Weisheit et al., 2003). It requires responsiveness to the community and a willingness to adapt to the culture of the area. In Pittsburg, if officers are not a good fit or cannot adapt to the southeast Kansas culture, they usually do not stay with the department. Weishet et al. (2003) argue that in many communities, the citizens expect the police to provide a range of services usually because other services are not available. Police are viewed as an integral and visible part of the community, as opposed to being separate from it. In rural areas, as in Pittsburg, officers often know the offenders, as well as the victims and their families. Officers may have less discretion because their work is more visible to the informal networks that exist within the community. This is frustrating to some officers because it inhibits their ability to "catch the bad guys." And because the approach is more informal, to some officers this means less control. Lack of control is more problematic to those who identify with a professional model of policing. Being responsive is a primary responsibility of the administrative officers. They must deal with the media, city commission, and other constituents. In effect, while police officers are accountable to the formal police hierarchy, they are also accountable to the community they serve.

Connecting with community members is mostly about making interpersonal contacts during the course of policing. It means stopping and talking with people, as well as taking the time to listen to their concerns. Police may behave differently because they know community members. They may be more patient and polite. This may not be a conscious decision, but something that evolves or emerges because community members are friends, neighbors, and local business owners. Patrol officers must take an active role in the process for it to be successful. There is no universal program of community policing; rather, each community adapts and applies the approach in its own unique manner. In Pittsburg, community policing is enacted in the three ways that Weisheit and his colleagues describe: responding to community concerns, connecting with individual community members, and problem-solving. While these three behaviors usually happen in tandem, for purposes of analysis I treat them as discrete categories and provide representative examples for each.

Responding and Connecting as Community Policing

I always wanted to be a cop . . . my mother thought I was crazy.

—Officer Becky Palluca, 32 years old,
LOS, seven years

Officer Becky Palluca embraces the community policing model. Her identity as a cop is closely tied to the community; she grew up in Frontenac, Kansas (five miles north of Pittsburg) and has spent her whole life in Crawford County, but that does not mean she is not interested in "trying to catch the bad guys."

ǁ ǁ ǁ

June 22, 2005, 5:40 a.m. It's foggy and very early. I'm barely awake as I walk into the police station for my ride-along with Becky. She greets me with a smile and leads me to the briefing room. At 6:00 we're ready to roll. Becky grabs her black canvas bag, which serves as a "portable office" and I follow her out the door. In the car, she does several checks, turns on the computer, fiddles with the radio and pushes some other buttons. It reminds me of watching an airline pilot go through the preflight checklist. We start talking, mostly small talk to try to get to know one another. She laughs and smiles a lot and I find her easy to talk to. And she swears like a mill worker. One officer who learned I was riding with Becky told me, "You can spend five years in the Navy or two days with Rebecca" to learn to swear like she does.

Soon she is dispatched to her first call. It is a report from a man who claims that his tools were stolen from a house he is remodeling. When we arrive, I feel more than a little out of place, almost like a voyeur, but I try to act as if I belong there. Becky politely asks him some questions, takes a detailed report, and then we get back into the car. We don't get a lot of calls, so we spend some time patrolling her beat. She waves and smiles at people. At one point she gets out of the car to talk to a man who works for the city and they hug each other, laughing. She seems to know almost everyone we pass. And they know her. "It's a fucking parade!" she says, laughing again. She's a female Andy Griffith, only she uses words that would make a sailor blush. She manages to turn this function off when in a professional mode. Either way, she is a role model for community policing. She enjoys connecting with people, and her youth, energy, and genuine enjoyment of the people and community she serves are directly related to her positive identity. Though she's young, she's not naïve about police work. She admits to being somewhat jaded about the people she deals with. "If you're talking,' you're lyin'" is her motto. This is a sentiment I heard expressed by every police officer I talked with during the time I spent at the PPD. As we are driving on Broadway, her cell phone rings. After a moment she says, "Just driving around in this car, trying to catch the bad guys," and smiles. It's her father, and he wants to meet her for breakfast. We go to a little home-style place called Bob's Grill, to meet Mr. Palluca and a friend of his. After the introductions, I ask her father how he feels about his daughter being a cop.

> He tells me, "If that's what she wants to do, then God bless her."
> "Do you worry?" I ask.
> "All the time," he says. After breakfast we walk to the parking lot. Becky gives her dad a hug. As we walk away, he shouts, "Hey, daughter, watch your ass!" We smile and get back into the patrol car.

"Boy, this has turned out to be a giant cluster!"

—Officer Rebekah Lynch, 28 years old,
LOS two years

Officer Rebekah Lynch laughed as she made the announcement quoted above. She said this after a long day of what she referred to as "clusters"—miscommunications, complicated problems, and a lot of time spent trying to get things resolved by the end of her shift. Although Rebekah joins in the good-natured (and sometimes off-color) camaraderie of the officers when she is hanging out on dispatch, her communication style with the public is respectful and professional. She is another cop who identifies with community policing.

‖ ‖ ‖

June 27, 2006, 5:45 a.m. I arrive at the PD to meet Rebekah for my ride-along. As we get settled in her patrol car, she punches the computer screen with her index finger, getting everything ready for her shift. We get rolling just before 7 a.m. It turns out to be a busy day.

As we respond to the various calls throughout the day, I find myself paying particular attention to *how* she talks to the people she interviews. Always professional, she empathizes with one man who had a stereo stolen from his car: "What a way to start the day," she says, shaking her head. In the same polite tone she says, "The chances of you recovering that are really slim; it does happen, and we *will* try, but you need to know this."

Later we go to an apartment to get a report from a man who supposedly wrecked his friend's car after drinking too much. As he tells his story, he backs up periodically, changing details. After listening to a couple of versions, Rebekah tells him patiently, "Run through your Sunday again with me." While she is firm and direct, her tone is still polite. When we get back in the patrol car, I make some comment about his contradictory accounts. She shakes her head, frustrated, and says, "I get lied to all the time."

At a little after noon we go to Subway for lunch. I insist on buying, though she objects at first. I tell her that I want to show my appreciation for her time, though I have had the same arguments with other officers. I ask, "Why is it so hard to buy you guys lunch?"

She says, "We're just not used to people being nice to us." I have no reply. The idea that she doesn't expect people to be nice to her is a way of managing the identity threats she receives in the form of rude behavior. Even more important, keeping your cool in the face of rudeness (or downright obnoxiousness) is a source of pride and self-esteem.

Problem Solving as Community Policing

Things are likely to get nasty; you should go back to the car.

—Officer Anne Scott, 33 years old,
LOS 9 years

The midnight shift (10 p.m.–6 a.m.) is usually when most of the "action" happens. The officers on this shift primarily answer domestic violence calls, reports of bar fights, and accidents due to drunk driving. On the night I rode with Anne Scott (from 10 p.m. to 2 a.m.), we responded to domestic calls exclusively. These calls require problem-solving skills and patience. Cops who do this kind of work take pride in preventing violence or in arresting an abuser.

‖ ‖ ‖

June 10, 2005, 10:00 p.m. I'm riding on the midnight shift, or "third watch" as it is sometimes called on television. Anne and I walk to her patrol car in the lot behind the police station. At her side she carries the black canvas bag that serves as her office. In it she has packed accident report forms, evidence bags, ticket forms, latex gloves, hand sanitizer, pens, pencils, a flashlight, and anything else she can think of that she might need. Because the officers might drive different cars each shift they work, these supplies go with the individual.

We patrol her beat for a short time, responding to some routine calls, stopping to talk to another officer, and talking about her work. Then at about midnight she gets a domestic call. She drives to the address, turning the lights off as we approach the house. "Don't want to warn potential suspects," she tells me. Because domestic violence calls are among the most dangerous to officers (and their ride-alongs), she parks several houses down the street and locks me in the car with the lights off. Two other officers are already at the scene; one in the house and one on the large and well-lit front porch. A young woman drives up and parks in front of the house. I am not sure who she is; my guess is that she's probably from the Crisis Resource Center. She walks up the steps to the porch and sits in a plastic chair next to the woman who is the reporting person, or RP. After several minutes, Anne comes out to the car and tells me I can join them on the front porch.

> "Is it okay with the woman who called? I don't want to invade her privacy."
> "Yes," Anne says, "I checked with her."

I walk up to the porch with her and pull up a chair. Anne introduces me to everyone. The woman who just arrived is a PRA, or police response advocate, and works in concert with the Crisis Resource Center. Her job is to talk to individual family members who have called the police to report abuse. As a PRA, she provides referrals for counseling or other services. She will help them leave their homes to go to a safe house if they wish to do so. Standing next to her and behind the RP is a young male officer. While the RP talks with Anne for a few minutes, the male officer and the PRA are talking about having recently graduated from Pittsburg State University; I realize how young they must be. He was a Criminal Justice major, and she was in Social Work. I am impressed that two such young people are handling such difficult situations, and I feel a sense of pride seeing how some of our graduates have "turned out."

Anne and the PRA talk with the woman on the porch (I only listen) while another officer tries to keep the husband calm and inside the house away from his wife. Should she want to leave, they want no interference from him. After a short time, she decides to leave. It won't be long now before one of the officers tells the husband.

"Things are likely to get nasty; you should go back to the car," Anne tells me. I do it without question. Soon after, she comes to the car and tells me we are moving on and letting the other officers finish up at this scene.

> *I'm always a cop but I can disconnect myself. I have a whole separate life outside of work. . . .*

—Sgt. Melanie Schaper, 25 years old,

LOS four years

Sgt. Melanie Schaper is the day shift supervisor, though she still works patrolling the streets. Her job as a supervisor is to provide support to the officers, solve problems, and act as a liaison between the officers and the higher administration. She seemed young to be a supervisor; however, I found her to be articulate and intellectually mature. She also struck me as very balanced. That is, although her life as a cop is important, she is just as dedicated to her life outside work.

‖   ‖   ‖

March 27, 2006, 6:00 a.m. An officer must perform several tasks while simultaneously patrolling the streets. As I get into the car with Melanie at a little after 6 a.m. on a June morning, I watch her get the car ready to roll. As we drive her quadrant of the town, she scans passing motorists and pedestrians, uses one hand to talk on the radio, operates the computer screen, watches street signs, and talks to me. For a while we just talk and patrol her area. She tells me about her background and her interests. She has a B.A. and M.A. in justice studies from Pittsburg State. She is very athletic; in fact her full-time hobby outside of work is competitive body building. She has a select group of friends and does not usually hang out with cops. Keeping her personal life separate from her work life is one way she manages the stress of being a cop.

Melanie enjoys the patrol duties. She has had some tough moments, like most cops. On two occasions she had to notify parents that their child had died. "They see you and they know," she tells me. She explains that you have to "be straight, no euphemisms. It reminded me how vulnerable we are. You know too much and you see too much." She remembers thinking, "I have a brother; it could've been him."

She likes the administrative side of police work too. She enjoys the autonomy and the opportunity to be creative and solve problems. But she says she has to know "when to take charge and when to hold back." A supervisor's job is to "lead and instruct."

I ask her, "What's it like supervising a bunch of men? How do they seem to feel?"

"Honestly, they seem okay," she tells me. "[I] haven't had a problem."

This fits with what I have observed and seen in her interactions with male officers. Since I have been hanging around for so long, I decide she's probably right. At least, if they do have any problems, it's not related to gender.

I think to some degree, the lying was surprising. Everybody lies—it's the saddest thing in the world.

—Officer Joe Noga, 36 years old,
LOS one year

Officer Joe Noga spent five years as a reporter for *The Morning Sun*, Pittsburg's daily newspaper, working the "cops and courts" beat. Eventually he realized he wanted to be a cop, not just write about them. He has only worked for the department for a year, so he is still trying to earn the respect and trust of his fellow officers. Not just because he's a rookie, but also because he was a reporter. "Cops . . . they have serious trust issues," he tells me, smiling. In spite of that, he says he loves being a cop. While he aligns himself with community policing, his "cop identity" clearly includes aspects of the professional model. He tells me that he thinks it is important to strike a balance between the two approaches. "If you're a good cop, you should," he says.

‖   ‖   ‖

July 5, 2006, 10:00 p.m. I meet Joe in dispatch and then we walk to the garage to join the briefing, already in progress. It's cut short; a report from dispatch sends us to an "injury-accident" call. All the officers on shift run to their cars. I run behind Joe and climb into his patrol car. On the way there, he calls dispatch, "Pittsburg 34, what's my beat?" "Rove, traffic enforcement." Joe likes working traffic.

"I did realize during the course of my studies [that] traffic is what we do . . . it's a point of contact [with the community]." Also, Joe says, "[you] write a ticket—you're done. I'm not real big on drinking and driving. . . . I like doing DUIs; I think it's important."

We arrive at the scene of the injury-accident. A college-age man has flipped his motorcycle; he looks basically uninjured, though he has a bad case of "road rash" (scrapes and bruises). After Joe does his work at this scene, we go to the next call. When we arrive, there's already another officer there. Joe turns off the lights and locks me in the car. Several minutes later he returns and I ask him,

> "What's going on here?"
>
> "Crazy people," he replies. Then he says, "Sometimes people just wanna talk."
>
> We start driving around and I notice "Bad to the Bone" is playing on the radio. He says, "Let's go ahead and make a car stop. I'm getting a little itchy."
>
> "Itchy?" I ask as he pulls a car over.
>
> "Was he speeding?"
>
> Joe shakes his head. "He's got a headlight out."

After the car stop we roll along and I ask him about the gender makeup of the department. What I really want is his reaction to the number of women in the department. He explains that the PPD is "by far the most progressive in that respect." He says that it is mostly a "nonissue." "Nobody ever talks about it." He believes that it would be unusual if there were not some feelings about it. This is no doubt true in any occupation that is historically male-dominated. But he insists that it does not interfere with the work.

He does three more traffic stops, two of them DUIs. We talk more about the job and he talks about how much he loves being a cop. He says that he knew it was right for him and he couldn't wait to finish the training. "When they let me go on my own, I felt like I was born."

‖ ‖ ‖

All of the officers in the examples above align themselves closely with the community policing approach. This was evident in everything they said and did. However, this does not mean they are not interested in enforcement; it is clear that they are. It is interesting to note that three of the four officers in the above examples are women. This implies that women are more often CP officers than men, though this is not necessarily so at the PPD. I only rode with eight of 39 total officers. Of the 39 sworn officers, seven are women, including the chief. In the following ride-along accounts, the officers I rode with use at least some community policing skills even though they align themselves more closely with professional policing.

Professional Policing

Officers at the PPD construct a dichotomy in terms of how they define the occupation. Officers are not assigned as CP officers or as PP officers. But most of them know how their coworkers think about and define police work. The dichotomy is constructed in how they talk about and do that work. While some talk about making contact with the community or solving problems, others talk more often about "getting the bad guys." And that is how they approach situations on the street. They manage the taint of being a cop by doing the job that they define as most important. If they are unable to do that job for any reason, it becomes more difficult to maintain a positive identity. In these cases, officers may suffer burnout, reconstruct their identities to more closely match what they do, or leave the job for another agency or another career altogether.

> *I got into this job to catch the bad guys.*
>
> —Officer Jarrod Lamborn, 26 years old,
> LOS, three years

I rode with Jarrod Lamborn on his last evening at the PPD. He was moving on to a bigger agency in Broken Arrow, Oklahoma. He said he thought he could be a more effective officer if he could focus on the kind of work that interested him most.

‖ ‖ ‖

June 23, 2006, 2:00 p.m. Jarrod is a 6'3" bald cop (he shaves his head very close) who takes what he does very seriously. When I first met him, I thought of him as "stoic." After talking with him a few times, I revised that view. He is serious, but not unfriendly. He smiles as he greets me: "Are you ready?" I nod. We walk down the hall to the briefing room where Lt. Farnsworth is sitting at his desk and the officers are standing around, laughing and joking. The lieutenant introduces me, and we all nod; I've met almost everyone in the room. I make some comment about so many bald officers, and Jarrod says smiling, "Yes, but I'm the *baldest*." Everyone laughs.

After the briefing we head out of the station, get into the patrol car, and go cruising for "bad guys." He taps the computer screen with his index finger a few times to find out if anything is happening yet. He tells me about the drug culture in Pittsburg. He talks about a group of "gang-bangers" from Kansás City with street names like

"Dark Side," who runs with "Frog," "Dirt," "Dash," "LaRay," "Hot Rod," and "Story T." Drugs are a serious problem in southeast Kansas. In fact, the Kansas Bureau of Investigation (KBI) has an office in Pittsburg for that very reason. Most crimes that are not directly about drugs are related indirectly. Theft within the drug culture is common, Jarrod explains. Most of those thefts are committed "so they can buy their next rock." His "thing," he explains, is to get drugs off the street. I remembered him saying in an earlier conversation that he didn't like traffic stops and giving tickets.

> "This is not a wealthy area; [citizens] can't afford to pay tickets . . . [so I don't stop speeders] unless it's just a blatant disregard for safety. I'd rather go out and find drugs." He explains that all cops are interested in different areas. He says that Sgt. Roughton and Officer Steffens are "traffic ninjas" and "all about running down DUIs." Besides getting drugs off the streets, "I enjoy hunting warrants, SWAT stuff [and] any kind of weapons work. I like being in armor."

At 6:30 the dispatcher calls Jarrod back to the station, "42, 10-84 please." We head back and as we pull into the parking lot, I notice that all the patrol cars are parked in their assigned spots. "Everyone seems to be here," I say. As we walk into dispatch all the officers are standing around laughing and joking. It's a going away party for Jarrod. After a minute I ask, "If you're all here . . . who's protecting the streets?" They just laugh. Well, I think, at least I'm safe.

Jarrod's next call is a burglar alarm at a liquor store on Fourth Street. We speed over there, but we don't run hot because a subject is "more likely to take hostages" if he or she is warned. We spot the reported car leaving the store's parking lot and follow it to a convenience store down the block. Jarrod pulls up behind the car and jumps out of the patrol car, locking me in. I watch the whole exchange from the car. Jarrod is standing in front of the suspect before the man has any idea about what is happening. The man looks to be thirty-something, and I notice he's wearing a wedding ring. He's dressed decently. I think, "This is not the guy." However, nothing is assumed until the subject is questioned—another thing I have learned from my ride-alongs. Jarrod asks the man if he can pat him down; I don't actually hear this, but I can see what is happening. The man nods, looking shocked and frightened, though not angry. Jarrod pats him down. They talk for a few minutes. Jarrod gets a call from dispatch—this I can hear—and, as it turns out, someone set off the store alarm accidentally. Both men seem to relax a little, talk a bit more and finally Jarrod smiles at the man and walks back toward the patrol car. As he climbs in, I say, "Well, he'll have a good story to tell his grandkids some day."

"Yeah," he says, smiling.

You can't do this job, and do it correctly, and not piss somebody off.

—Officer John James, 50 years old,
LOS, 28 years

Officer John James "came up" in the professional policing days and still aligns himself closely with that style. He has constructed and reconstructed his cop identity over the years, mostly due to new chiefs of police and new ideas about policing. Cops who do not fit the community policing role are sometimes perceived as rude.

‖   ‖   ‖

June 28, 2006, 6:15 p.m. John starts our ride-along by announcing that the dispatchers and supervisors are a little hacked at him because he questions calls. "What do you mean?" I ask. He tells me that he hates the "dog calls." Dispatchers often send officers to "dog-at-large" calls after the animal control officers go off duty, but John does not see this as police work. I ask him why he decided to work in law enforcement.

"Some days I wonder," he says, laughing. "I grew up in Arma [five miles north of Pittsburg]. I've been playing policeman since I was a little kid."

He tells me that some people think he is rude and admits that he has had some complaints from the public. "My voice is forceful . . . and I'm direct. If you don't want my opinion, don't ask for it," he says, laughing again. I mention community policing and he nods. He knows treating people well is important, though he is more focused on doing the job as he views it. He tells me that policing has changed a lot since he came on the job.

We spend a busy four hours answering routine calls. At the end of the evening, we go visit Mary. Mary is an 87-year-old woman who calls several times a week, complaining that someone named Karen is in her backyard or has stolen something from her house. John and I head over so he can "shine my spotlight real bright in [her] backyard so she'll know [he] was there." Then we cruise around to the front of the house to check it out. No one seems to be there, so we head back to fuel up since the shift is ending. He tells me that Mary's son lives in

Tulsa. John says he "wishes there was some way we could make [the son] come here and take care of her." He says he's afraid she will fall and hurt herself and no one will know about it. As we finish fueling, dispatch radios that Mary called again. "Well," he says smiling, "Let's go visit Mary. This time I'll use my BIG spotlight."

|| || ||

Officers who identify most closely with a PP approach have clear ideas about what counts as police work and what does not. Officer John Steffens is another officer who seems to prefer the professional approach to policing. I rode with him in June of 2006. His "thing" is getting drunk drivers off the street; he says he hates "anything to do with alcohol." The identities of PP officers are closely tied to their abilities to "get the bad guys," and sometimes they are frustrated with the department's focus on community service and problem solving. However, they still perform the community service functions, though they might prefer a more traditional approach. They do it because Chief Hulvey clearly identifies the PPD as a community policing department, and this theme is evident in her communication with her officers and staff.

Managing Taint at the Pittsburg Police Department

Private Strategies

To manage the taint associated with their jobs, police officers at the PPD employ both private and public strategies. Privately, they construct positive social (i.e., personal and occupational) identities. Ashforth and Kreiner (1999) argue that dirty work "threatens the ability of occupational members to construct an esteem-enhancing social identity" (p. 413). Officers accomplish this with social validation. This includes interactions with coworkers, friends, and family that allow them to maintain an identity of "good people doing dirty work." Nearly every officer I spoke with talked about the importance of attending to their relationships with family and/or friends as a way to mitigate the stresses associated with the job. Much of the stress comes from the way people treat them in their roles as police officers. Several officers told me that drivers frequently "flipped them off" when they passed them on the street.

They are hesitant to have their meals in public while in uniform. Without exception the officers I rode with preferred a place where they could either see the food prepared or where they knew the people who worked there well enough to feel comfortable. They believe that restaurant personnel spit in food if they know it's going to a cop. This attitude produces a "we versus them" attitude that creates cohesiveness between officers. They often talk about instances of suspects lying to them. Becky Palluca's "if you're talking', you're lyin'" is a common attitude among officers. There is an inherent lack of trust between them and the people they deal with daily. As Joe Noga said, "Cops . . . they have serious trust issues." This reminded me of what one of our Citizens' Academy instructors, Lt. Henry Krantz, told us: "In God we trust; all others we run through NCIC" (National Crime Index Center).

For the officers of the PPD, identity construction is related to how individuals define their role as police officers, i.e., what counts for them as "real" police work. Aligning themselves with community policing, professional policing, or some hybrid of the two influences how officers construct and enact their occupational roles. For the community policing officer, occupational identity is constructed based on his or her ability to serve the community and to solve problems. For the professional policing officer, identity is more closely related to traditional police work—getting the "bad guys" off the street. Officers who embrace the opposite approach sometimes challenge their coworkers' identities. This is evident in the way they talk about what they like to do (get DUIs or drugs off the street) or by saying that dog calls are not "police work." This creates factions or cliques within the group as a whole. However, there doesn't appear to be much (if any) overt conflict on the job at the PPD. Good-natured ribbing is more commonly practiced.

Police identity is closely tied to the material culture and artifacts associated with the occupation. These aspects are crucial in expressing the uniqueness of the culture. In police work, this includes, but is not limited to, patrol cars, uniforms, badges, service weapons, and all the other gear that is part of the job. No matter what the weather is, most officers wear 30 to 38 pounds of gear daily. This includes the uniform, heavy shoes, a Kevlar vest, service weapon, baton, radio, handcuffs, notebook, pens, a flashlight, and whatever else seems necessary. But it is a badge of honor to be able to do the job with the extra weight and in extreme temperatures. Plus, the gear itself is considered "cool." During the Citizens' Academy classes, Lt. Craig Farnsworth introduced us to the gear used by the Special Response Team (SRT), or what many people refer to as SWAT. While showing us the gear, he said that the purpose was "not just to look cool, but that's a perk." Jarrod Lamborn, who served as a SRT officer before he left Pittsburg, admitted, "I like being in armor." Each officer is responsible for the care and maintenance of his or her gear, so it becomes part of that individual's identity and work. They often talk about the gear, the cars, and the other "toys" that come with their work. This strong material culture creates an exclusive group with a cohesive membership.

The PPD's strong culture is supported by the shared values and beliefs; this is demonstrated in the languages, humor, and stories. The language is a unique combination of military terms, commonly used law enforcement "10-codes," and slang that is particular to this group. During my first few ride-alongs, I could only decipher one in ten words I heard from dispatchers and other officers. By the time I finished my last ride, I could decipher almost all that I heard, and I was beginning to understand about 25 percent of the codes.

Humor is an integral part of the police subculture that supports group values, beliefs, and behavior. Pogrebin and Poole (1988) explain that it creates group solidarity, allows coworkers to laugh at each other with no ill will, and serves as a coping strategy. This allows officers to normalize crises and to laugh at their dilemmas. Both members and organizations benefit from institutionalized humor because it preserves the status quo. It's a means of transmitting group culture to new members. Officers tell jokes and stories about the situations they deal with daily, as well as about past events. I heard many stories during the ride-alongs, and I saw much of this kind of interaction while sitting in dispatch waiting to meet with an officer or supervisor. But humor and storytelling usually remain within the boundaries of the occupational community. Most outsiders would not necessarily understand, nor would they likely appreciate, the intent or value in these private exchanges.

Public Strategies

Community Policing

A reoccurring theme in this chapter has been community policing. This is an explicit public strategy for managing taint, though from the viewpoint of occupational members, that is only one of many benefits. In this context, Hulvey says her role as chief is to "provide officers with everything they need to do their jobs . . . [but it's] far more challenging than I thought it would be." She must balance the needs of the department and officers with the needs of the community. Some officers are more enforcement oriented (i.e., professional policing), but the community expects service. Hulvey says, "We truly are just a mirror image of our community." In her opinion, the police department needs to reflect the values of the community and provide needed services in addition to law enforcement, but the "services should always tip the scale." Not all people appreciate her perspective on community service and involvement, but the Pittsburg community as a whole has responded positively. Personnel from the police department are involved in many community service organizations, activities, and events.

Citizens' Academy

> *In 2006, the police department was able to successfully implement the department's first Citizens' Academy. This effort was a decade-long dream that eventually came to fruition.*
>
> —Chief Mendy Hulvey

Chief Hulvey charged Sgt. Roger Rajotte and Maj. Brent Narges with organizing the first PPD Citizens' Police Academy. They recruited members of the community whom they thought would be "friendly" to the idea and who would provide useful feedback regarding both process and product. Because I had been hanging around off and on for over a year and the officers were familiar with me, I was invited to attend. The academy classes were ten weeks long, meeting for three hours one night each week. We began on April 4 and had a formal graduation on Saturday evening, June 6, 2006.

The Citizens' Academy was an effort to educate the community about policing in Pittsburg. In addition, it was an attempt to provide a more accurate (and positive) image of the policing profession as a whole. On the day that we graduated from this course, Sgt. Roger Rajotte gave a speech to the Pittsburg Noon Rotary Club, explaining the purpose, development, and implementation of the academy: "This is a program that was talked about for ten years and never got off the ground. Chief Hulvey told us to do whatever we had [to do] to make the program a reality." He explained why it became important:

> In the past, police departments felt the need to keep what they do a mystery and not share the inner workings of a police officer or department. . . . That is how departments used to think: "The public won't understand us." As different people have told me, there is a natural curiosity about police officers and what they actually do on a day-to-day basis. How do we solve crimes? Do we really just drink coffee, eat doughnuts, and just drive around all day? . . .

> So the purpose of the academy is "understanding through educa-
> tion" . . . We want people to understand just what we do . . . Police
> work is not like TV. The Citizens' Academy reminded us that we
> are all members of the same community.

The community and police department have created an ongoing
working relationship that has engendered mutual support. In
August of 2006, "voters overwhelmingly approved a half-cent sales
tax Tuesday night for the public safety center by a margin of 1,542 to
528" (*Pittsburg Says Yes*, 2006).

"It's almost surreal," Hulvey said over the phone. "This has been
needed for so very long . . . now we can move forward."

Conclusions

Wrapping Up

In this chapter we have tried to describe the ways in which police
work is physically, socially, and morally tainted. When Sgt. Roger
Rajotte read a preliminary draft of this chapter, I received an e--mail
from him pointing out that I had not mentioned specific examples of
the physically dirty aspects of the job at the PPD. Other than potentially dangerous situations, I hadn't observed any. He shared with
me some specifics in his e-mail:

> Nobody thinks about police having to deal with a dead body that
> has been dead for three or four days in a house or outside with
> high temperatures, and we have to deal with that smell. Also when
> the body fluids rupture and go all over the place when you have to
> move them. This is a job no one wants, but the public rarely hears
> about. At a crime scene you have to work for hours around the
> body. That smell will linger with you for days (R. Rajotte, personal
> communication, August 23, 2006).

I replied with, "Thanks, Roger, I just had my lunch." But he
made a good point. My experiences with the PPD were clean for the
most part, and so I did not get a real sense of what the physically
dirty aspects of the job are like. And in a small town like Pittsburg,
there is no separate crime scene unit. That means the officers on
duty are responsible for collecting the evidence, unlike the officers
in CBS's *Crime Scene Investigation*, who only stand respectfully to the
side. The only exception to this rule is cases of homicide. In those
situations, the detectives at the PPD are called into the scene, and

the official evidence officer, Detective John Colyer, is in charge of the evidence collection.

Chief Hulvey and I met a couple of days later to talk about the chapter. I told her about Roger's e-mail and so she elaborated on his point, talking about murder scenes she had worked as a patrol officer: "You live and breathe and smell those experiences for days. It's in your nose, it stays there, and you can taste it." Message received. Still, I know that understanding the experience is not the same as *having* the experience. It's the same with fieldwork in general. We might think we can understand the experiences of others, but it is not the same as *having* those experiences. All the same, I hope that what we have provided is a *sense* of the experiences of the officers we represent here. And with their help, I like to think that we have approached that goal.

In that same conversation Chief Hulvey asked me, "What are your conclusions and what do they mean?" I told her that although the PPD has some officers who practice a community policing approach and some who practice professional policing, many seem to integrate the two approaches in their work. I said that this combination seems to work well for the PPD. She agreed, explaining that a police department is a "paramilitary structure" and so it is natural for some cops to identify with the professional approach, since it is a structured way of doing police work. However, many of the officers (not all) have grown up in small towns very much like Pittsburg. In a rural community it is harder for them to detach, because the people they deal with daily are local business owners, neighbors, and sometimes even friends or relatives. It is difficult to take an "enforcement only" attitude under these circumstances. It is easier and more natural for these officers to integrate the two approaches.

As a communication professor I am naturally drawn to an approach that emphasizes good interpersonal and problem solving skills. But during the course of this research I acquired a better understanding and appreciation for the professional policing model. This is due in part to the time I spent with officers who explained to me *why* and *how* do their work. It is also because I came to know more about the history of the policing profession as well as about the corner of the world where I live and work. My hope is that I have done an adequate job of representing these approaches in a fair or at least balanced manner.

10

The Death Doctors

Bob M. Gassaway

Introduction

The dead human bodies arrive at the back door of the New Mexico Office of the Medical Investigator day and night, about 3,000 times a year, each one a puzzle with medical, social, and legal ramifications that need the careful analysis of a forensic pathologist. The Office of the Medical Investigator—better known to police officers as OMI—has jurisdiction by state law over any death that is "unattended," meaning OMI investigates any death that is sudden, violent, untimely, and unexpected; or where a person is found dead and the cause of death is unknown.

A lot of the cases reported to OMI—almost 2,000 a year—come as no real surprise. A local physician who has been caring for the person in recent months may conclude that the circumstances of the death are what might be expected in this situation, and that physician will agree to sign the death certificate. So these cases can be handled locally if an OMI investigator finds nothing to suggest that a more detailed investigation should be conducted. But the 3,000 dead bodies that arrive at the back door of OMI reflect the cases in which the police, family members, or physicians call on forensic pathologists to make sense of the unexpected, usually sudden, death of a human being.

I undertook an ethnographic study of forensic pathologists' work over a three-month period in 2005, during which I observed portions of about 30 autopsies. I wanted to try to understand the work of forensic pathologists. I was interested in how they handled daily contact with dead bodies. Merely being in contact with dead bodies often establishes some level of social, physical, or moral taint among people in a variety of occupations (Ashforth & Kreiner, 1999; Hughes, 1951).

The Background

The forensic pathologist is trained to deal with dead bodies. Other pathologists may examine samples of blood or urine or other body fluids or bits of tissue removed from surgical patients or removed for biopsy, but the forensic pathologist is trained to examine whole, dead bodies and answer two vital questions: 1) What was the cause of death? and 2) What was the manner of death? For example, a gunshot may be the cause of death. But how was the gunshot inflicted? The forensic pathologist must try to determine from the available evidence whether the gunshot was self-inflicted or inflicted by someone else and whether the shooting was suicide, murder, accidental, or not known.

These specialists spend four years becoming medical doctors, three to five years in residency programs in pathology, and an additional year in a fellowship where they focus on the legal implications of their work and how to present their findings in court—the aspect of their training that qualifies them to put the word *forensic* in front of pathologist. Some of the people I observed were experienced forensic pathologists working at OMI where they also were members of the faculty of the adjacent School of Medicine of the University of New Mexico; others were fellows studying with the experienced pathologists at OMI.

When they examine a body, forensic pathologists work at two levels. They begin with a gross examination. At OMI, each body usually is presented naked, lying on its back in a stainless steel tray that is placed atop a wheeled cart called a gurney. A field investigator who is not a physician briefs the pathologists on each case and points out injuries or other problems that were noted where the body was found. The body often is rolled onto its side so the back can be examined, then it again is placed on its back.

The half-dozen or so pathologists on duty on a given day choose the cases that interest them; any leftover cases are assigned by the pathologist who is the "attending" physician for the day. One or two morphology technicians, called "morph techs" around OMI, work with each pathologist. They move each body from its gurney to an autopsy table.

The primary autopsy suite at OMI has four autopsy tables. Each table is L-shaped and made of stainless steel. Each has a 2 $1/_2$-foot-deep stainless steel sink in the corner of the table where the long and short legs of the "L" meet. The body to be examined is placed on the long leg of the "L," which is eight feet and three inches long, including the sink. Raised lips along both legs of the "L" make the table into two sinks $2^1/_2$ inches deep. Thin streams of water flow constantly from two-dozen holes in the raised lip at the head of the table—the end away from the deep sink—to wash away blood and other waste generated in the autopsy. The pathologist spends a great deal of time working on the short end of the "L," which is five feet long, at a raised table called a cutting board. The white cutting board, manufactured from a durable, man-made material, is raised about five inches off the stainless steel. The cutting board's feet allow water to flow down the table into the sink. The water comes from a small diameter hose the pathologist can use periodically to rinse blood and other waste from the cutting board. A light fixture as big as a man's hat, which holds three bright bulbs, hangs from a movable arm above the autopsy table; the pathologist can position it as needed.

About 450 to 500 times each year, the pathologist on a case determines that an external examination will answer the necessary questions. In these cases, if the pathologist sees no reason to open the body, or the report from the field suggests no suspicious circumstances surrounding the death, the pathologist elects a minimally invasive procedure called a "closed examination." In these cases, a technician uses a series of sterile syringes to take several samples: blood from the femoral artery in the thigh, blood directly from the heart, urine from the bladder and vitreous fluid from each eyeball. These samples will be tested for toxic substances, the level of sugar in the blood and the levels of electrolytes, or basic, normal chemicals, in the body. The body is returned to a gurney and put into its white plastic body bag. A morph tech zips the bag closed, attaches a seal and wipes the outside of the bag with a disinfectant to remove any blood or other body fluids. The body is wheeled out of the autopsy suite and another usually takes its place. The fluids removed from the body during the closed examination are injected into sterile vials and submitted to a medical laboratory for analysis.

If the pathologist concludes that a conventional autopsy is necessary, he or she typically directs the technicians to open the body, using a standard, Y-shaped autopsy incision. The technicians make an incision at each shoulder that leads across the chest to the middle of the trunk with a modest curve in the incisions so they miss the breasts. The incisions continue to just below the breastbone at an anatomical landmark called the zyphoid process. From there a single incision continues down to the pubic bone, making a slight curve to the left or right around the navel.

The technicians use parrot-beak "loppers," the long-handled, curved-bladed devices gardeners use to remove limbs from trees, to cut ribs so the breastbone and several inches of ribs can be removed to expose the lungs, the heart and other organs in the chest cavity. Medical catalogs offer cutters that will do the same job, but they are more expensive, so OMI opts for the less costly tree loppers to save on its state budget.

Depending on the case, the technicians may remove the organs from the chest and abdominal cavities, or the pathologist may elect to handle the task. As the organs are removed, they are placed near the cutting table where the pathologist will work. The doctor moves each organ onto the cutting block and begins a process called "sectioning." This means each organ is cut into ribbons less than a half-inch wide and the pathologist examines each section, checking for injuries, tumors, or other abnormalities.

Even this detailed examination of organs is still part of the gross examination, so the pathologist is using the unaided eye and experienced hands that may have handled hundreds or even thousands of organs. As the pathologist examines each organ, he or she snips a small amount of tissue from each. One segment of tissue, usually smaller than a grape, goes into a plastic container filled with a preservative fluid; it can be used later for a reexamination in the event the pathologist's conclusions are questioned. A slice of tissue usually *less than half the size of a postage stamp goes into a plastic con*-tainer called a "cassette." This sample goes to a laboratory where a technician infuses it with melted paraffin, allows it to cool, and then cuts it into slices thinner than a sheet of paper. These slices of tissue, which are so thin they are transparent, are chemically stained to make their cells more visible and then made into slides that the pathologist can examine under a microscope—the second aspect of the autopsy.

The Mix of Cases

Drawing from a state population of 1.8 million people scattered over 121,593 square miles of space, New Mexico produces a complex mix of cases each year for the OMI pathologists to unravel. For example, I observed the autopsy of an elderly man who was killed when he was thrown from a pickup truck.

Dr. Ian Paul, who at that time was nearing the end of a fellowship at OMI and now is on the faculty, was the pathologist on the case. He was clad in scrub pants and a scrub shirt, a cloth surgical gown with ties in the back, a full-length plastic apron, white plastic sleeve protectors, paper shoe protectors and safety glasses. In addition, he was breathing through a high-filtration mask that covered his nose and mouth. The mask met the federal government's N-95 standard, meaning it filtered out 95 percent of particles that were three-tenths of a micron in size or larger. (A micron is a unit of length equal to one-millionth of a meter, which measures 39.37 inches. For the sake of comparison, a human hair is about 75 microns in diameter.)

Paul prepared for the autopsy by putting on multiple pairs of gloves. He put on rubber gloves first, sprinkled those with talcum powder, then pulled on a pair of woven gloves and added another pair of rubber gloves. He said the woven gloves were made of Kevlar, a material widely used in making bullet-proof vests. "They are relatively sharp resistant," he said, meaning they are good at deflecting sharp objects, such as needles and knives he would be using in the autopsy.

Paul performed a detailed external examination of the body before morph techs opened the body at 9:30 a.m. Two technicians were moving quickly, one on each side of the autopsy table, using scalpels to separate the skin of the chest from underlying tissue and ribs. Quickly they gained access to the ribs and used long-handled pruners to clip the ribs so they could remove the breastplate. Dr. Paul examined the breastplate before returning it to the autopsy table for later replacement.

Paul had a pencil at the cutting board and was labeling the board with abbreviations for the major organs along the top left side of the board. He said he records weights for the organs there. He drew a line and added a section below that where he could write comments and observations about the organs. Although decidedly low-tech, a pencil will write on a wet surface, unlike many more expensive writing instruments.

The morph techs began removing organs from the trunk and placing them near the cutting board for Paul to examine. Holding up the man's stomach with a pair of curved, surgical scissors, he emptied a fairly viscous, yellow-white fluid from the stomach into a measuring pitcher. He said the color and consistency of the stomach contents can change, depending on what the dead person has eaten and how recently "and how much bile is refluxing." Later, after examining the stomach, he read the pitcher to see how much fluid was in the stomach, poured out the fluid and rinsed the measuring pitcher with a water hose.

Paul said he had performed between fifty and sixty autopsies during his five-year residency and estimated he would complete about 250 autopsies during his fellowship, doing an average of two autopsies a day, four days a week.

The bodies in the autopsy suite are highly variable in size and weight. Dr. Paul was conducting an autopsy on a man who appeared to have been frail. He was lying on his back with his mouth gaping open, revealing that he had no teeth. The man on the next table was a beefy, strong-looking man who was somewhat obese. A woman was on the table in the back left corner of the room. A man of average height and build was on the fourth table.

The elderly man's face was only minimally visible. The flap of skin at the top of the Y-shaped autopsy incision, plus skin from the man's throat, were folded back to cover the lower half of the man's face. The technician had made an incision across the man's scalp from ear to ear; the technician slid the front part of the scalp forward over the man's upper face and slid the back of the scalp down below the back of the skull, preparing to open the skull.

After examining the brain, Paul completed the final details of the autopsy and transcribed his notes from the cutting board on the dissection table to a clipboard he was holding. By 11:05 a.m., Paul was gathering papers from the autopsy, preparing to leave the autopsy suite. I asked if he had any preliminary impressions. He said: "He has some pretty bad coronary artery disease, and there may be pneumonia as well. It's not a very complicated case." However, he added, "I'm not going to sign the death certificate yet until we find out more about the traffic accident." He excused himself, saying he had to go to a meeting.

Later, he said he telephoned the man's family and received a full account of the accident that killed the man. He said the family reported that the latch on the pickup's right door had not been working, so the family assumed that it would not open. However, when the elderly man leaned against the door during a slow-speed turn, the door opened and the man fell to the pavement. Paul said he had concluded the death was accidental and had signed the death certificate.

By 11:09 a.m. the technicians had transferred the man's body back to the open body bag on the gurney. A technician then wheeled the gurney through a set of double doors onto the loading platform in a garage-like area where transport vehicles drop off bodies that will undergo autopsies and pick them up when the autopsies are finished. If no one is there to pick up this body, however, the morph tech wheels it into a walk-in refrigerator. This body will wait here, among a collection of other bodies in white plastic bags, until someone claims it.

|| || ||

A persistent problem for the pathologists is to determine whether a death actually occurred as reported. For example, several weeks later, Dr. Merrill Hines was called on to document the death of a man in his forties whom police believed was murdered. He was found dead in his son's mobile home in a small New Mexico town on a Sunday morning.

Hines did a careful external examination, examining the head of the victim, opening and examining each eye in turn, asking the techs to roll the body so he could examine the back, and then having the techs remove the man's pants and his colorful boxer shorts, which had a large blood stain on them, apparently a drip from the head wound.

As a technician removed his outer rubber gloves to replace them with fresh gloves, he used the elasticity of one glove to fire it into the trash barrel six feet away.

The attending physician that day, Dr. Rebecca Irvine, had taken the case of a Native American woman in her late forties who was on the autopsy table next to the one where Hines was autopsying the gunshot victim. The woman was found dead in her outhouse in a rural area. Police said they found no signs of violence on the body. However, the woman probably had been dead for a number of hours before her body was found.

Everyone was asked to leave the autopsy suite while an X-ray was made of the woman. All the physicians and technicians filed out of the autopsy suite and waited in a hallway briefly while the X-ray was made. After the all-clear, when everyone returned to the autopsy suite, Irvine walked over to the table were Hines was working and discussed the head wounds of the body Hines was autopsying. The man's head had two wounds, one about $2^1/_2$ inches above the right ear and another above and slightly behind the left ear.

Irvine asked Hines which wound he thought was the entry wound. He said he thought the bullet entered on the right side of the head. Dr. Irvine says she thought the wound on the left side of the head was the entry wound. Irvine returned to her table briefly to retrieve a scalpel and used it to deftly shave away the hair around the wound on the right side of the man's head. The shaving made it easier to discern the edges of the wound. A short time later, Hines rolled the head to the right and used his own scalpel to shave the hair from the wound on the left side of the head. Hines at first knelt on one knee as he shaved; a few minutes later he dropped to both knees, fully kneeling at the head of the autopsy table as he shaved. The full plastic face shield that Hines was wearing was only six or eight inches from the wound he was working on. Both wounds were much more clearly outlined after the hair was shaved away. Rolling the head back to the right, Hines continued to clean around the wound, using a 4x4 gauze pad to remove blood a couple of inches away from the wound. The wound on the left side of the head was "stellate," as physicians say, which is a Latin-based word meaning star-shaped.

As Dr. Hines worked on the dead man, a small amount of blood bubbled from the man's mouth, and some of it spilled out the right corner of the mouth and made a streak done the right side of the man's face.

Hines was new to the state, so he asked where the town is where the man was killed. A police officer who was there to observe and photograph the autopsy said it is a couple of hours southeast of Albuquerque. One of the technicians mentioned that the high school in the town has good football teams. The police officer said the town also has good players in other sports, but he said football is the dominant sport in town. "On Friday nights, 7 to 9, we get no calls for service whatsoever," the cop said. "Everybody is at the football game. I'm not kidding you, they breed football players there." The other three men around the table laughed. "They start playing in the seventh grade. My son's going to start football next year."

Hines placed a ruler (called a *scale* in medical parlance) just above the right-side wound to measure tearing around the wound. He rolled the head to the right and repeated the process on the left side. When Hines completed his external evaluation of the wounds, the technicians prepared to open the body. They brought two rubber or plastic blocks to the table, one black and one white. The technicians lifted the upper portion of the torso and placed the white block between the man's shoulders. This threw the shoulders back and caused the chest to protrude, making it easier to open the chest cavity.

Hines was now examining the lower portion of the body and pointed out blemishes on the man's skin. Hines asked if the man had been skin popping, meaning taking drugs, particularly heroin, via superficial subcutaneous injections.

The police officer suggested the skin blemishes more likely were the result of "crank bugs." He said that people who take methamphetamines—often called "crank" on the street—sometimes claim they feel bugs crawling under their skin, and they scratch at them so vigorously that the skin begins to bleed and the scratching leaves a scar. Hines said people who take methamphetamines sometimes develop blemishes on the skin caused by the body trying to remove the impurities in the drug. Sometimes bumps are raised on the skin where the body has gathered some of the impurities.

"Methamphetamine is the drug of choice in our town," the police officer said. I asked him whether the drugs are made in local labs or whether they come in from Mexico, which shares a long border with New Mexico. He answered, "All of the above."

Hines used a gloved finger to probe the man's mouth, explaining as he did it, "The mouth is an easy place to miss a bullet wound, an entrance wound or an exit wound. The mouth and the ear—the ear is also an easy place to miss a bullet wound."

Fifty-one minutes into the autopsy, the technicians started the Y-shaped incision to open the body. One of the technicians was training the other technician who was new to the job. The senior technician had the newer technician continue the incision to the pubis. The new technician began snipping ribs to allow removal of the breastplate and thus expose the thoracic organs. When he finished, he handed the tree pruner to the senior tech, who snipped the ribs on the left side of the body. The new tech used a scalpel to cut away soft tissue so the breastplate could be removed. The technicians began removing organs in rapid succession and placing them on the drain board next to the pathologist's cutting board. Hines said, "We're rocking and rolling now." Soon one of the technicians made an incision from the right side of the scalp to the left side in preparation for opening the skull. He makes the incision behind both bullet wounds.

The technician then slipped the scalp forward over the face and backward over the back of the head before inviting Hines over to examine the fractures in the skull. The skull had four major fractures radiating from the bullet wounds. In addition, two bone chips, each the size of a nickel, were visible adjacent to the left wound. The pressure of the bullet penetrating the skull apparently had blown away a couple of small pieces of skull, leaving a hole in the skull on the left side.

When he examined the multiple fractures in the skull, Hines observed: "The bullet must have had a great deal of residual velocity." Hines examined the skull carefully and swabbed away blood on the skull. Hines fetched his clipboard, measured the fragments of bone and the fractures in the skull. He diagramed the fractures onto his clipboard. Hines already had ordered an X-ray of the dead man's head, and it was in place on a lighted box for him to view. The X-ray showed no bullet remaining in the head, consistent with a through-and-through shot.

Hines and the senior technician discussed where to make the Stryker saw cut so the top of the skull could be removed as much intact as possible. First the technician shot additional photographs of the bare skull showing the fractures. When he was ready to use a Stryker saw to cut the skull, he used a scalpel to score the skull, creating a line to follow with the saw. He then retrieved the Stryker saw from a nearby countertop and plugged its cord into an electrical outlet on the right side of the autopsy table and began to cut the skull along his scored line.

In the meantime, Hines returned to the cutting board and resumed examining internal organs.

The senior technician finished his cut and retrieved a Virchow skull breaker from a nearby counter. The skull breaker looks a bit like a T-shaped screwdriver. The handle is about $3^3/_4$ inches long and has a shaft about three inches long protruding from its center. The lower end of the shaft forms a blade about a half-inch wide that can be inserted into the cut made by the saw and used to gently separate the top of the skull, called the calvarium, from the lower skull to expose the brain and its soft-tissue coverings.

In most cases, a morphology technician removes the top of the skull for the pathologist and may even remove the brain. However, in this case, Hines moved over to the autopsy table to remove the skull. First, Hines freed a large section of the skull on the right side of the head. With the skull removed, Hines stopped to examine the brain while it was still in the head. Next he removed a large section of the skull on the left side of the head and a section of skull from the back of the head.

A radio on the other side of the autopsy suite played upbeat, cheery music, its sound pervading the room as Hines worked.

The brain of the man on the autopsy table was cherry red, caked with blood. Hines said later that the gunshot probably had knocked the victim unconscious, and he bled into the skull for some period of time, putting a lot of pressure on the brain.

I moved over to ask Dr. Irvine how her case was coming on the woman found dead in an outhouse.

"This is not the freshest case," Irvine said. "We'll have to wait for the toxicology report to see if she had alcohol in her system or an alcohol alternative." Relatives said the woman drank alcohol everyday. Irvine added that some alcohol abusers who cannot get normal beverage alcohol will drink alternative forms of alcohol; some will drink mouthwash containing alcohol and some will mix hairspray that contains alcohol with water before drinking it.

The technicians on Hines's case took two pieces of bone from the left side of the skull to a stationary film camera. They carefully fitted the pieces together in their original positions before they shot a close-up of the bullet hole penetrating the left side of the skull. They later did the same thing with the right side of the skull, photographing the hole in it.

Hines pointed out that the bullet hole on the left side of the skull cut cleanly through the outside of the bone. By contrast, the edges of the bullet hole were beveled inside the skull, meaning the bullet entered from the left side. Similarly, there was no beveling inside the skull on the right side; the edges of the bullet hole were clean where the projectile had punched its way through. But there was beveling on the outside of the bone, marking that as the exit wound.

At 11:15 a.m., an hour and 41 minutes after the autopsy began, the police officer who had been observing the autopsy had what he was looking for: The bullet entered on the left side of the head and exited on the right. The officer gathered up his camera and camera bag and left the autopsy suite to change out of his scrubs into his street clothes. Before he left, the police officer said, "This was a walk-by shooting. Somebody walked up and shot into the car and the mobile home and walked away."

Hines observed, "This is a good reason to keep your kids off drugs."

One of the technicians gave Hines a puzzled look, and Hines added, "So their friends don't come by and shoot up your house."

When I walked over to Irvine's table, she announced she had found the cause of death for the woman who collapsed in the outhouse. "She's been working on this all her life," Irvine said. She added that the woman died of a subarachnoid aneurysm, a congenital defect in the brain.

Hines walked over to concede that Irvine was right—the bullet hole on the left side of the man's head was the entry wound.

Irvine was gracious, saying only: "After you've seen a thousand autopsies, it gets easier."

The Dangerous Cases

Some of the OMI cases are potentially dangerous to the physicians and technicians. The chief medical investigator, Dr. Ross Zumwalt, took one of those cases one day when he was teaching as well as performing an autopsy. He had with him a medical student, Sally Palmisano, who was between her second and third years of medical school. She was on a rotation in forensic pathology, learning what it was like. She was scheduled to study other specialties in pathology in the future—hematology, serology, and surgical pathology. Dr. Zumwalt noted that all of that day's cases were at least initially believed to be the result of natural deaths.

"We run in cycles," he said. "Tuesday (two days previously) we had traffic accidents. Yesterday we had three gunshots."

By 9:50 a.m. the first case of the day was finished—the external examination of a balding, obese man with white hair and a white beard. The morph techs used syringes to draw vitreous fluid from both eyes, blood from the femoral artery, blood directly from the heart, and urine from the bladder. Zumwalt explained,

> Vitreous is particularly good for glucose (measurement) because after death the glucose slowly decreases in the vitreous. So if you draw vitreous and do a glucose level and it's low, it doesn't mean anything, but if it's high, it's a good indicator of diabetes or diabetes out of control. The blood is not a good indicator because the levels of glucose go up after death because of the release of glucose from the liver.
>
> Peripheral blood from the femoral artery is a better sample to test for drugs. Often a central sample from the heart may have an elevated level of drugs because some of the drug that has been accumulated in the liver is released back into the interior vena cava and into the heart blood. So a peripheral blood level for many drugs is much more indicative of pre-mortem values than a central blood sample. We try to get a peripheral level and we also take a central level because it's easy to get a lot of blood there, so if you run out of blood, you have some left. And urine also is a good sam-

ple to screen. You can take a urine sample, which is easy to work with, and screen for a lot of drugs and get a qualitative answer of what drugs are present. Then you go to the blood with specific tests to get a quantitation of how much drug is there. So toxicology is a complicated process; it's not just one simple test. It's different tests for different drugs and qualitation versus quantitation. We submit those to toxicology. What they are looking for and what's present will determine which samples they will use and how much of those samples.

The body was returned to the white plastic body bag in which it was shipped to OMI. The morph techs zipped the body bag, and the tech near the head of the body wiped down the exterior of the body bag near the head to avoid contaminating other people. Then the tech resealed the body bag.

When Dr. Zumwalt entered the autopsy suite, Palmisano was attempting to sharpen one of Zumwalt's knives. She said, "I think it's interesting that they use regular kitchen knives for autopsies."

When Zumwalt arrived at the table, he took the knife and sharpening steel from Palmisano. He turned the upper side of the knife at a slight angle to the sharpening steel, touched the heel of the knife to the sharpening steel and drew the knife across the steel toward himself as he swept the blade down the sharpening steel almost to the base of the steel. He broke the knife's contact with the steel and lifted the knife again toward the top end of the sharpening steel. This time he lifted the knife above the sharpening steel, shifted the knife a fraction of an inch to put the lower side of the blade at a slight angle to the top of the sharpening steel, touched the heel of the blade to the sharpening steel and swept the knife downward toward the base of the sharpening steel as he again drew the length of the blade across the steel. He established a steady rhythm, sharpening each side of the knife in turn. His movements had the smoothness of frequent practice. He quickly sharpened three butcher knives.

"The secret to knives is to use the sharpener every one or two cases so they stay kind of sharp," Zumwalt told Palmisano.

Zumwalt said the man on the autopsy table was in his forties and had a prior medical history of AIDS, intravenous drug use, and alcohol use. He was living with a long-time male companion at the time of his death. Marijuana paraphernalia was found near the body. The man also had been known to abuse prescription pain medications. This autopsy was requested to determine whether the man died of natural causes or a drug overdose.

"I was working in Cincinnati when the AIDS virus was discovered," Zumwalt said later. "The transcriptionists were so panicked over AIDS that they wouldn't even type our reports about it. We had to put all our documents dealing with the autopsy in plastic folders so no one had to touch them. Then they found out the AIDS virus doesn't have wings or springs" to spread it.

Zumwalt announced to the morph tech and to Palmisano, "What I do with AIDS cases is I only have one person have a sharp instrument in his hands at one time."

Palmisano used a syringe to draw blood from the heart and carefully covered the needle with a plastic shield before handing it to the morph tech to inject into a test tube for later laboratory analysis.

Zumwalt also wanted a sample of blood from the spleen. The morph tech swabbed the spleen with a dark, reddish-orange liquid. Zumwalt said it was a double Betadine swab; an iodine-based disinfectant.

Referring to the spleen, Zumwalt said, "There is so much blood in it, the spleen is a good place to get a culture."

A kitchen ladle was used to remove fluid from the man's abdominal cavity.

When Zumwalt looked at the man's bladder, he said: "He's got a full bladder. That's always a concern for an overdose. If they're in a coma, they lay around and get a full bladder (because their kidneys are still producing urine). If they aren't in a coma, they want to get up and go (urinate)."

Zumwalt snipped a small hole in the top of the bladder so the morph tech could use a syringe with a plastic snout on it, but no needle, to remove urine. The tech first took some urine for laboratory analysis, then he removed the remainder of the urine to keep the body cavity clean.

By 10:40 a.m. the *post mortem* examination of the man whose body was open on another autopsy table was finished and he was put on a gurney in preparation for removal to the walk-in refrigerator.

Zumwalt worked quietly but rapidly in the thoracic cavity and the abdominal cavity for several minutes to cut away the connective tissues that held the organs in place and cut through the arteries and veins to remove the thoracic and abdominal organs.

"He's removing the organs in a single bloc," Palmisano observed. "It's called the Rokitansky method." The organs, except for the stomach and bowel, were moved onto a separate table for examination.

The technician emptied the stomach contents into a glass container. The stomach contents were dark, almost black. The technician held the container up for Zumwalt to examine. "I don't see any problem here with the stomach," he said.

"Running the gut" was a job for the technician. He placed the many feet of bowel into a pink plastic dishpan six inches deep. Although the man was slender, when his bowel was removed, numerous globules of yellow fat were attached to it. The technician took his plastic pan—available in any hardware store—over to the sink and opened the bowel under running water. The technician slit the bowel with a knife and removed partially digested food, washing the bowel as he went. The technician, who was new to his job, put the newly cleansed bowel into a plastic sack and placed it back into the body cavity.

In a gentle voice, Zumwalt corrected him: "We like to examine the bowel." Sheepishly, the technician said, "Sorry," and put the bowel back into the freshly washed pink pan for examination. The chest and abdominal cavities now were empty except for the spinal column rising perhaps four inches into the man's trunk.

When all the internal organs were on a separate adjacent table for examination, Zumwalt and Palmisano moved to opposite sides of that table and Zumwalt reached up to focus a bright, three-lens light fixture on her work area as Palmisano began examining each organ. Palmisano was working at a cutting board and Zumwalt washed away blood every few minutes.

Zumwalt was quiet, but his practiced eyes evaluated organs and tissues as Palmisano handled them. Occasionally he would reach out to touch an organ, assessing its firmness and general physical consistency, obviously comparing it against his years of experience with healthy and diseased organs. Nothing escaped his notice. "The ureters are normal size," he observed.

After watching Palmisano work for several minutes with scissors, Zumwalt told her, "When you're cutting with scissors, they work much better if you cut with the middle third (of the blades) rather than the tips." She thanked him.

Palmisano examined the pancreas and took small sections for analysis before she moved on to the adrenal glands. When they reached a kidney, Zumwalt took the knife and demonstrated the way he opens an organ. He placed one hand on top of the organ on the cutting board, applied a bit of pressure and used his knife in long, graceful, sliding cuts that split the organ in half. Then Palmisano took a turn, trying to duplicate his movement with the knife. "That's a lot better," Zumwalt observed.

After she split each organ on its flat dimension, Palmisano cut it into strips a half-inch wide for closer examination.

Zumwalt selected the man's testicles from among the organs. "They look alike," he observed. "I don't feel any nodules" that would suggest unusual growths.

The lungs and liver followed. When the gallbladder was sliced, it spilled greenish-yellow bile onto the cutting board, which Zumwalt washed away.

Because this man had AIDS, he was susceptible to a variety of infections. Zumwalt told Palmisano, "If there's going to be an infection, it's most likely going to be in the lungs."

Palmisano opened the back of the trachea, the windpipe. And she paused to examine what she saw. Zumwalt explained, "That's froth: probably from pulmonary edema." He noted that the man's lungs were heavy for their size, also probably from pulmonary edema, which meant the tissues were overly full of fluid.

Later, I noticed the point had been broken off the largest of the knives Zumwalt was using. Mindful of Zumwalt's expressed concern about safety at the autopsy table, I asked if he broke the point off the knife purposely.

"No," he said. "That used to be one of my kitchen knives. I was carving a pumpkin one year and broke the point. I decided to bring it in and use it here."

As Palmisano and Zumwalt worked on the abdominal and thoracic organs, a morph tech prepared to remove the brain. The technician told Dr. Zumwalt that he had the skull open, and Zumwalt walked around the table to examine the brain. He first felt the consistency of the brain, then began to loosen it from the lower skull. Gently he eased the brain out of the lower skull a short distance and then used a scalpel to detach the brain from the meninges, blood vessels and the spinal column.

Zumwalt explained that the brain is examined in different ways, depending on the type of autopsy being conducted. For a death from a traffic accident or some other form of physical trauma, the pathologist may examine the brain immediately after removal from the skull when the brain is relatively soft and spongy. The doctor can cut it in half and then cut it into thin sections, examining each section for injuries to the brain, tumors, or other abnormalities. In other cases where the brain needs to be examined in greater detail, the brain may be put into a "brain bucket," a five-gallon plastic bucket filled with a solution called formalin, which is 20 percent formaldehyde and 80 percent water. Formalin makes the brain firmer and facilitates some kinds of examination. Pathologists prefer to leave the brain in the formalin solution for about ten days before examining it, but three days in formalin provides sufficient firming in some situations. If the pathologist thinks the brain exam should be conducted after the brain has been firmed up, OMI requests permission from the family.

> We ask if we can keep the brain ten days and then we can cremate it. If they are not comfortable with that, we'll either cut the brain fresh and put it with the rest of the organs, or we will keep it for a couple of days and get a better exam and return it to the funeral home for burial. We don't keep any organs out unless we have family permission.

A woman dressed in street clothes opened the door to the autopsy suite a couple of inches and called Dr. Zumwalt's name. He turned, recognized the woman, stripped off his rubber gloves to reveal another pair underneath, and walked to the door. After a conversation of a minute or so, he returned to the autopsy table, pulling on fresh outer gloves as he arrived.

As Palmisano prepared to open the heart, she removed the used blade from her scalpel and replaced it with a fresh blade, putting the old blade into a black plastic box the size of a cigarette pack to render it safe. Her scalpel had a long handle to allow the pathologist to reach into the body cavity with the blade while removing organs. Palmisano weighed the heart before she opened it. She removed clotted blood from the heart and weighed it again before examining the heart. She moved on to the bladder and the prostate gland.

The man's body seemed relaxed on the autopsy table, its feet splayed outward in repose. The skin was a dark purplish-red color in some areas on the lower side of the body, marking where blood pooled after death. This is called livor mortis.

Another pathologist came to the autopsy suite door and reported to Zumwalt on the case of a man who had a cardiac pacemaker in place at the time of his death. The pathologist said his team used a special computer to "interrogate" the pacemaker and found the man had ventricular fibrillation, a common cause of death.

"They shocked him, and he really didn't come out of it," the pathologist reported.

Palmisano moved to the autopsy table sink to examine the bowel of the man she was working on. She used her left hand to slide the opened bowel between her right thumb and index finger, feeling for abnormalities as she examined it visually.

Palmisano had finished with all the organs. The technician put the bowel into a clear plastic bag and placed that into the abdominal cavity. He added the plastic bag containing the man's other organs to the abdominal cavity.

At 12:22 p.m. Zumwalt announced, "Okay, I think we're done. This man had AIDS, but he was in good shape otherwise. I don't see anything else. It probably was an overdose." This is a preliminary observation, however. He will wait until he receives the toxicology report on the fluids removed from the man's body and he completes his own analysis of the slides made from autopsy tissue before rendering a formal decision on the cause of death. The man is believed to have overdosed on hydrocodone, a powerful narcotic chemically related to codeine. It suppresses the central nervous system.

Zumwalt said: "It's one that has recently been abused a lot. It is sold illegally out on the street and abused a lot."

"That was fun," Sally Palmisano announced.

The morph tech began cleaning the autopsy table as Zumwalt and Palmisano took off their protective clothing.

At 12:30 p.m. Palmisano left the autopsy suite.

The morph tech returned the body to its white body bag on a gurney, preparing it for storage in the walk-in refrigerator until it was claimed.

Later I asked Palmisano if taking a lead role in the autopsy was stressful for her.

"No, it wasn't," she said. "I enjoy working with Dr. Zumwalt because I sort of have a direction with him. He guided me the whole way, which was nice. I can apply that to my next autopsy."

The Public Health Concern

The work of the OMI pathologists stretches far beyond individual autopsies. They say they are ever alert to public health issues that may arise in their work. By investigating every unattended death in the state, they watch for outbreaks of disease or patterns of death that may need public attention. Even when they are conducting an autopsy that seems straightforward, such as that of a woman who died when her car collided with a train, they consider public health issues. They look for signs that the person may have had an underlying disease or genetic abnormality that her siblings, offspring, or other relatives may need to be told about; they may need treatment to protect their health or even to save their lives. Zumwalt said,

In monitoring deaths in any sort of jurisdiction, you're monitoring the illnesses and the injuries and the hazards that the citizens in that jurisdiction have. And if you do a good job of that, you're able to identify clearly what sort of natural disease or what sort of accidents or what sort of violence the citizens of that jurisdiction are susceptible to. If you can identify the sources of the injuries and deaths, then you can make plans to address those hazardous conditions.

OMI also has a grant from the U.S. Centers for Disease Control and Prevention for bioterrorism surveillance.

We . . . monitor deaths in the state for those that have symptoms or syndromes that would be compatible with a bioterrorism agent, such as anthrax or plague or tularemia. And when somebody dies that has fever or other symptoms that might be a result of a bioterrorism agent, we take jurisdiction and do that autopsy and determine if the person has an infectious disease or a toxic disease.

The pathologists impose strict safety standards in the autopsy suites because they are never sure what they are dealing with when they begin an autopsy. In addition to AIDS cases, the pathologists encounter deaths from a variety of contagious illnesses, including tuberculosis and hepatitis. So they treat each case as if it may be dangerous to the people at OMI and the larger public. In addition to requiring anyone entering the autopsy suites to wear multiple layers of protective clothing, OMI uses a negative-pressure air conditioning system to maintain a constant flow of air through the autopsy suites. A powerful fan removes the air so it can be carefully filtered to remove any impurities before it is released into the atmosphere.

Conclusion

The pathologists at the New Mexico Office of the Medical Examiner had many other options open to them when they finished medical school. For example, one of them, Rebecca Irvine, is also trained in internal medicine. Another, Ian Paul, was trained in emergency medicine and worked in hospital emergency departments for several years before quitting his job to undertake a five-year residency in pathology and then a fellowship in forensic pathology, a dramatic career change.

The head of OMI, Dr. Ross Zumwalt, answered readily when asked about his career choice:

> I think that I chose it because I like solving problems. When I was
> doing clinical years and treating patients (in medical school), I
> couldn't wait to get down to the laboratory to see what the results
> of the laboratory tests were so I could sort out what problem the
> person had and what abnormality it caused. I got exposure to an
> autopsy when I was a medial student and found it fascinating. I
> like to solve problems.

Sociologist E. C. Hughes (1951) and philosopher Al Gini (2001)
tell us that the jobs that people do contribute significantly to establishing their identities, but like other human endeavors, the meaning that people derive from their work is filtered through their
perceptions of the world around them. I found that the forensic
pathologists interpret their work very positively because they see
themselves as performing tasks that are essential to the well-being
of society. By solving the parallel puzzles of how and why someone
died, discovering and preserving facts that will be pertinent to the
prosecution of people who commit crimes, and acting as watchdogs
protecting public health, the pathologists seem to reframe the
potential taint to create a definition of their work that leaves little
opportunity for taint to attach itself to them.

Although the focus of this study was on the forensic pathologists, I saw some evidence that the morphology technicians at OMI
may be less successful in fending off taint, but that is beyond the
scope of this study.

The pathologists, as physicians, are members of a prestigious
professional group who apply scientific knowledge and scientifically
based techniques to their work, and that further enables them to
fend off implications of taint. Indeed, even the multiple layers of
protective clothing strengthen their ties to medical science; the
pathologists dress essentially the same way surgeons do, and the
selection of clothing and masks is based on science. Similarly, their
work is parallel to that of surgeons and internists and other medical
specialists. All are seeking to make a diagnosis based on the evidence available to them. The dramatic difference is that the pathologists are making the final diagnosis, and they do not develop a
treatment plan for the patient. Instead, they focus on how they may
help prosecute a killer or how they can contribute to public health,
thereby helping society at large protect itself from illness and
injury.

Part III

CONCLUSION

11

Ethnography as Dirty Work

Shirley K. Drew & Melanie Mills

An ethnography is written representation of a culture (or selected aspects of a culture). It carries quite serious intellectual and moral responsibilities, for the images of others inscribed in writing are most assuredly not neutral"

—John Van Maanen, *Tales of the Field*, p. 1

Goodall (2000) defines the "new ethnography" as "creative narratives shaped out of a writer's personal experiences within a culture and addressed to academic and public audiences" (p. 9). Ethnographers aim to "reveal the multiple truths apparent in others' lives" (Emerson, Fretz, & Shaw, 1995, p.3). But there is more to the work than "revealing" social "truths." Ethnography is the written representation of a coconstruction of interpretations between the ethnographer and the members of the culture or site studied. "There is no direct correspondence between the world as experienced and the world as conveyed in a text, any more than there is a direct correspondence between the observer and the observed" (Van Maanen, 1988, p. 8). Ethnography is a way of seeing, but we believe that it is also a way of being.

‖   ‖   ‖

In the process of constructing and coconstructing this volume about dirty work, Shirley and Melanie had several conversations about "ethnography as dirty work." The catalyst was an article we'd both read by Gary Fine, entitled *Ten Lies of Ethnography* (1993). We decided to construct a list of questions that would address some of the relevant issues. The following is a set of e-mail correspondences between Melanie and Shirley. In some cases they have been edited for clarity.

Melanie's Thoughts [M], *Shirley's Reactions [S]*

- What makes doing ethnography dirty work? In what ways is ethnography a tainted pursuit? How do we know it is tainted?

[M]: Ethnography involves rolling up your shirt sleeves and getting involved in the field. As a "field hand" there is occasional physical taint, especially with dirty workers. Dirty work ethnographers "enjoy" the same taint as their subjects, by virtue of their association (social), as well as the work environment (physical). The moral dimension of taint can also be a factor—as evidenced in questions from colleagues like "whatever do you want to study (fill-in-the-blank) as your occupation for?" which suggests that there are better (more appropriate, more worthy, less filthy, less "questionable") objects of study "out there." I've gotten a lot of variations on the "What's a nice girl like you doing studying truckers?" theme question over the years.

[S]: *Yes, I seem to recall reacting the same way when you first started studying truckers back in grad school. I was more concerned for your safety than anything. But I also remember thinking, "Where is this going?"*

[M]: Ethnographers in general (aside from studying dirty workers) are tainted in my field (communication) because qualitative work is marginalizing. One way I know this is from participating in extended discussions at national meetings and in my department about ethnographic research and Institutional Review Boards (IRBs). The emergent nature of the research makes it impossible (indeed, inappropriate and undesirable) to generalize outcomes, to control for variables, or to predict events. Many IRBs have items on their forms that assume these things. Ethnographers do not "fit." They often cannot even fill out the permission forms to do their research. Or alternately, we are told that we do not need to go through the IRB because "your stuff" is "autobiographical" and, as such, not research. To be told your work does not count as research is pretty marginalized. Further, research work that predicts and controls is professionally rewarded more than work that describes and evokes situational understandings. Look at grant awards at research institutions.

This is not to say that ethnographic work is never valued. If that were the case, we would not survive. But sometimes it does feel like pushing a big rock uphill. One of my colleagues who taught research methods regularly invited me to guest lecture for a couple of days of "qualitative crap" (token attention to my "kind" of research) in his class. The minimal time devoted to qualitative methods alone sent students a message. Fortunately, my department has evolved since then and now offers two research methods classes, one quantitative and one qualitative.

[S]: *I have had similar experiences in my department. One of my colleagues equates qualitative methods with content analysis . . . and I'm talking about quantitative content analysis. He thinks that since you use words, it must be qualitative. Actually I think he's revised his view a bit. For the last several years I've been teaching a qualitative methods class in our department and I do go to his grad class and talk about the variety of approaches. Still, he asked me once why NCA needed a whole division for a method. I tried to tell him that ethnography is a subject as well as a set of methods, but I'm not sure he believed me.*

[M]: Several years ago, there was a highly critical (as in hatchet job, not critical theory) article on the topic of autoethnography published in *Communication Monographs* (Shields, 2000), ironically a journal that, especially under that editor, would likely not publish an ethnography. Responses to it on the NCA ethnography listserv expressed frustration that ethnographers' voices weren't valued, and that Shields's voice was privileged to speak about them in a forum where they were not invited or welcome to respond. For example, Chris Poulos wrote,

> These kind of debates have often reminded me of the "English Only" debate that has taken place here in Colorado over the years. The dominant group (English-speaking Republicans) says to the non-dominant group: "Do not speak your language. It is illegitimate. Speak only ours." To which, it seems sometimes, the only viable reply is "Vaya con dios."
> I, for one, have not read the Shields article. So I won't (yet) comment directly on it. This *unfortunate* turn of events is due

to the fact that I cancelled my Comm Mono subscription shortly after Beatty took over as editor. And that was because I simply do not have time to pore over statistical tables. They are not written in my language. They hold very little interest to me; from my (obviously biased and admittedly uneducated) perspective, they do not have anything like, as Bud Goodall puts it, the soul of ethnographic (and I STRONGLY include here autoethnographic) writing.

My response is probably similar to the response of at least some of my Spanish-speaking neighbors. I grew up speaking my language (ethnography, phenomenology). It is mine. I may learn others, but my language will always be my language. And it shapes who I am. It IS who I am. Take away my language and you remove me. . . . And though I might someday learn your language, I CANNOT lose mine. (C. Poulos, personal communication, February 20, 2001).

Nick Trujillo wrote,

I wish that Shields could have found a bigger base of autoethnographic studies in communication journals to critique, but we haven't had—and still don't have—many opportunities to publish such work; and I don't think we truly will until we have a QUALITATIVE journal in communication. It's kind of hard to find ample "seeds of destruction" as Shields concluded about critical autoethnography, when only a few kernels are allowed to be planted in the first place. There are, of course, many seeds in other disciplines, though Shields did not review that literature (N. Trujillo, personal communication, February 20, 2001).

[S]: *I have not read Shields' article either. I probably should before I say anything else, but I won't. I trust the assessments of Poulos and Trujillo. The real point here is that we still live in a time where the communication field mutes the voices of those they don't agree with. Until we either start making our way into some of the field's journals (certainly not all would be a good fit) and/or start our own, we'll still be forced to go outside the discipline.*

[M]: Shields responded to a well-written letter (in my opinion and that of others on the listserv) by Larry Frey, which very diplomatically suggested that the piece had been harsh, that he had received many more positive than negative responses to the article, which to a statistician counts as "right." To an ethnographer, it counts as taint. To me, it seemed like shooting a wild tiger in a cage, hardly a noble pursuit.

[S]: *Love the image . . . it "resonates."*

[M]: Being an ethnographer makes you more vulnerable—to your subjects (responding to your humanity) to criticism professionally (because of research methods and also misunderstandings about its rigor), and to failure (because of limited publication opportunities in our academic journals and also because of an inability to—along with a responsibility not to—hurt our subjects). Ethnography is a clearly biased way of knowing. Ethnographers believe that's OK (with appropriate reflexivity). Many others don't (although I no longer believe in absolute objectivity anyway). Unfortunately, the "others" have better access to public expression. And that is how I know ethnography is tainted.

[S]: *Criticisms about methods (particularly rigor) are usually, if not always, based on lack of understanding. All the criteria used to evaluate our work are lifted directly from positivism. While criteria do exist that are parallel to our purposes, they are often dismissed out of hand.*

• What strategies do you use to manage the taint associated with doing ethnography?

[M]: Ethnographers are cautioned against the vulnerability of "going native" (see, e.g., Van Maanen, 1988). While one of the reasons for this is to guard against hyper-subjectivity related to the research, another is to protect the researcher from the hurt that can accompany caring about your subjects. Sometimes subjects don't like the way your writing presents them. This affects your relationships. Striking a balance is a critical part of surviving ethnography.

[S]: *I am very sensitive to potential ethical dilemmas because I've been faced with them (and they're not fun). I'm sensitive to them for the sake of my participants and because I believe that attention to ethics will protect me from the moral taint of the pursuit.*

[M]: Professional criticism is an acknowledged part of the choice to be an ethnographer in my field. Fortunately, there is now some formal social support for those who make that choice. In 1999, ethnographers organized a division of the National Communication Association (NCA). For me, this was a very welcome move because it gave me a way of calling myself legitimate in my home field. Before that time, I felt like a nomad, attending a variety of conferences in other related disciplines where ethnographic writing has more credibility (namely American and Popular Culture and Sociology). I even questioned my choice to be a communication professional at times, because I was drawn both to ethnomethodologies AND social construction of realities through message choices and strategies, a combination that was difficult to reconcile in my field for awhile. I now wear my taint as a badge of honor, having survived for over 20 years in the field without compromising myself too much in the pursuit of tenure. It feels like an accomplishment.

Not everyone makes it. Some academic departments set ethnographers up for failure with strict publication quotas, tight time frames, and rigid rules for promotion and tenure. Good ethnography takes time. I've been studying truckers for over 20 years. Fortunately, it is possible to find places to fit that do value the richness that immersion in a culture over time provides. Reasons for these "failures" include what I would term semi-legitimate concerns (e.g., cost of journal space—no room at the inn, so to speak—rich ethnographies are generally long articles) and illegitimate ones (e.g., suffering "science" as the default way of doing things in the academy—see the special issue of *Communication Theory* that addresses disenchantment in academe). Fortunately (again), there are publication outlets other than journals: this book, for example. Unfortunately, some review committees require journal publication.

[S]: *You make some excellent points about the social (professional) taint. I've always wanted to do this kind of work. I avoided it until I got tenure and became a full professor. It was just too time-consuming. I teach at a university where the load is twelve hours (four courses) each semester and I just wasn't willing to work the number of hours I needed to in order to do the research that interested me. I hate to admit this, but it's true.*

[M]: Ethnographers can help each other by getting actively involved in taint management. This often involves pointing out the taint in the first place, since academic discrimination is sometimes invisible to those in dominant positions. Standpoint theory tells us that marginalized groups are much more likely to "speak the language" of the dominant group than the other way around (Griffin, 2006). Some of us need to teach our ways to the folks we need to understand and value us. This means serving on IRBs and grant awarding boards.

Finally, good humor is a critical survival tool in any profession. Lightening the load of taint with some well-placed laughter is important. This is true among ethnographers and also between them and their subjects in the field. There's always a better "fit" when there are ways to share smiles.

[S]: *Yes, humor is critical. When one of my colleagues described ethnography as "witchcraft" I said, "Yes, that's one of the things I like best about it."*

- How do you transition from the field back to your everyday life ("clean up" physically, emotionally, mentally)?

[M]: Transitioning from the field is important to understand. By this, I mean that at first it is sometimes difficult to recognize how you are affected by the field, along with how the field is affected by you. It's also important to respect your differences. In other words, your "way" might not work for them. Don't go into the field trying to "fix" things. Shut up and learn first.

I notice my language varies from the field to home. For example, I've had to recover my "mom mouth" on occasion after returning from places in the field where the language is a little more "colorful." Sometimes, I need to physically transition—for example, clean my fingernails and/or take a bath. And I mean a bath, not a shower, because sometimes I need to feel like a girl, to literally become softer. Sometimes this is because I've been in a psychologically rough place, perhaps where I've had my guard up a lot, and I need to simply relax. Sometimes, I'm cleaning up physical dirt.

To transition effectively, it is critical to develop good reflexivity skills so that you can differentiate "you" from your subjects. While it is important to see the world from the others' perspectives, it is just as important to recognize what is theirs and what is yours. Of course, what is theirs will affect you. It will change you. You would otherwise not be a very good ethnographer. You SHOULD be moved by your work. You SHOULD NOT lose yourself in it.

[S]: *Good advice and it's vital that we do it. While we don't claim objectivity (nor do we want to) I think it's hard to be fair (or balanced, if you prefer) if we don't step back periodically. And easing back into our identities outside the field is the only way to do it.*

- Why do you do it?

[M]: It is interesting as hell! I love learning about how others walk in the world we share. I NEED to know how they do it, what they think, who they are, and how we all fit together. People are fascinating. How we construct, coconstruct, and reconstruct our social systems is amazing to study. That we do it all with language is very powerful. That we can do it better keeps me going.

Ethnography DRIVES me.

As others have more eloquently put it, ethnography is a way of being (Goodall, 2000). It is not just what I do. It is who I am. I do it to embrace life and living, to know a variety of ways of being, to appreciate and share my many blessings and gifts, and cheesy as it sounds, to leave the world a better place for having walked this way.

[S]: *And it provides us access to people and places that most people will never see—and wouldn't know about without an ethnographer's work.*

Shirley's Thoughts [S], *Melanie's Reactions [M]*

- We assume that ethnography is dirty work. So, in what ways is ethnography a tainted pursuit? How do we know it's tainted?

[S]: As ethnographers, we can be physically, socially, and morally tainted. We are sometimes physically tainted, both in terms of actual dirt and physical danger. I haven't experienced any physical taint while hanging out with lawyers. Physical dirt and danger is much more likely when you hang out with cops. During my police department ride-alongs, I was told that some situations might be physically dirty (exposure to blood or other body fluids, such as suspects vomiting in the patrol car, spitting, etc.), though I never experienced this first hand. I was warned that some situations during the ride-alongs could be dangerous, particularly domestic violence calls. Though I never *felt* unsafe (the Pittsburg PD has very strict ride-along rules to protect citizens), there were situations that might have proved unsafe had the officers I rode with not handled them as well as they did.

Association with the people we study sometimes socially taints us. In my research the people I studied are tainted because of the people they serve. Reactions from the public about what we choose to study can be interesting. During a ride-along in June of 2005 with Officer John Steffens, we answered a burglar alarm call. It happened to be a false alarm, but when we drove up to the house, I realized the house belonged to someone I know. When she walked over to talk to the officers she saw me sitting in the patrol car. Clearly surprised, she said, "Shirley, what are you doing here?" I found myself stumbling over my words to explain. I was a little embarrassed; I wanted her to know immediately that I was not under arrest—I was "doing research."

Moral taint is not unusual within our own discipline (communication) and outside of it—by other colleagues as well. We are morally suspect because we don't use traditional social scientific methods of study. Critics don't approve of the subjective nature of our relationships with our participants. Many of our colleagues simply don't understand what we do. More disappointing is that they don't even want to know.

Ethical dilemmas are common in ethnographic work, as they are in all social research. This is a taint that's difficult to deflect. A contemporary (and familiar) example of this is Humphreys's (1970) study of homosexual encounters in public restrooms in parks (called tearooms). Humphreys posed as a "watch queen" or lookout for participants while they engaged in anonymous sexual encounters. As he did this, he noted license plate numbers of those he observed. Then he located some of these individuals' addresses through the DMV and went to their homes posing as someone conducting research. Doing so, he was able to collect more information about these individuals and describe the kind of people who engaged in these encounters. After he published his work, there was a huge backlash. The public accused him of invasion of privacy and misrepresenting his researcher's identity, as well as deception in the name of research—and they were right. Issues raised by Humphreys's research are ethical concerns faced by any ethnographer. Fine (1993) says that engaging in impression management is inherent in every occupation, including ethnography. In fact, he argues that we must choose among many possible roles. And any role we choose is still "based on only partial truths or even self deceptions" (p. 268). He recognizes the need to manage our impression for the people we study; "Illusions are necessary for occupational survival" (p. 267). But he urges us to critically examine these roles and be fully aware of the choices we make. The only way to avoid these dilemmas is to stop doing the work. That's not an option I care to consider. Still, I believe that we're obligated to consider what actions can be justified in the interest of research and then weigh the potential benefit of that research against the potential harm to the participants and their lives.

Another ethical dilemma is commonly referred to as "going native." Going native may compromise the data as well as potentially harm the participants. Historically, "going native" has implied a lack of objectivity on the part of the observer. In the "new ethnography" (see e.g., Goodall, 2000), subjectivity is a natural part of the process of studying and writing about culture. But subjectivity does not mean advocating a particular viewpoint. According to Anderson (1987), "Going native limits one's ability to be analytically descriptive because of confusion over the purpose of writing . . ." (p. 321). The problem "appears in the field notes and in the ethnographic text when the analyst becomes an *advocate* for membership rather than an interpreter" (p. 321). This is one of the major ethical mistakes I made as a beginning ethnographer. In one study, I allowed myself to privilege *and adopt* some members' viewpoints over others; I became sympathetic to a viewpoint and expressed it openly in my writing. That paper has never been presented in its original form, and I have since abandoned the project.

How do we to protect the participants and still safeguard the data? A related issue concerns what information to include or exclude in the final report. This occurred when I sent a draft of a paper to participants to do a member check. I gave them two weeks to respond. One participant sat down with me and meticulously went through each page, making corrections in the use of the technical language as well as in my interpretations of stories he'd told me. I found this discussion extremely helpful in the revision process. I received feedback and suggestions from other participants as well. I was encouraged, because the general responses indicated that I'd accurately captured a slice of their lives at work.

One response surprised me, however. One participant wrote a lengthy e-mail to me explaining that she did not want a particular conversation included between her and a coworker. I sent an email back to her immediately and told her that I would remove that excerpt from the paper. I remember thinking that I had told everyone what I'd be doing and what my purposes were for the project. However, "strained relations and ethical dilemmas are not completely avoided by informing others of one's research purposes. While participants may have consented to the research, they might not know exactly what the research involves or what the researcher will do to carry it out" (Emerson et al., 1995, pp. 21–22). And so I deleted that portion from the text, even though I believed the conversation illuminated a part of the culture that was important for readers to understand. It was a typical example of how this group interacted when they were "offstage." I had other examples of offstage behaviors that I knew would compensate for what I'd eliminated. Still, something had been lost from the narrative, and I couldn't recover it. But it was more important to me to maintain a good working relationship with her. The research is ongoing, and I don't want to burn bridges. And I want to establish a reputation as someone who respects the people and the communities I study.

I continue to struggle with the issue of when and how to represent some viewpoints and not others. I make this decision on a case-by-case basis; that decision is informed by my general purpose for being there, the multiple contexts of the study, and which participants will be able to give me the information I need; the decision about what's "needed" is also quite subjective. These aren't the only things to consider, but it's a place to start.

Finally, we try to represent what and who we observe as fairly as we can. But Fine (1993) asks, "What does it mean to be fair? Is fairness possible?" (p. 276). He argues that two meanings are possible. Either we mean objectivity or we mean balance. He claims objectivity is an illusion and I agree, though I've always used the word "myth." His solution is that we must admit to ourselves that we cannot be objective; perhaps fairness is not possible either. This doesn't mean we don't try. So maybe "balance" is the right word.

I like to think we've come a long way since Humphreys's (1970) study. As we move forward in our research of lived experience, we must balance (there's that word again) our obligation to "the truth, the whole truth, and nothing but the truth" (Goodall, 2000) with our obligation to the people whose stories we tell. Certainly this advice oversimplifies the problems encountered by ethnographers. But it's still good advice in general.

[M]: *We all comment on the social taint by association, especially when we study dirty work. I think the taint from the communication discipline (that we also both address) is both social and moral. The social taint creates an access problem to "legitimate" scholarship which is critical to our survival as university professors. The moral taint comes from misunderstandings (e.g., "witchcraft") and from ethical issues, some of which you've raised in your responses (e.g., Humphreys's research). It's like the section in your cops paper where you talk about "bad cops" portrayed in media. There are "bad" (unethical) ethnographers too, although I'm not convinced they are any more prevalent than other kinds of unethical social scientists.*

One issue that affects our credibility that we both identify is the subjective nature of ethnography (this is where going native fits). Differentiating subjective reporting and advocacy is important and you've done that. Balance (protecting the integrity of our data while also safeguarding our subjects) is another place we are vulnerable to ethical questions (moral taint).

• What strategies do you use to manage the taint associated with doing ethnography?

[S]: I talk to students and colleagues about ethnography, and what I'm convinced of is the inherent value of the work. I let people read what I write and recommend other ethnographies as well; I think the work speaks for itself. I depend on social support from like-minded colleagues with whom I can discuss the work as well as sometimes commiserate with about the lack of understanding regarding what we do. But I try not to focus on the negatives because whining doesn't get the work done.

[M]: *Letting others read and respond to our work before we make it public is a good comment. I agree and have done this too. I can remember meeting Jack (a primary informant in the trucking study) in Effingham and doing his laundry while he sat in the truck and read drafts of my research. Having good entrée and including subjects in the construction of their stories is good practice. I think highlighting supportive social practices (communities of ethnographers or like/open-minded people) is healthy taint management. Your point about avoiding the negative (or not getting mired down in it) is good advice too.*

[S]: We have to be careful who we let read our work, though. Member checking is a good thing to do. But letting too many people outside the participants read the work can be "crazy-making." You may get so many different kinds of comments that they aren't helpful at all. I always choose two or three people who I know understand what I'm trying to do. They aren't all ethnographers, but they do understand qualitative work. I also have a good friend in the English department who will do a technical edit on a manuscript if I give her enough lead time. That's incredibly valuable.

[M]: *If you establish good boundaries about what is and what isn't "on the record" in your interactions with participants, you can more fairly address questions about what to include or exclude. You need to have the freedom to write it as you see it, and you need to be honest up front. Not every representation is flattering. Fairness is more critical than flattering. I count it good writing if one of my informants responds to my question of whether I've represented them accurately with, "That's true, but I never thought of it that way before." Pretty cool.*

How do you transition from the field back to your everyday life? ("clean up" physically, emotionally, mentally)

[S]: Sometimes I just take a hike. And I mean this both literally and figuratively. I have some favorite hiking trails and I go to work my body and relax my mind. I believe what Stephen King says: ". . . eighty-five percent of what goes on in a novelist's head is none of his business" (1998, p. 176). I think this is true for all writing. So I just hike along and let my mind go in any direction it wants to go. I like to relax by watching a movie or by reading something completely unrelated to what I've been writing about. I talk about my work with my husband; though he's a biologist, as academics we similarly construct the "writing experience." Spending time with students always brings me out of my head—and that can be a good thing.

Finally, if I'm in the middle of a project and need a break, I take a few days away from the field. This might sound easy, but often it isn't. Sometimes I don't necessarily *want* to leave the field, even for a short time, particularly with the occupational research. In part because I'm afraid that if I do, I'll miss something, or worse, forget the "story." And sometimes I don't want to leave because I'm so wrapped up in what I'm doing that I forget I'm not really a part of those groups or communities.

[M]: *As I read this, I thought "this is taint management, too," so we might rethink it as a separate "category." We both physically enact good separation metaphors (taking a hike or walking away from it, or literally cleaning up). This kind of ritual behavior serves a taint management function for us. I also love the Stephen King quote here! So appropriate . . . and it also highlights the simmering time that is critical for good thoughtful ethnography (can't be "thought-full" if you don't take time to think!).*

Why do you do it?

[S]: I sometimes think that the best thing about doing ethnography is that we get to vicariously experience so many different lives. Some might consider this a selfish reason, but it gets me out there doing the work. But I also do it because I believe it's the best way to provide a window into the lived experiences of others; it's a way of seeing what we might never achieve with any other method of inquiry.

[M]: *The "sight" metaphor is nice (a window for "seeing" the world). Actually, I like ethnography because it doesn't marginalize the senses or privilege one over another (i.e., ethnography makes us taste, hear, feel, smell—even gag!—which makes it closer to where people live than more "sanitized" research). Both of us have reasons beyond professional practice to be ethnographers, which is likely characteristic of a lot of people who choose it. I think you have to have this added motivation to survive the professional taint.*

[S]: Sometimes I fantasize about quitting my teaching and doing this full time. But for now I'm just happy being what Van Maanen (1988) refers to as a "recidivist ethnographer."

Conclusion

Bob Gassaway participated in this conversation at points as he reviewed our writing for this chapter. His view differs from ours. He says,

> I don't agree that ethnography per se is dirty work. I presented a paper at NCA last year on a family-operated restaurant as a performance. I researched that paper by eating in the restaurant two to five (or more) times a week for a little over a year. I didn't feel the slightest bit tainted from that experience, and I certainly didn't feel the need to shower, change clothes or otherwise engage in any sort of ritual to "return" to my normal life. That was a part of normal life for me; I simply ate there rather than somewhere else. So I think the taint derives from the place you're doing research and the phenomenon you are studying (B. Gassaway, personal communication, August 20, 2006).

What he seems to be saying is that while some situations and people might make the pursuit physically, socially, and/or morally tainted, this is not inherent in ethnographic work. Later that day we (Melanie and Shirley) discussed this on the phone. Bob is an ex-journalist and a recently retired journalism professor, with degrees in both journalism and sociology. His professional experience has been different from ours. Some disciplines (particularly anthropology and sociology) do not suffer the taint aspects associated with this kind of work at the level or to the degree that we do in communication. Putting Bob's answer in that context provided clarification about why his experiences differ so greatly from ours. It is our hope that one day "taint management" will also become a non-issue for us.

In the meantime, we hope our conversations in this chapter give you some insight into ethnography as a tainted practice in our lives, along with some encouragement to support this kind of work. Because we are also social constructionists, we offer this writing as a move toward changing (or constructing more positive) scholarly perceptions of ethnography in communication. Truly, as we endeavor to understand human interaction, there is unique value in ethnographic theories and methods, which examine people at length where they live, love, and work. Indeed, we do more than look at them. We look with them.

12

Concluding Thoughts

Melanie Mills, Shirley K. Drew,
& Bob M. Gassaway

No labor, however humble, is dishonoring.

—The Talmud

Over the years that we have been studying occupational cultures, we have often been asked why dirty work? There are a number of answers to that question. First, we are fascinated by the work itself and what it takes to do it. Part of this is plain curiosity and enjoying learning about jobs through vicarious experiences of what others do for a living (just being nosy!). Second, we are intrigued by the systemic nature of professional work and how occupations meet and intersect in interesting ways in everyday life. Dirty work may be stigmatized, but it is critical for the success of our social system. Taint management then becomes a survival issue—for all of us. Finally, we feel that uncovering occupational mysteries can lead to better appreciation of dirty work and dirty workers, which has the potential of making taint management easier (and survival more likely). It may improve the "curb appeal" of the job for prospective workers. While this is true of all kinds of work, we feel it is particularly crucial for tainted work that may be overlooked or taken for granted. It is at risk in our social system. And we need it. We also need good people doing it. We intend our work to honor dirty workers.

In this chapter, we will address methodological and substantive issues we think are important in this book. Methods issues include using ethnographic approaches to data collection, reporting, and interpretation. Content issues include discussions of power, personal responsibility, public and private identity work, taint barriers, environmental (material and space) issues, occupational rituals and traditions, and humor as they relate to taint management strategies. We will also take up the "so what, now what?" question before we leave you.

Methodological Issues

If we knew what it was we were doing, it would not be called research, would it?

—Albert Einstein (physicist)

Ethnographic research is a naturalistic, interpretive, and multilayered approach to understanding the social realities of specific situations and the people who inhabit them. We don't know what we will find when we set out. We go, we observe, we record, and then we ponder. The focus on culture, including language, rituals, norms, and roles—in effect, the human experience itself—is the heart of the approach. As researchers, our goal is to understand, from multiple viewpoints, the constructed and coconstructed realities of particular people that might otherwise remain hidden. In the process, we, too, are constructing, coconstructing, and reconstructing what we study *along with* the people we study.

In many cases, we have used the real names of participants in this book, including full names, first names only, or "other" names (e.g., CB handles). Individuals' names are usually chosen with great care and they are an integral part of our identity construction. In traditional positivism, names of "subjects" are never used. They are only "subjects," sometimes identified by gender, age, or other demographic and psychographic characteristics. In ethnography we prefer to use names; this makes the people we study "people." They are not always politically correct, and they do have a sex. For that reason, our pronoun use in this volume follows the sex of our participants, rather than APA rules. For us, in this volume, individual lived experiences are valued over the aggregate. It's not always possible (or even desirable) to use real names. In Goodall's (2000) example of his ethnography with the band Whitedog, he points out that using participants' real names might put them at risk within their own culture or maybe in ours. Some of our dirty workers are referenced by pseudonyms (as noted in individual chapters) to respect their privacy, either by our choice or their preference. Considering the outcomes for our participants is crucial. But if they're comfortable with it, then actual names enhance the credibility of the research. Names also include professional titles. In the "Doing Justice" chapter, attorneys (and others) address the judge as either "Judge Noland" or simply "judge." The title defines the position and authority of that individual, which is the primary part of his occupational identity.

How we collect data, whether through observations, interviews, conversations, examination of artifacts or material culture, or some combination of these, affects what meanings are made. Our job is to try to make sense of at least some of these meanings created in the social realities we study. We can only do this by spending time hanging out and immersing ourselves in their everyday lives. Still, we must maintain enough distance that we can distinguish between meanings of the participants and the ones that we help make. This is what we have presented to our readers, at which point they become participants (albeit once removed) in the construction process, too.

Hanging around is essential in most ethnographic research. It takes time to make the unfamiliar familiar, to learn the routines, relationships, rules, and patterns of interaction. Hanging around gives us time to keep our minds open; we can take a "wait and see" attitude. It allows us to better define the parameters of our research and helps us to determine if the site will be a feasible one for our purposes. All of our authors spent considerable time hanging out with members of their occupations, both in their work spaces and in third places away from the work environment. Hanging around might or might not be a first step; fieldwork methods are rarely if ever linear in their application. Moving between hanging around to participant observation to interviews to analyzing material artifacts to historical/archival research or to other methods allows for the research to evolve and change.

We strongly recommend getting to know research subjects' third spaces. We are using the term "third spaces" intentionally instead of Oldenburg's (1999) term "third places" because the latter excludes places on the work site. A "third place" is away from work or home. We have found that there are also "third spaces" that are away from actual work places, yet still on the work premises (e.g., break rooms, cafeterias, locker rooms, etc.). The working talk, and talk about work, in these environments is illuminating.

While participant observation is not used in all fieldwork, it usually is in ethnography, though at varying levels. It gives us "an intuitive as well as an intellectual grasp of the way things are organized and prioritized . . . the ways in which social boundaries are defined . . . and other cultural patterns that are not easily addressed or about which discussions are forbidden" (Schensul et al., 1999, p. 91). We selected authors who valued participant observation because we do. We believe it is critical to roll up your sleeves and "get dirty," so to speak.

We have included chapters that have both micro and macro approaches to studying occupational cultures (see Chambers, [2000] for a discussion of micro/macro approaches to applied ethnography). While ethnography typically involves a localized experience in the field, we have also tried to include a broader focus at times, too, to show how the local affects the larger social system and vice versa. The result is a zooming in, zooming out experience for our readers. For example, in terms of defining the field, the nurse chapter is a very broad occupational view of the direct work in multiple job descriptions, while the chapter on AIDS workers zooms in on a very specifically targeted group of health-care workers. We have included multiple occupations related to criminal justice to provide insights into the relationships among these different jobs at a more systemic level (the criminal justice "system"). Methodologically, all the chapters use language (occupational talk) as a source of information, however, how they do that varies from conversational analysis at a particular job site (examining more micro-features of the talk) to analysis of broader (macro) occupational narrative themes across a number of workplaces.

The use of these methods over time implies immersion in the site. Immersion in a research site reveals the "taken-for-granteds" and provides the groundwork for thick description, a key characteristic in ethnographic research. All of this leads to interpretation in our ethnographic writing. We have, along with our participants, constructed and revealed something about their lived experiences, in this context, at this point in time. Van Maanen (1988) says that "Fieldwork is then a means to an end" (p. 3). It is enough.

Content Issues

Language exerts hidden power, like a moon on the tides.

—Rita Mae Brown, Social Activist

While we have focused on reporting taint management and the experience of a number of dirty jobs, we also recognize that this book serves a broader reflective critical purpose as well, which is to consider how our stories about work frame and privilege certain ideologies about class, gender, ethnicity, education, and labor. While this is not a prominent, explicit theme in the book, it is an assumption that underlies the concept of taint. Without social privilege, there is no taint. Social systems are hierarchical, which implies an inequitable power and status distribution that impacts occupational identity. This book argues that the everyday discourse of dirty workers negotiates tainted identities derived from the broader social discourse related to their occupations.

One interesting feature of our chapters is how this social powerlessness is managed. Some ways of "doing" powerlessness include submission to the dominant ideologies in the culture (e.g., "just following the rules" or "just doing my job" comments in the legal professions and from prison workers). Humor is another strategy that mediates helplessness related to unpleasant job conditions. This is especially evident with the crime scene investigators, nurses, and truckers. It is also interesting to notice who does what kind of work. Traditionally marginalized people often do marginalized work, or their work is trivialized. For example, we have noted the feminized nature of some work as contributing to its taint (secretaries and nurses), along with immigration issues that affect the historical development of job identities (cops).

These chapters confirm and illustrate taint negotiation strategies of reframing, recalibration, and refocusing as identified by Ashforth and Kreiner (1999). Reframing entails defining the work as valuable (wearing the "dirt" as a badge of honor), focusing on the positive aspects of the work. Recalibrating involves adjusting evaluation criteria to magnify non-stigmatized parts of the job. Refocusing shifts attention (vs. changing values or transforming meanings). Personal autonomy in the job seemed to mitigate taint. Those who have more autonomy have more freedom to choose among a wider variety of taint management strategies.

Some chapters also provide examples of passing off the stigma, a "blame the victim" strategy of taint management. This approach involves rejecting social taint derived from whom dirty workers must interact with by virtue of their job descriptions, and passing it back to them (e.g., the "shit bums" EMTs work with). Name-calling is one identifying characteristic of this tactic, which is more successful when there is social validation from other workers to confirm the conclusion that the taint "belongs" elsewhere. Dirty workers who are isolated from other members of their profession do not have good access to this strategy. For example, it was more difficult for prison workers to manage their taint this way because they did not have as much social or community time with their peers as some of our other workers.

The issue of social responsibility for taint is relevant to dirty work because a lot of physical, social, and moral taint is derived from factors people are assumed to have some personal control over. This includes things like educational achievements (or lack thereof), health status, homelessness, decisions to obey rules (or not), or even occupational choice in the first place. How responsibility for taint is assigned will affect the success of taint management strategies (or whether others "buy" the identity work of the subject). Resisting social responsibility for taintedness and resisting resistance to dirty jobs are taint management strategies worth investigating further. The willingness or unwillingness of tainted clientele to accept personal responsibility for their stigma may affect how dirty workers interact with them. Perceptions of personal responsibility may also relate to their ability to find their dirty work rewarding. For example, it is presumably more rewarding to help the helpless than to help the stupid. This is delicate taint management because there are so many choices for how to understand the derivation of stigma. As a social construction, taint "comes from" many places and perspectives. Is a "shit bum" a victim of social structures or an idiot? Does the answer vary according to circumstance? How do you differentiate them? Should you? Are all perceptions equally valid? Tough questions.

Additional study might look beyond describing taint management strategies to examining further what conditions affect the likelihood that particular strategies will be effective in particular kinds of work. For example, why doesn't bitching work for secretaries? Does it work for other workers? What preconditions, emergent conditions, and interpretive choices make it likely a particular strategy will succeed or not?

Dirty workers construct and coconstruct identities that protect them from (or at least mitigate) taint. They do this both privately and publicly. For example, in private, they take pride in doing what they consider their "real work," however they might define it in a particular profession. We often found this contrasted with "paper work." It may involve internal status hierarchies to negotiate divi-

sion of taint related to specific job descriptions within an occupation (e.g., forensic pathologists and morphology technicians).
Whether this is an accepted in-house or public perception, taint is
not the same for every worker in each occupational area. This is a
function of how individual identities are socially constructed,
negotiated, and interpreted.

Workers share common experiences with coworkers, sometimes developing a specialized language, sometimes telling jokes
and stories. For example, "RN" standing for "real nurse" instead of
"registered nurse," or looking at the community policing model as
inferior to "real" police work. Many of these exchanges are not for
public consumption; most people would not understand or appreciate the value of this interaction to the dirty workers. In fact, the
public would likely negatively evaluate or misunderstand the function of some of this talk. Calling brain parts "goobers" is an example.
Some words in the context of the work are not meant to be as disrespectful as they might sound to outsiders. For this reason, dirty
workers may publicly put on a different face and use a different
vocabulary. This guards against unintended consequences of language choices.

Dirty workers sometimes use protective barriers to shield themselves from danger and from those (outsiders) who would taint
them and those (clients) whose association taints them. For example, police work puts officers in a servile relationship to stigmatized
groups. In order to maintain some distance, police officers construct
barriers between them and the bad guys. Patrol cars are equipped
with cages between the officers in the front seat and the offenders
in the rear seat; entrance into the inner sanctum of the department
offices and interrogation rooms requires codes. Some dirty workers
create strict boundaries between their personal and professional
lives, and do not "hang out" with their colleagues outside of work.
Many do not publish their phone numbers or even live near their
workplace in order to create further distance—not just from the
tainted group, but also from the people in the community who taint
them. In prisons, correctional officers distance themselves from
inmates in order to distance themselves from the social dirt associated with the job. They physically distance themselves by keeping
their booths locked so inmates cannot enter without permission,
they may avoid interaction with them, or just ignore them altogether. Sometimes they blame the inmates for their incarceration,
creating psychological as well as physical distance between themselves and the inmates. Emotional distance is sometimes cited as a

necessary part of survival in caring or helping professions (like nursing). So taint management may involve constructing protective physical, psychological, and emotional barriers.

Some of these are available for material study. Social construction of the meanings of material culture and space are under studied (Leeds-Hurwitz, 2006). We believe that both of these areas could be taken into account more often, not only to understand protective barriers, but also other aspects of work cultures. Material culture includes physical features of the world (such as objects, clothing, food, or tools). The social negotiation of the meanings of "stuff" provides ideas about their role in identity management. We have done some of this work in this volume by including tools of the trades in our discussions. We believe it is illuminating and gives our work more rich description and depth. Similarly, studying how space functions as a part of interaction reveals additional insights about what taint management "looks like." These things are worth noticing.

Organizational rituals and traditions are human performances that constitute and reveal cultural realities to us. Rituals provide members ". . . access to a particular sense of shared reality" (Pacanowsky & O'Donnell-Trujillo, 1983, p. 129). They serve positive and negative functions in the professions we studied. One positive function is initiating new members to the profession. This kind of rite of passage serves to bond individuals to their jobs. Another positive function is to clarify and perpetuate an occupational rule system. In the criminal justice system, rituals both maintain and strengthen the infrastructure. The judge's and attorneys' prescribed behaviors and speeches are links to the courtroom traditions and maintain the current system of rules and roles. Legal traditions are a form of civilized behavior codes that bring order to the courtroom. Rituals create and maintain bonds between members, reinforcing and strengthening the cultures. On the other hand, traditions can outlive their usefulness. For the firefighters included in this volume, hanging on to some traditions led to safety hazards—for example, using wooden ladders that are inferior to their aluminum counterparts, and using protective clothing passed down from previous generations of firefighters that do not meet current federal safety standards.

We would be remiss not to note the value of humor as a taint management tool in all our chapters. Humor does some serious taint management work. It provides a way to defend dirty workers from those who would taint them by "beating them to the punch line." It provides tension release and diffuses some of the emotional struggles associated with more extreme taint. Finally, it bonds us

together in laughter and keeps us from taking our taint (or ourselves) too seriously.

So What, What Next?

The honest work of yesterday has lost its social status, its social esteem.

—Peter F. Drucker, management specialist

The shift from "honest work" to "dirty work" was lamented by many
people we encountered in the production of this book. There is a tension between the value of honest labor and the physical, social, and
moral taint socially imposed upon the professions highlighted in this
volume, along with other jobs that qualify as "dirty work." Taint
management, as a means of recovering occupational social esteem, is
critical to the survival of these workers and these jobs. The survival
of these jobs is vital for the continuation of some things we like in the
larger social system, namely a number of the comforts or services
many of us have come to take for granted that it will provide.
Somebody has to do the dirty work. Without it, we will suffer—
indeed, we may not survive. There are identifiable survival predic-
tors (Gonzales, 2005). Being able to accept certain realities (taint) as
part of the experience is one of them. This answers the question of
why it is important to know more about dirty workers and their taint
management strategies. Further, it also strikes us as a good reason to
ask ourselves, now that we know more about the work and the workers, how can we improve the social esteem of this work?

   We have endeavored to take you to the workplaces of a number
of dirty jobs in the hope that knowing more about these occupations
will help you more fully appreciate these workers. Perhaps we will
introduce you to more dirty workers in a subsequent volume. In the
meantime, smile at a police officer, wave to a trucker, or write a secretary a thank you note. Remember that we live in the social worlds
we create. Examine your assumptions about the work of others, bite
your tongue on unkind comments, and be thankful somebody is
doing the dirty work. Pay attention to work issues when they become
a matter of public discussion and public policy. When we value our
differences and each others' work, we socially construct a friendlier,
fairer, and more productive world. Let's pay attention to how we are
constructing our selves (and by extension, our society), and who we
become in the process. Henry J. Kaiser, U.S. industrialist, noted,
"When your work speaks for itself, don't interrupt." We have
reached the time for all of us to listen to the voices of the workers.

Bibliography

Achterberg, J. (1991). *Woman as Healer.* Boston: Shambhala.

Adams, A., and Ryder, A. (2003). *A Survival Guide for Truck Drivers: Tips from the Trenches.* Clifton Park, N.Y.: Thomson/Delmar Learning.

Adelman, M. B., and L. R. Frey. (1997). *The Fragile Community: Living Together with AIDS.* Mahwah, N.J.: Lawrence Erlbaum.

Alexian Brothers Salus Place (n.d). [Brochure].

Anderson, B. J. (2000). *Doing the Dirty Work: The Global Politics of Domestic Labour.* London: Zed Books.

Anderson, J. A. (1987). *Communication Research: Issues and Methods.* New York: McGraw-Hill.

Anionwu, E. (2006). *Reflections. Nursing Standard* 2 (34): 26.

Arnoldussen, B. (2004). *Training Wheels for Nurses: What I Wish I'd Known My First 100 Days on the Job.* New York: Simon & Shuster.

Asbury, K. E. (1988). "Social Control in a Local Community: Role of the Apartment Superintendent." *Journal of Research in Crime & Delinquency* 25 (4): 411–26.

Ashcraft, K. L., and M. E. Pacanowsky. (1996). "'A Woman's Worst Enemy': Reflections on a Narrative of Organizational Life and Female Identity." *Journal of Applied Communication Research* 24: 217–39.

Ashcraft, K. L., and D. K. Mumby. (2004). *Reworking Gender: A Feminist Communicology of Organization.* Thousand Oaks, Calif.: Sage.

Ashforth, B., and G. Kreiner. (1999). "'How Can You Do It?': Dirty Work and the Challenge of Constructing a Positive Identity." *Academy of Management Review* 24 (3): 413–34.

Averting HIV and AIDS. "AIDS Statistics—2005." Retrieved November 2006, from www.avert.org.uk/usastata.html.

Barker, J. R., and P. K. Tompkins. (1994). "Identification in the Self-Managing Organizational Characteristics of Target and Tenure." *Human Communication Research* 21 (2): 223–40.

Barrett, C. (1983). *Practical Handbook of Private Trucking.* Washington, D.C.: Traffic Service Corporation.

Beck, C. S. (2001). *Communicating for Better Health: A Guide through the Medical Mazes.* Boston, Mass.: Allyn & Bacon.

Belman, D. L., and K. A. Monaco. (2005). *Sailors of the Concrete Sea: A Portrait of Truck Drivers' Work and Lives.* East Lansing: Michigan State University Press.

Berger, P. L. (1964). *The Human Shape of Work.* South Bend, Ind.: Gateway.

Bergmann, J. R. (1993). *Discreet Indiscretions: The Social Organization of Gossip.* (J. Bednarz Jr., trans.). New York: Aldine de Gruyter. (Original work published 1987.)

Bippus, A. M. (2000). "Humor Usage in Comforting Episodes: Factors Predicting Outcomes." *Western Journal of Communication* 64 (4): 359–84.

Blake, J. A. (1974). "Occupational Thrill, Mystique and the Truck Driver." *Urban Life and Culture* 3: 205–220.

Blau, J. R., S. C. Light, and M. Chamlin. (1986). "Individual and Contextual Effects on Stress and Job Satisfaction." *Work and Occupations* 13: 131–56.

"Book Explores Kansas Meth Industry." (2003, November 10). *The Morning Sun*, 7.

Bordwin, M. (1995). "Don't Ask Employees to Do Your Dirty Work." *Management Review* 84: 53–55.

Bormann, E. (1972). "Fantasy and Rhetorical Vision: The Rhetorical Criticism of Social Reality." *Quarterly Journal of Speech* 58: 396–407.

———. (2001). *The Force of Fantasy* (2nd ed). Carbondale & Edwardsville: Southern Illinois University Press.

———. (1983). "Symbolic Convergence: Organizational Communication and Culture." In L. Putnam and M. E. Pacanowsky (eds.), *Communication and Organizations: An Interpretive Approach* (99–122). Beverly Hills: Sage.

Brodsky, C. M. (1982). "Work Stress in Correctional Institutions." *Journal of Prison Jail Health* 2: 74–102.

Brown, C. (dir.). (1936). *Wife vs. Secretary.* Hollywood, Calif.: MGM.

Bruder, P. (1999). "Nursing Unions: The Prime Time for Organizing Is Now." *Hospital Topics* 77 (2):36–39.

Brunacini, A. V. (2002). "Fire Command." Washington: National Fire Protection Association.

Bureau of Labor Statistics, U. S. Department of Labor. (n.d.) *Occupational Outlook Handbook*, 2006-07 edition, Registered Nurses. Retrieved August 13, 2006, from http://www.bls.gov/oco/ocos 083.htm.

Center for Disease Control and Prevention. "AIDS Statistics—2002." Retrieved November 20, 2002, from http://www.cdc.gov/hiv/ topics/surveillance/resources/reports/2002report/commentary. htm.

Cesnik, J. A., and E. Coleman. (1989). "Use of Lithium Carbonate in the Treatment of Autoerotic Asphyxia." *American Journal of Psychotherapy* 43 (2): 277–86.

Chambers, E. (2000). "Applied Ethnography." In N. K. Denzin and Y. S. Lincoln (eds.), *Handbook of Qualitative Research* (2nd ed.), (389–418). Thousand Oaks, Calif.: Sage.

Cheek, F. E. (1984). *Stress Management for Correctional Officers and Their Families.* College Park, Md.: American Correctional Association.

Cheney, G. (1983). "The Rhetoric of Identification and the Study of Organizational Communication." *Quarterly Journal of Speech* 69: 143–58.

Cheney, G., and P. K. Tompkins. (1987). "Coming to Terms with Organizational Identification and Commitment." *Central States Speech Journal* 38 (1): 1–15.

Chiarella, M. (1995). "The Magic of Nursing." *Australian Nursing Journal* 3 (3): 22–25.

Clair, R. P. (1998). *Organizing Silence: A World of Possibilities.* Albany: State University of New York Press.

———. (1996). "The Political Nature of the Colloquialism, 'A Real Job': Implications for Organizational Socialization." *Communica-tions Monographs* 63: 249–67.

———. (1993). "The Use of Framing Devices to Sequester Organizational Narratives: Hegemony and Harassment." *Communication Monographs* 60: 113–36.

Coates, J. (2000). "Small Talk and Subversion: The Female Speakers Backstage." In J. Coupland (ed.), *Small Talk* (241–63). Harlow: Pearson.

Cockerham, W. C. (1995). *Medical Sociology.* Englewood Cliffs, N.J.: Prentice-Hall.

Collinson, D. L. (2003). "Identities and Insecurities: Selves at Work." *Organization* 10: 527–47.

———. (1992). *Managing the Shopfloor: Subjectivity, Masculinity, and Workplace Culture*. Berlin: DeGruyter.

Communication Books (1976). *The Official CB Slang Dictionary Handbook*. Retrieved December 18, 2006, from http://seattletimes.nwsource.com/html/living/2002070339_third-place24.html

Conquergood, D. (1984). "Drama, Cosmology, and Culture in Organizations." Paper presented at the annual meeting of the Speech Communication Association, Chicago, Ill.

Cooper, R. (1995). "The Firemen: Immaculate Manhood." *Journal of Popular Culture* 28: 139–71.

Cragan, J. F., and D. C. Shields. (1995). *Symbolic Theories in Applied Communication Research*. Cresskill, N.J.: Hampton Press.

Dannefer, W. D., and J. H. Kasen. (1981). "Anonymous Exchanges: CB and the Emergence of Sex Typing." *Urban Life* 10: 265–87.

Dannefer, W. D., and N. Poushinsky. (1977). "Language and Community." *Journal of Communication* 27: 122–26.

Davis, A. Y. (1998). "Masked Racism: Reflections on the Prison Industrial Complex." *ColorLines* 1: 11–17.

Davis, D. S. (1984). "Good People Doing Dirty Work: A Study of Social Isolation." *Symbolic Interaction* 7 (2): 233–47.

Deal, T. E., and A. A. Kennedy (1982). *Corporate Cultures: The Rites and Rituals of Corporate Life*. Reading, Mass.: Addison-Wesley.

DeLaHunt, B. (2005). "Portable Documentation Comes to Resident Care." *Nursing Homes: Long Term Care Management* 54 (9): 44–46.

Denzin, N. K. (1997). *Interpretive Ethnography: Ethnographic Practices for the 21st Century*. Thousand Oaks, Calif.: Sage.

Douglas, C. (1994). "The Barber Trembles." *British Medical Journal* 309: 545.

Douglas, M. (1966). *Purity and Danger: An Analysis of the Concepts of Pollution and Taboo*. London: Routledge.

Drory, A., and B. Shamir. (1988). "Effects of Organizational and Life Variables on Job Satisfaction and Burnout." *Group and Organization Studies* 13: 441–55.

Duff, C. (1993). *When Women Work Together*. Berkeley: Conari Press.

du Pré, A. (2005). *Communicating about Health: Current Issues and Perspectives* (2nd ed.). New York: McGraw-Hill.

———. (1998). *Humor and the Healing Arts*. Mahwah, N.J.: Lawrence Erlbaum.

Edds, K. (2004, June 1). "Truckers Warm to Wireless Hot Spots: Technology Offers an Online Link in Comfort of Cab." *Special to the Washington Post*, p. A03.

Eff, E. (1978). "Truckstop: The Research, Presentation, and Interpretation of Occupational Folk Culture." Unpublished master's thesis, State University of New York, Oneonta. New York.

Ehrenreich, B., and D. English. (1973). *Complaints and Disorders: The Sexual Politics of Sickness*. New York: The Feminist Press.

Eisenberg, E. M. (2001). "Building a Mystery: Toward a New Theory of Communication and Identity." *Journal of Communication* 51: 534–53.

Eisenberg, E. M., and H. L. Goodall. (2004). *Organizational Communication: Balancing Creativity and Constraint* (4th ed.). Boston, Mass.: Bedford/St. Martin's.

Emerson, R. E., R. I. Fretz, and L. L. Shaw. (1995). *Writing Ethnographic Fieldnotes*. Chicago: University of Chicago Press.

Emerson, R. M., and M. Pollner. (1976). "Dirty Work Designations: Their Features and Consequences in a Psychiatric Setting." *Social Problems* 23 (3): 243–54.

Ewens, G., and M. Ellis. (1977). *The Cult of Big Rigs and the Life of the Long Haul Trucker*. New York: Quarto Publishing.

Farmer, B. C. (1996). *A Nursing Home and Its Organizational Climate*. Westport, Conn.: Greenwood Publishing.

Federal Bureau of Invesigation. (2004). *Crime in the United States*. (Uniform Crime Reports). Washington, D.C.: U. S. Department of Justice.

Feldman, M. S., and J. G. March. (1981). "Information in Organizations as Signal and Symbol." *Administrative Science Quarterly* 26: 171–86.

Fensch, T. (1976). *Smokeys, Truckers, CB Radios, & You*. Greenwich, Conn.: Fawcett Publications.

Fields, W. C. (quote retrieved August 12, 2006 from chatna.com/theme/nurses.htm).

Fine, G. A. (1993). "Ten Lies of Ethnography: Moral Dilemmas of Field Research." *Journal of Contemporary Ethnography* 22 (3): 267–94.

"Firefighter Jobs for Minorities." (1971, August 14). *The Sun Reporter*, 7.

Fisher, B. A. J. (2000). *Techniques of Crime Scene Investigation* (6th ed.). Boca Raton, Fla.: CRC Press.

Foucault, M. (1977). *Discipline and Punish: The Birth of the Prison*. New York: Vintage Books.

Geertz, C. (1973). *The Interpretation of Cultures*. New York: Basic Books.

Geertz, C. (1976). "From the Natives' Point of View: On the Nature of Anthropological Understanding." In K. E. Basso & H. A. Selz (eds.), *Meaning in Anthropology* (221–37). Albuquerque: University of New Mexico Press.

Geist, P. (1999). "Surreal Illusions, Genuine Realities: Disenchantment and Renewal in the Academy—Introduction." *Communication Theory* 9: 365–76.

Gergen, K. (1991). *The Saturated Self.* New York: Basic Books.

Gilmore, V. (2005). "Getting Education Right for Enrolled Nurses." *Australian Nursing Journal* 13 (4): 13.

Gini, A. (2001). *My Job, My Self: Work and the Creation of the Modern Individual.* Boca Raton, Fla.: Taylor & Francis.

Glaser, B., and A. Strauss. (1967). *The Discovery of Grounded Theory.* Chicago: Aldine.

Godin, P. (2000). "A Dirty Business: Caring for People Who Are a Nuisance or a Danger." *Journal of Advanced Nursing* 32 (6): 1396–1403.

Goffman, E. (1961). *Asylums.* Garden City, N.J.: Anchor Books.

———. (1974). *Frame Analysis: An Essay on the Organization of Experience.* Boston: Northeastern University Press.

———. (1959). *The Presentation of Self in Everyday Life.* Garden City, N.Y.: Doubleday.

———. (1963). *Stigma: Notes on the Management of Spoiled Identity.* Englewood Cliffs, N.J.: Prentice-Hall.

Gold, R. (1958). "Roles in Sociological Field Observations." *Social Forces* 36: 217–23.

Gonzales, L. (2005). *Deep Survival.* New York: W. W. Norton.

Goodall, H. L. (1989). *Casing a Promised Land: The Autobiography of an Organizational Detective as Cultural Ethnographer.* Carbondale: Southern Illinois University Press.

———. (2000). *Writing the New Ethnography.* Lanham, Md.: Rowman & Littlefield.

Gossett, L. M. (2002). "Kept at Arm's Length: Questioning the Organizational Desirability of Member Identification." *Communication Monographs* 69 (4): 385–405.

Griffin, E. (2006). *A First Look at Communication Theory.* (6th ed.). New York: McGraw-Hill.

Grossman, H. Y., and A. J. Stewart. (1990). "Women's Experience of Power over Others: Case Studies of Psychotherapists and Professors." In H. Y. Grossman and N. L. Chester (eds.). *The Experience and Meaning of Work in Women's Lives.* Hillsdale, N.J.: Lawrence Erlbaum Associates.

Guendouzi, J. (2001). "'You'll Think We're Always Bitching': The Functions of Cooperativity and Competition in Women's Gossip." *Discourse Studies* 3: 29–51.

Gutek, B. A. (1989). "Sexuality in the Workplace: Key Issues in Social Research and Organizational Practice." In J. Hearn, D. L. Sheppard, P. Tancred-Sheriff, and G. Burrell (eds.), *The Sexuality of Organization* (56–70). London: Sage.

Hafferty, F. W. (1988). "Cadaver Stories and the Emotional Socialization of Medical Students." *Journal of Health and Social Behavior* 29: 344–56.

Harrison, L. (1996, May 30). "Love, Hate or Apathy: Minority Firefighters Debate the Correct Responses to Racism." *The Sun Reporter*, 16.

Hendley, W. C. (1979). "What's your Handle, Good Buddy? Names of Citizen's Band Users." *American Speech* 54: 307–10.

Heinsler, J. M., S. Kleinman, and B. Stenross. (1990). "Making Work Matter: Satisfied Detectives and Dissatisfied Campus Police." *Qualitative Sociology* 13: 235–50.

Heron, E. (1998). *Tending Lives.* New York: Ballantine.

Heumann, M. (2003). "Adapting to Plea Bargaining: Prosecutors." In M. R. Pogrebin (ed.), *Qualitative Approaches to Criminal Justice: Perspectives from the Field* (204–18). Thousand Oaks, Calif.: Sage.

Hichins, M. (1999). "Pros Shouldn't Do Dirty Work." *Manage-ment Review* 88 (2): 7.

Higgins, C. *Nine to Five* (film). Century City, Calif.: Twentieth-Century Fox and IPC Films Production.

"History of Nursing Resources." (n.d.) Retrieved June, 5, 2006, from http://www.library.vcu.edu/tml/bibs/nsghis.html/.

Hoban, S. (2006). "CNAs Are Speaking—But Are You Listening?" *Nursing Homes: Long Term Care Management* 55 (3): 38–41.

Hochschild, A. R. (1983). *The Managed Heart: Commercialization of Human Feelings.* Berkeley: University of California Press.

hooks, b. (1989). *Talking Back: Thinking Feminist, Thinking Black.* Boston: South End Press.

Hooper, E. (1999). *The River: A Journey to the Source of HIV and AIDS.* Boston: Little, Brown.

Howe, L. K. (1977). *Pink Collar Workers: Inside the World of Women's Work.* New York: Avon Books.

Hughes, E. C. (1962). "Good People and Dirty Work." *Social Problems* 10 (1): 3–11.

———. (1958). *Men and Their Work.* Glencoe, Ill.: Free Press.

Hughes, E. C. (1951). "Work and the Self." In J. H. Rohrer and S. Muzafer (eds.), *Social Psychology at the Crossroads* (313–23). Oxford: Harper.

Humphreys, L. (1970). *Tearoom Trade: Impersonal Sex in Public Places.* Chicago: Aldine.

Huntington, A. D., and J. A. Gilmour. (2001). "Re-thinking Representations, Re-writing Nursing Texts: Possibilities through Feminist and Foucauldian Thought." *Journal of Advanced Nursing* 35 (6): 902–8.

Ignatiev, N. (1995). *How the Irish Became White.* New York: Routledge.

International Association of Administrative Professionals (IAAP). *Why Certification?*, March 5, 2006. http://www.iaap-hq.org/cert/advantage.htm.

James, D. H. (1995). "Humor: A Holistic Nursing Intervention." *Journal of Holistic Nursing* 13 (3): 239–47.

Jervis, L. L. (2001). "The Pollution of Incontinence and the Dirty work of Caregiving in a U.S. Nursing Home." *Medical Anthropology Quarterly* 15 (1): 84–99.

Jones, D. (1980/1990). "Gossip: Notes on Women's Oral Culture." In D. Cameron (ed.), *The Feminist Critique of Language: A Reader* (242–50). London and New York: Routledge. (Reprinted from Jones, D. [1980]. "Gossip: Notes on Women's Oral Culture." In C. Kramarae [ed.], *The Voices and Words of Women and Men* [193–98]. Oxford: Pergamon Press.)

Junion-Metz, G. (May 2006). "A History of Caring for Others." *School Library Journal*, 26.

Kanter, R. M. (1977). *Men and Women of the Corporation.* New York: Basic Books.

Kaprow, M. L. (1991). "Magical Work: Firefighters in New York." *Human Organization* 50: 97-103.

Katriel, T. (1986). *Talking Straight: Dugri Speech in Israeli Sabra Culture.* Cambridge: Cambridge University Press.

King, S. (1998). *Bag of Bones.* New York: Scribner.

Koller, M. R. (1988). *Humor and Society: Explorations in the Sociology of Humor.* Houston: Cap & Gown Press.

Kvale, S. (1996). *InterViews: An Introduction to Qualitative Research Interviewing.* Thousand Oaks, Calif.: Sage.

Lawler, J. (1998). "Nursing and the Virtual World of the Next Era." *Nursing Inquiry* 5: 203.

Leeds-Hurwitz, W. (2006). "Social Constructionism: Moving from Theory to Research (and Back Again)." Paper prepared for Catching Ourselves in the Act: A Collaboration to Enrich our

Discipline through Social Constructionist Approaches, a summer institute sponsored by the National Communication Association and Crooked Timbers Project, Albuquerque, N.M.

Lembright, M. F., and J. W. Riemer. (1982). "Women Trucker's Problems and the Impact of Sponsorship." *Work and Occupations* 9: 457–74.

Lindlof, T., and B. Taylor. (2002). *Qualitative Communication Research Methods.* (2nd ed.). Thousand Oaks, Calif.: Sage.

Lofland, J., and L. H. Lofland. (1984). *Analyzing Social Settings: A Guide to Qualitative Observational Research.* Belmont, Calif.: Wadsworth.

Lynch, O. H. (2002). "Humor Communication: Finding a Place for Humor in Communication Research." *Communication Theory* 12: 423–45.

MacLeod, A. E. (1992). "Hegemonic Relations and Gender Resistance: The New Veiling as Accommodating Protest in Cairo." *Signs* 17: 533–57.

Martinez, S. P. (2003). "Crack Pipes and T-Cells: An Ethnography of Communication in a Residential Community for People Living with HIV/AIDS and Addiction." Unpublished doctoral dissertation. (Dissertation Abstracts International).

Matthaei, J. (1983). *An Economic History of Women in America: Women's Work, the Sexual Division of Labor and the Development of Capitalism.* New York: Schocken.

McCarl, R. S. (1984). "'You've Come a Long Way. And Now This Is Your Retirement': An Analysis of Performance in Fire Fighting Culture." *The Journal of American Folklore* 97 (386): 393–422.

McKee, M. B. (1990). "A Cultural Study on the Lifestyle of Long Haul Truckers." Unpublished doctoral dissertation, Bowling Green State University, Ohio.

McIntyre, L. J. (1987). *The Public Defender: The Practice of Law in the Shadows of Repute.* Chicago: The University of Chicago Press.

McTavish, D. (2001). *Big Rig: Comic Tales from a Long Haul Trucker.* Edmonton, Alberta: Lone Pine.

Meade, M. (1973). *Bitching.* Englewood Cliffs, N.J.: Prentice-Hall.

Miles, M., and Huberman, A. (1994). *Qualitative Data Analysis.* Thousand Oaks, Calif.: Sage.

Mills, M. B. (2007). "Miles of Trials: The Life and Livelihood of the Long Haul Trucker." In DeGenaro, W. (ed.), *Who Says? Working Class Rhetorics, Class Consciousness, and Community* (127–43). Pittsburgh: University of Pittsburgh Press.

Mumby, D. K., and L. L. Putnam. (1992). "The Politics of Emotion: A Feminist Reading of Bounded Rationality." *Academy of Management Review* 17: 465–86.

Nightingale, F. (Retrieved August 12, 2006, from http://chatna.com/theme/nurses.htm).

"Nurses Tend to Use Individual Behavioral and Visual Cues to Assess Pain in Nursing Home Residents." (2005, October). *Nursing* 14 (5): 324.

O'Brien, P. G., and K. J. Peak. (1991). *Kansas Bootleggers.* Manhattan, Kans.: Sunflower University Press.

O'Halloran, R. L., and P. E. Dietz. (1993). "Autoerotic Fatalities with Power Hydraulics." *Journal of Forensic Sciences* 38 (2): 359–64.

Oldenburg, R. (1999). *The Great Good Place: Cafés, Coffee Shops, Bookshops, Bars, Hair Salons and Other Hangouts at the Heart of Community.* New York: Marlowe.

O'Leary, V. E., and J. Ickovics. (1990). "Women Supporting Women: Secretaries and Their Bosses." In H. Y. Grossman and N. L. Chester (eds.), *The Experience and Meaning of Work in Women's Lives* (13–34). Hillsdale, N.J.: Lawrence Erlbaum Associates.

Ouellet, L. J. (1994). *Pedal to the Metal: The Work Lives of Truckers.* Philadelphia: Temple University Press (Labor & Social Change Series).

Pacanowsky, M. E., and N. O'Donnell-Trujillo (1983). "Organizational Communication as Cultural Performances." *Communication Monographs* 50: 126–47.

Page, R. M. (1984). *Stigma.* London: Routledge.

Pappassun, J. (2006, March 20). "National Survey Ranks Firefighter as Sexiest Job." *Sun Herald.* Retrieved March 21, 2006, from http://www.sunherald.com.

Payne, B. K., B. L. Berg, and I. Y. Sun. (2005). "Policing in Small Town America: Dogs, Drunks, Disorder, and Dysfunction." *Journal of Criminal Justice* 33: 31–41.

Penelope, J. (1990). *Speaking Freely: Unlearning the Lies of the Fathers' Tongues.* New York & London: Teachers College Press.

Perry, S. E. (1998). *Collecting Garbage: Dirty Work, Clean Jobs, Proud People.* New Brunswick: Transaction.

Peters, T. J., and R. H. Waterman. (1982). *In Search of Excellence: Lessons from America's Best-Run Companies.* New York: Harper & Row.

Pogrebin, M. R., and E. D. Poole. (2003). "Humor in the Briefing Room." In M. R. Pogrebin (ed.), *Qualitative Approaches to Criminal Justice: Perspectives from the Field* (80–93). Thousand Oaks, Calif.: Sage.

Powell, J. T., and D. Ary. (1977) "Communication Without Commitment." *Journal of Communication* 27: 118–21.

Pringle, R. (1988). *Secretaries Talk: Sexuality, Power and Work.* London: Verso.

Ragan, S. L. (1990). "Verbal Play and Multiple Goals in the Gynecological Exam Interaction." *Journal of Language and Social Psychology* 9: 67–84.

Ramsey, R. D. (1999). "How to Enjoy Your Job More (10 Steps to Greater Job Satisfaction)." *Supervision* 60 (9): 15–17.

Rawlins, W. K. (2000). "Teaching as a Mode of Friendship." *Communication Theory* 10: 5–26.

Romano, M. (2006). "The New CNO." *Modern Healthcare* 36 (16): 24–47.

Ronai, C. R. (1995). "Multiple Reflections of Child Abuse: An Argument for a Layered Account." *Journal of Contemporary Ethnography* 23 (4): 395–426.

Runcie, J. F. (1969). "Truck Drivers' Jargon." *American Speech* 44: 200–209.

Ruscoe, D. (2006). "Education, Education, Education." *Practice Nurse* 31(4): 7.

Ryan, E. B., D. E. Kennaley, M. W. Pratt, and M. A. Shumovich. (2000). "Evaluations by Staff, Residents, and Community Seniors of Patronizing Speech in the Nursing Home: Impact of Passive, Assertive, or Humorous Responses." *Psychology and Aging* 15 (2): 272–85.

Schensul S. L., J. J. Schensul, and M. LeCompte. (1999). *Essential Ethnographic Methods.* Walnut Creek, Calif.: Altamira Press.

Schlosser, E. (1998). "The Prison-Industrial Complex." *The Atlantic Monthly* 282 (6): 51–77.

Scott, C. R. (1997). "Identification with Multiple Targets in a Geographically Dispersed Organization." *Management Communication Quarterly* 10 (4): 491–522.

Scott, C. W., and K. K. Myers. (2005). "The Socialization of Emotion: Learning Emotion Management at the Fire Station." *Journal of Applied Communication Research* 33: 67–92.

Scott, J. B. (2003). *Risky Rhetoric: AIDS and the Cultural Practices of HIV Testing.* Carbondale, Ill.: Southern Illinois University Press.

Scott, J. C. (1991). *Domination and the Art of Resistance: Hidden Transcripts.* New Haven: Yale University Press.

Sherrod, B., D. Sherrod, and R. Rasch. (2005). "Men at Work." *Nursing Management* 36 (10): 46–51.

Shields, D. C. (2000). "Symbolic Convergence and Special Communication Theories: Sensing and Examining Disenchantment with the Theoretical Robustness of Critical Ethnography." *Communication Monographs* 67 (4): 392–422.

Shiminoff, S. B. (1980). *Communication Rules: Theory and Research.* Beverly Hills, Calif.: Sage.

Shinn, M., S. Lehmann, and N. W. Wong. (1984). "Social Interaction and Social Support." *Journal of Social Issues* 40: 55–76.

Sibbson, J. B. (1991). "USA: Dirty Work in the Drug Industry." *Lancet* 337 (8735): 227.

Smith, A. C., III, and S. Kleinman. (1989). "Managing Emotions in Medical School: Students' Contacts with the Living and the Dead." *Social Psychology Quarterly* 52: 56–69.

Smith, H. W. (1980). "The CB Handle: An Announcement of Adult Identity." *Symbolic Interaction* 3: 95–108.

Smith, J. J. (1981). "Gender Marking on Citizen's Band Radio: Self-Identity in a Limited-Channel Speech Community." *Sex Roles* 7: 599–606.

———. (1979). "Male and Female Ways of Speaking: Elaborately Restricted Codes in a CB Speech Community." *Papers in Linguistics* 12: 163–84.

Sotirin, P. (2000). "All They Do Is 'Bitch, Bitch, Bitch': Political and Interactional Features of Women's Office Talk." *Women & Language* 23 (2): 19–25.

Sotirin, P., and H. Gottfried. (1999). "The Ambivalent Dynamics of Secretarial 'Bitching': Control, Resistance, and the Construction of Identity." *Organization* 6: 57–80.

Sotirin, P., and D. Miller. (1994). "Secretarial Positioning: Gender Ambivalence and Harassment." In A. Taylor and J. B. Miller (eds.), *Conflict and Gender* (93–112). Cresskill, N.J.: Hampton Press.

Spradley, J. (1979). *The Ethnography Interview.* New York: Holt, Rhinehart & Winston.

Stern, J. (1975). *Trucker: A Portrait of the Last American Cowboy.* New York: McGraw-Hill.

Stevenson, R. (n.d.). *Old Truckers Never Die, They Just Take Another Pill.* Self-published.

Stradling, D. (2001). "Dirty Work and Clean Air: Locomotive Firemen, Environmental Activists, and Stories of Conflict." *Journal of Urban History* 28 (1): 35–55.

Strauss, A., and J. Corbin. (1998). *Basics of Qualitative Research: Techniques and Procedures for Developing Grounded Theory.* Thousand Oaks, Calif.: Sage.

Stripling, S. (2004, October 24). "Conversation Starters: 'Third Places' Provide Havens for Diverse Discussion." *Seattle Times.*

Strom, S. (1992). *Beyond the Typewriter: Gender, Class, and the Origins of Modern American Office Work.* Champaign: University of Illinois Press.

Talbot, L. A. (2000). "Burnout and Humor Usage among Community College Nursing Faculty Members." *Community College Journal of Research and Practice* 24 (5): 359–73.

Tebeau, M. (2003). *Eating Smoke: Fire in Urban America, 1800-1950.* Baltimore: The Johns Hopkins University Press.

Thomas, E. M. (1975). "A Century's Progress in Law Enforcement." Unpublished manuscript.

Thompson, T. L., A. M. Dorsey, K. I. Miller, and R. Parrott. (2003). *Handbook of Health Communication.* Mahwah, N.J.: Lawrence Erlbaum.

Thorson, J. A., and F. C. Powell. (1993). "Relationships of Death Anxiety and Sense of Humor." *Psychological Reports* 72 (3): 1364, 3.

Tompkins, P. K. (1983). "On the Desirability of an Interpretive Science of Organizational Communication." Paper presented at the Speech Communication Association Annual Meeting, Washington, D.C.

Tracy, K., and J. Naughton. (1994). "The Identity Work of Questioning in Intellectual Discussion." *Communication Monographs* 61: 281–302.

Tracy, S. J. (2000). "Becoming a Character for Commerce: Emotion Labor, Self Subordination and Discursive Construction of Identity in a Total Institution." *Management Communication Quarterly* 14: 90–128.

———. (2004a). "The Construction of Correctional Officers: Layers of Emotionality behind Bars." *Qualitative Inquiry* 10: 509–33.

———. (2004b). "Dialectic, Contradiction, or Double Bind? Analyzing and Theorizing Employee Reactions to Organizational Tensions." *Journal of Applied Communication Research* 32: 119–46.

———. (2005). "Locking Up Emotion: Moving beyond Dissonance for Understanding Emotion Labor Discomfort." *Communication Monographs* 72: 261–83.

Tracy, S. J., K. K. Myers, and C. Scott. (2005). "Transforming Complexity and Absurdity to Comedy and Identity Affirmation: A Grounded Multisite Analysis of Humor and Organizational Sensemaking." Presented at the meeting of the National Communication Association, Boston.

Tracy, S. J., and C. Scott. (2006). "Sexuality, Masculinity and Taint Management among Firefighters and Correctional Officers: Getting Down and Dirty with 'America's Heroes' and the 'Scum of Law Enforcement.'" *Management Communication Quarterly* 20: 6–38.

Tracy, S. J., and A. Trethewey. (2005). "Fracturing the Real-Self ↔ Fake-Self Dichotomy: Moving toward Crystallized Organizational Identities." *Communication Theory* 15: 168–95.

Treiman, D. J. (1977). *Occupational Prestige in Comparative Perspective.* New York: Academic Press.

Trethewey, A. (1997). "Resistance, Identity, and Empowerment: A Postmodern Feminist Analysis of Clients in a Human Service Organization." *Communication Monographs* 64: 281–301.

Troll, L. E. (1988). "Rituals and Reunions." *American Behavioral Scientist* 31 (6): 621–31.

Trujillo, N., and G. Dionisopoulos. (1987). "Cop Talk, Police Stories, and the Social Construction of Organizational Drama." *Central States Speech Journal* 38 (3 and 4): 196–209.

Twigg, J. (2000). "Carework as a Form of Bodywork." *Aging & Society* 20 (4): 389–411.

Turnbull, J. M. (1998). "10 Steps to Staying Sane." *Family Practice Management* 5 (1): 65–68.

United Nations Program on HIV/AIDS. "AIDS Epidemic Update—2004." Retrieved from http://www.unaids.org/wad2004/report.html.

U.S. Department of Health & Human Services (2002). *Projected Supply, Demand, and Shortages of Registered Nurses.* Health Resources and Services Administration, Bureau of Health Professions, National Center for Health Workforce Analysis.

Van Maanen, J., and S. R. Barley. (1984). "Occupational Communities: Culture and Control in Organizations." In B. M. Staw and L. L. Cummings (eds.), *Research in Organizational Behavior.* Greenwich, Conn.: JAI Press.

Van Maanen J. (1988). *Tales of the Field: On Writing Ethnography.* Chicago, Ill.: University of Chicago Press.

Van Wormer, K., and M. Boes. 1997. "Humor in the Emergency Room: A Social Work Perspective." *Health & Social Work* 22 (2): 87.

Waters, A. "Only 60 practitioners." *Nursing Standard* 20 (32): 6.

Weedon, C. (1997). *Feminist Practice and Poststructuralist Theory* (2nd ed.). Oxford: Blackwell.

Weick, K. E. (1995). *Sensemaking in Organizations.* Thousand Oaks, Calif.: Sage.

Weisheit, R. A., L. E. Wells, and D. N. Falcone. (2003). "Community Policing in Small Town and Rural America." In M. R. Pogrebin (ed.). *Qualitative Approaches to Criminal Justice: Perspectives from the Field* (128–40). Thousand Oaks, Calif.: Sage.

Weiss, W. H. (1997). "Humor on the Job." *Supervision* 58: 9–11.

Williams, A., L. Phillips, and Z. Ahmed. (2000). "Assessment and Management of Autoerotic Asphyxiation in a Young Man with Learning Disability: A Multidisciplinary Approach to Intervention." *British Journal of Learning Disabilities* 28 (3): 109–13.

Will, F. (1992). *Big Rig Souls: Truckers in America's Heartland.* West Bloomfield, Mich.: Altwerger & Mandel Publishing.

Witkin, S. L. (1999). "Taking Humor Seriously." *Social Work* 4 (2): 101–4.

Wise, M. F., and B. Di Salvatore. (1995). *Truck Stop.* Jackson: University Press of Mississippi.

Wolin, S. J., and L. A. Bennett. (1984). "Family *Rituals.*" *Family Process* 23 (3): 401–20.

About the Contributors

SHIRLEY K. DREW is a professor of communication and director of graduate studies at Pittsburg State University in Pittsburg, Kansas. She has been teaching and living in the Sunflower State since 1989. She completed her Ph.D. at Bowling Green State University in 1985. Before moving to Kansas, she worked for three years as an internal management trainer and consultant for a 650-bed hospital in Toledo, Ohio. Her teaching areas include interpersonal, group, and organizational communication and qualitative research methods. Her research is primarily qualitative (ethnographic) and includes ritual, group culture, and occupational culture. When not hanging out with lawyers and cops, Shirley enjoys hiking, reading sci-fi and mystery, and camping. She also likes hanging out with her field biologist husband, who's glad he found an "outdoor girl."

BOB M. GASSAWAY is a professor emeritus of the Department of Communication and Journalism at the University of New Mexico. Bob covered his first homicide at the age of 17 as a reporter for a television station in Texas. As a journalist for 20 years, he frequently covered police and crime stories and was a war correspondent in Vietnam. He earned graduate degrees in sociology, focusing much of his study on death and dying, and on occupations and professions. He has taught courses in journalism, mass communication, and research methods, particularly ethnography. He accompanied crime scene investigators in the Albuquerque Police Department to more than two dozen death scenes as he studied their work. Last year, he observed about 30 autopsies while studying the work of forensic pathologists. He recently retired from the University of New Mexico to write a series of mystery novels focusing on crime scene investigators.

CHIEF OF POLICE MENDY HULVEY grew up in southeast Kansas. She has a bachelor's and a master's degree in Criminal Justice. She has been in law enforcement since 1985. She joined the Pittsburg, Kansas, police department in 2000 and was promoted to chief of police in 2005. She is a FBI National Academy graduate and is one of only 203 female police chiefs in the United States. Mendy is a fitness enthusiast and enjoys running, boating, camping, and various other outdoor activities.

STEPHANIE POOLE MARTINEZ is assistant professor of communication and basic course director at St. Edward's University in Austin, Texas. Recent studies focus on various aspects of addiction communication, including communication over the Internet, in support groups, and in counseling. She also conducts and is interested in service learning. In her free time, she enjoys the company of her partner, Chris, and her daughter, Anya.

MELANIE MILLS is a communication practitioner dedicated to collaborative improvement of social conditions in challenging situations, focusing on emergent communication and organizational problems. She is a professor in the Communication Studies Department at Eastern Illinois University, where she teaches undergraduate and graduate level courses in interpersonal and organizational communication, research methods, and communication theories. She is co-coordinator of the interdisciplinary Health Communication Program, and also on the Women's Studies faculty. Her scholarship examines the ways employees construct and manage issues of stigma, crisis, and identity in occupational work groups. Research projects have analyzed humor, occupational cultures, gender relationships, dirty work, social support, women's friendships, personal responsibility, and crisis communication in corporate, health, religious, and government systems. Melanie's favorite moments are sharing good music, good food, good conversation, laughter, and great life adventures with the "other" Dr. Mills (Tim) and their daughters, Martha, Katie, and Lauren.

AMY SCHEJBAL is a recent graduate of Eastern Illinois University in Charleston, Illinois. She has spent the past year completing a master's degree in communication studies while teaching Introduction to Public Speaking. Currently, Amy is living and working in the Chicago area as a medical representative for Merck & Co. As the youngest of nine children, Amy loves spending as much time as possible with her many nieces and nephews. In her free time Amy also likes to travel, cheer for the Cubs, and enjoy her family and friends who have supported her throughout all her endeavors.

CLIFF SCOTT is an assistant professor of communication studies and an assistant professor of organizational science at the University of North Carolina at Charlotte, where he also serves as a consultant for health, public safety, and educational organizations through its Organizational Science Consulting and Research unit. Appearing in *Management Communication Quarterly*, *Journal of Applied Communication Research*, *Communication Monographs*, the *Peking Business Review*, and the *Handbook of Gender and Communication*, his research concerns occupational identity, organizational diversity, and qualitative research methods. Prior to his current position, he completed his Ph.D. in organizational communication at Arizona State University (2005), an M.A. in organizational communication at Northern Illinois University (2001), and a B.S. in speech communication at Bradley University (1997). Before joining the academy, he worked as a field sales manager, supervising a team of geographically dispersed employees and overseeing large corporate accounts for a major manufacturer of resilient flooring (a.k.a., "linoleum"). It was during his rather rough (and in many ways accidental) transition from college to flooring sales ("wood is good, but vinyl is final!") that he became personally interested in how organizations, occupations, and the ways we talk about them shape both our sense of self and the flesh and blood practices of public and private life. When he's not working on his occupational identity as a masculine, scientific intellectual in public, he enjoys exploring the mystery of manliness in his private life, which lately includes the consumption of junk food, a jeep, a camouflage steering wheel-cover, and a commercial-grade brush cutter. Cliff and his partner/spouse Jill enjoy living in the woods with their two black Labrador Retrievers.

PATTY SOTIRIN is an associate professor of communication in the Department of Humanities at Michigan Technological University. Her research interests include women's office talk,

mundane workplace struggles over power and resistance, and quali-
tative feminist methods. She has published in such journals as
Organization, Women and Language, Text and Performance Quarterly, and
Cultural Studies-Critical Methodologies.

SARAH J. TRACY is an associate professor and director of The Project
for Wellness and Work-Life in the Hugh Downs School of Human
Communication at Arizona State University in Tempe. Her scholarship examines the ways employees construct and manage issues of
emotion and identity in organizations. Her research projects have
analyzed emotion, labor, humor, sexuality, burnout, dirty work,
work-life balance, contradiction, and workplace bullying with 911
emergency call-takers, cruise ship personnel, prison/jail correctional officers, and workplace bullying targets. Sarah attempts to do
"use-inspired" research by focusing on emergent communication
and organizational problems in the field. She generally uses qualitative methods along with social constructionist and poststructuralist
epistemological approaches to shed light on research issues and, in
the best of cases, provide space for action, change, or transformation. In her free time, Sarah enjoys cooking good food, watching
"Dirty Jobs" on television, playing with her two cats, laughing, and
training for 5ks and triathlons.

Author Index

Subject Index